CW00546573

The Exmoor Pony
CHRONICLES

SUE BAKER

HALSGROVE

First published in Great Britain in 2017

Copyright © 2017 Sue Baker

All rights reserved. No part of this publication may be reproduced, stored in a retrieval system, or transmitted in any form or by any means without the prior permission of the copyright holder.

British Library Cataloguing-in-Publication Data
A CIP record for this title is available from the British Library

ISBN 978 0 85704 315 3

HALSGROVE
Halsgrove House, Ryelands Business Park,
Bagley Road, Wellington, Somerset TA21 9PZ
Tel: 01823 653777 Fax: 01823 216796
email: sales@halsgrove.com

Part of the Halsgrove group of companies
Information on all Halsgrove titles is available at: www.halsgrove.com

Printed and bound by Parksons Graphics, India

Contents

Exmoor Pony Tales Pages 72 - 87

Old Farmer Mole/Making Merry/Travelling to Bampton/By Train to Islington/School Days/
The Rabbit-Catcher/Exmoor Versatility/The Winter of 1947/Bampton Fair/Tommy the Pony/
Good Companions/Shipping Exmoors to Canada/Let the Train Take the Strain/Outsmarted/
Assembly/Student Days/Tax Evasion/Inspecting Exmoor Ponies/Exmoor Pony Society/
Public Relations Ponies/Pony Racing/Racing 'Up-Country'/An Unexpected Encounter/Call of the Wild.

Warfare
Chariot Ponies 7 - 10
West Somerset Yeomanry 43
The Exmoor Mounties 93 - 95
Exmoor Pony Targets in WWII? 100

Archaeology
The Bolham Roman Intaglio 11
General Pitt Rivers 31

Moorland Breeders
The Withypool Miltons 12 - 14
The Hawkridge Westcotts 17 - 21
The Thornes of Twitchen 25 - 26
The Crockfords and Westerns 45 - 46
The Williams of Great Ash 53 - 54
The Porlock Westcotts 55 - 56
The Green Family 60 - 61

Celebrity and Royal Encounters
Sir Walter Scott 15 - 16
Roy Rogers 117
Princess Anne 118

Artists and Illustrators
John Leech 22
Joan Wanklyn 64
Allen Seaby 68 - 69
Sir Alfred Munnings 90 - 91
Michael Lyne 106
Hope Bourne 121 - 122

Exmoor Pony Breeding
Exmoor Pony Twins 92

Moorland Misadventures
World War II – Dark Times 96
Gate-crashing 128
Grounded and Adders 138
The Will to Live 147

Globetrotting
New Zealand 23 - 24
India? 24
Australia 29
Denmark 97 - 98
Canada 108 - 109
Germany 110 - 113
Norway 123
Sweden 125 - 126
United States of America 131 - 132
The Philippines 132
The Falklands 141 - 142
The Netherlands 145

Exmoor Crosses
Robert Smith 27 - 28
Arab x Exmoor 38 - 39
Wild Ass and Zebra x Exmoor 40
Quarter Horse x Exmoor 146
Lusitano x Exmoor 148
Takhi and Konik x Exmoor 154
Exmoor x Haflinger 157

Pony Sales
Bampton Fair 1881 30
Molland Pony Sale 32
Bampton Fair 1937 88 - 89
Brendon Pony Fair 124
Bampton Fair 1974 - 2014 133

Pony Personalities
South Hill 33
Fisherman 119 - 120
Royal Mantle 134 - 135

Exmoor Pony People
Daniel Evans 34 - 35
Sophia Best 70 - 71
Lilo Lumb 103

Conservation
The Acland Herd after 1818 36 - 37

Exmoor Ponies in Music
There Goes Old Tom 41

The Exmoor Pony Society
The Need for a Society 42
Founding the Society 47 - 48
Honorary Secretaries 49 - 52
The Breed Show 105

Exmoor Pony Photographers
Charles Reid 44
Alfred Vowles 59
Richard Kingsley Tayler 66 - 67
Annie Dent 144

Gathering and Droving
Porlock to Bampton 57 - 59

Exmoor Ponies in Literature
Eleanor Helme 62 - 63
Fay Weldon 149

Exmoor Ponies in Poetry
Exmoor Ponies/Gay 65
An Exmoor Lane/Munnings 99
Winter Journey/Spottiswoode 140
Physician of Olympus/Young 151 - 152

Exmoor Ponies in Zoos
Regent's Park Zoo, London 101 - 102
North Holland Zoo 104
Edinburgh Zoo 107
Crystal Palace Zoo, London 114 - 116

Exmoor Ponies in Family Life
Love & Marriage – 20th Century 127
Birth and Childcare 137
Fetching and Carrying 143
Love & Marriage – 21st Century 155

Exmoor Pony Collectables
The Beswick Exmoor 129
The Royal Worcester Exmoor 136
The Poole Pottery Exmoor 139

Exmoor Pony Snippets 130

Agricultural Workers
The Milton Pony Plough 150

Exmoor Ponies in Arts and Crafts
Stained Glass 153
Quilting 156

Epilogue 158

Acknowledgements

There is a long list of people who have contributed to this book through providing illustrative material: each image is attributed within the caption; where there is no attribution, these are my own photographs. My special thanks to the many who have sought nothing in return. I am especially grateful to Alma Swan for bringing the Pony Tales to life with her paintings. My thanks also to the Exmoor National Park Authority for their grant towards commercial image reproduction fees.

In some cases, despite extensive searches, I have been unable to locate a copyright holder: if anyone knows how I can contact the heirs of John Keene, Michael Lyne, Richard Kingsley Tayler, Alfred Vowles or Joan Wanklyn, please contact me (details on page 158).

So many people have provided information for this book and some must be brought into the limelight: my thanks go to Jackie Ablett, Penny Beattie, Gill Langdon, Muriel Mason, the late Fred Milton, Margaret Rawle, Gay Seguro, Val Webber, Mary Werner, Linda and Julian Westcott, the late David Westcott, John and Anne Western and Robert Williams for their invaluable help in telling the stories of the moorland breeders; to Bill Adams and David Buxton, the Exmoor charioteers; to Anne Le Bas and Robert Gillmor for for sharing their memories of their grandfathers; to Doreen Whitney for telling the whole story of Crystal Palace Zoo; to Merrilyn Thomas and Toby Young for allowing me to write about Megan Young; to David Brewer, Melissa Coyner, Eline Falch, Neil Gowing, Ann Gugler, Anne Holmes, Hans Hovens, Sandy Roede, Louise Rundell, Iben Tjelum and Melanie and Bob Wright for their help with the Globetrotting stories; to Janet Blakeney, Henri Kerkdijk-Otten and Hilary Pittam for their stories of Exmoor crosses; to the wonderful staff at the Somerset Heritage Centre in Taunton and Devon Record Office in Exeter; to Dr Helen Blackman at the Exmoor Society; and to Sandra Mansell and Sue McGeever at the Exmoor Pony Society.

Inevitably I will have left someone out and if that is you, then my heartfelt apologies – my forgetfulness in no way detracts from my gratitude.

Foreword

In her first book about Exmoor Ponies, Sue Baker laid out the natural history and place of these intriguing and lovable animals in the ecology and landscape of the British Isles. How biologically interesting they are and how crucial that their natural history – a critically important part of our natural heritage – was documented.

Now Sue takes things further. In this book she turns her attention to the cultural heritage of these ponies, and what a heritage that turns out to be. It was obvious, really. Humans cannot interact with a particular animal type for thousands of years without the development of deep, significant and interdependent links. And so it has proved as the people and the ponies of Exmoor have lived, worked and played alongside one another over time.

For many of those years these interactions were undocumented and are too long ago to have been passed through the oral traditions. Sue has, however, delved deeply into more recent, accessible history, tracing stories through reports, newspaper articles and the papers of families whose lives were intimately connected with the ponies. She has also tracked and recorded oral histories from people who have lived part of those stories.

As a result of this painstaking research, in this book we have a rich, informative and entertaining trove, a cultural history as important to record as the natural history recounted in Sue's previous volume. By itself, it fulfils a role in collecting together and presenting a story that enriches our knowledge and understanding of the ponies and their role in our own history.

I suspect, however, that this book may prove to have one more role, which is to stimulate the recalling and reporting of yet more memories in its readers, the unearthing of yet more evidence of the bond between the people of Exmoor and their equine companions. Bring it on, if this book reminds you of a tale of your own or one told in the family, I'm sure Sue is ready to put together the follow-up volume!

Dr Alma Swan
Exeter, 2017

Sue Baker with Sutcombe So Charming (Mini).
Photo: Ian Baker.

Introduction

The first steps towards this book were taken many years ago, when I walked into the White Horse Inn in Exford. Sitting in the bar, an elderly gentleman at a neighbouring table engaged me in conversation. He thought I was a visitor but I explained that I was studying the Exmoor ponies. 'Well,' he said, 'I got some tales I can tell 'e 'bout they!' – and he did. From then on, whenever I could, I asked people to tell me their stories about the ponies: sometimes we would be leaning on gates at gatherings or inspections; sitting in a farmhouse kitchen or chatting at the Exmoor Pony Society exhibition unit. There were many other visits to Exmoor hostelries as well! Frequently, when giving talks, a member of the audience would approach me afterwards and say 'I remember my grandfather …' and such like. So part of this book is a selection of these Pony Tales.

I loved exploring the Exmoor pony world from the moment I began studying their ecology in 1974. After I finished my Ph.D., I evolved from ecologist to historian as their past fascinated me more and more. This book celebrates the stories and images that have emerged from old books and magazines, photos and oral recordings and various archives. It has been like being a detective, following up clues and sometimes it has taken years to find the full 'back story' of some snippet of information that set me wondering. When you finally make a breakthrough, it's a real 'buzz'.

Researching has been revolutionised by the amount of material that is searchable online: a significant proportion of *The Exmoor Pony Chronicles* would not have been possible before the advent of the Internet. We researchers and readers owe such a debt to those unsung heroes and heroines who undertake the often thankless task of digitising material for online archives. Hard to believe that I once said that I couldn't imagine I would ever make much use of the Internet!

One of the most enjoyable parts of exploring the history of the ponies has been visiting families who run moorland herds on Exmoor: hearing about their family histories and poring over old family photos has been such a privilege. Writing their stories has brought home to me that this book is as much about people as ponies; their histories are indivisible.

So, here is the result of following all those leads, heading off at tangents, being side-tracked – a miscellany of all things Exmoor pony: warfare, archaeology, family histories, celebrity and royal encounters, artists and illustrators, globetrotting, Exmoor crosses, pony sales, personalities – both human and equine, herd management, the Exmoor Pony Society, photographers, pony droving, the ponies in literature and poetry, Exmoors in zoos, at weddings and funerals, at risk and in arts and crafts. Enjoy your journey from 55 B.C. to the end of the twentieth century (with just a few glimpses of the twenty-first). I fervently hope that there will be someone amongst the readers of my book who will be inspired to continue the chronicling of the Exmoor Pony and Exmoor pony people.

Chariot Ponies

Their mode of fighting with their chariots is this: firstly, they drive about in all directions and throw their weapons and generally break the ranks of the enemy with the very dread of their horses and the noise of their wheels; and when they have worked themselves in between the troops of horse, leap from their chariots and engage on foot. Thus they display in battle the speed of horse, [together with] the firmness of infantry; and by daily practice and exercise attain to such expertness that they are accustomed, even on a declining and steep place, to check their horses at full speed, and manage and turn them in an instant and run along the pole, and stand on the yoke, and thence betake themselves with the greatest celerity to their chariots again.

From 'War Commentaries' by Julius Caesar, The Gallic Wars *Book 4 (55 BC)*

Julius Caesar's account of the speed and manoeuvrability of the British chariots gives rise to the question – what sort of horses were used to pull the chariots? They would have been ponies but there was no Latin word specifically for a pony, hence 'horse' in the accounts. If the British charioteers had tamed and trained the indigenous British ponies, then those that pulled the chariots into battles with the Romans probably looked virtually the same as today's Exmoor ponies.

This must have been the thinking behind the BBC deciding to have Exmoor ponies feature in their series for schools *Out of the Past*, in the episode *Immigrants to Britain* about the Celts; it was broadcast three times in October/November 1969. Students of the Royal (Dick) Veterinary College in Edinburgh were involved – who were the two ancient Britons in the chariot? Which ponies were used? How had the ponies been trained for their starring role on television?

Finding the answers to these questions meant following up a trail of clues that led me to an archaeologist, Professor John Coles, who was there on the day of filming and to the archive of archaeologist Professor Stuart Piggott; the archive yielded a letter from the BBC identifying both the warrior and the charioteer as Dave Buxton and Bill Adams: a 'eureka' moment. Eventually, I managed to trace Dave and he and Bill told me the full story.

The story of the chariot filming really starts in 1962, when James and Mary Speed decided to sell their ponies: a group of the veterinary students who had been running treks for them at Snoot Youth Hostel bought some of the Herd 2 mares and carried on. A staff member provided oversight of the project and in the latter part of the 1960s, this was Mr Bobby Jones.

1. Royal (Dick) veterinary students and two of Herd 2 Exmoor ponies recreated charioteering for the BBC. This photograph by Robin Fairweather was published in The Exmoor Pony *by Anthony Dent in 1970.*

2. Professor Terence Powell (left) and Professor Stuart Piggott with the Celts. Photo: Professor John Coles.

Around Easter time in 1969 Bobby Jones was

3. A trek fording the burn in front of the Snoot Youth Hostel. Photo: courtesy of Dave Buxton and Bill Adams.

4. Bill Adams having a practice run. Photo: courtesy of Dave Buxton and Bill Adams.

contacted by Felicity Kinross, a producer from the BBC, who wanted to film a Celtic chariot drawn by Exmoor ponies, as they resembled, as near as possible, the small pre-Roman ponies of Britain. Before taking the ponies down to Snoot in July 1969, ponies Cahoola and Fitchett were chosen as the best matched pair to be trained to pull the chariot. Students Bill Adams and Dave Buxton agreed to train the ponies.

An authentic Celtic chariot, with harness, was made by the coach-builders at the Edinburgh Co-operative stables. The stables housed the many horses that pulled the Co-op milk carts through the city in those days and also cared for the Queen's carriages and horses used on state occasions in Edinburgh. Horses were housed in loose boxes on two levels with a long concrete ramp for the horses to reach the upper storey. To guide them, the coach-builders were supplied with details of Celtic design by Professor Stuart Piggott, from the Department of Archaeology, at Edinburgh University. They constructed the chariot from the axle and front wheels of a horse-drawn hearse sitting under an oak platform. A long oak pole extended forwards with an oak yoke bolted to its far end. The two semi-circular sides were constructed of oak and woven basket work, the latter made by the Royal Edinburgh School for the Blind.

Dave and Bill recalled training the ponies to accept the chariot:

> *'Training of the ponies was for three weeks before filming and started with getting the two ponies used to long reins with the trainer walking behind. After this Fitchett and Cahoola were introduced to the yoke which was strapped*

5. The chariot ponies yoked together and about to be put to the chariot. Photo: Professor John Coles.

6. Bill Adams training the ponies to accept the yoke. The harness used consisted of a webbing girth with leather straps stitched on to it sitting just behind the forelimbs and this was combined with a webbing and leather breast strap to prevent the girth from being pulled backwards. The yoke was laid across the withers and buckled on to the girth strap. The reins were then attached to the bespoke bridles and fed back through rings on the topside of the yoke, after which the two nearside reins were combined into one as were those on the offside so that the driver could hold the appropriate ones in his left and right hands. Photo: courtesy of Dave Buxton and Bill Adams.

to the two girths. They both took quite a while to get used to this procedure and initially were inclined to turn outwards and rear up. When they were more at ease with the yoke it was bolted to the chariot and the ponies harnessed in place and led by the head to get them used to having the chariot behind them. Along the way there were quite a few moments of "excitement".

As the training progressed the ponies became more accustomed to the procedure but they were inclined to rotate their backsides out and away from the centre pole which caused them to panic and rear up.

On one occasion they broke the yoke's attachment to the centre pole. We felt that fitting traces may have helped to prevent Cahoola and Fitchett from swinging out and panicking. Liz Torbet, a fellow student who had just graduated, called in along with her parents. Her father, a farm worker, had ploughed with horses when a young man and agreed that traces could help. However, Professor Piggott was adamant that there was no archaeological evidence for their existence. It is interesting to speculate as to whether the fitting of traces might have made it easier and also whether early pre-Roman chariot harness did or did not employ them. With hindsight three weeks was not really long enough to sufficiently train the ponies but that was the schedule set by the BBC.'

7. During training – Dave Buxton and Liz Torbet (leading) with Bill Adams (driving). Photo: courtesy of Dave Buxton and Bill Adams.

On the first day of filming, archaeologists Professor Piggott, Professor Terence Powell and Dr John Cole were present. The BBC contingent included Felicity Kinross, the cameraman, sound man, wardrobe man and make-up lady. These last two were of course vital as they had to transform Dave and Bill into convincing Celts.

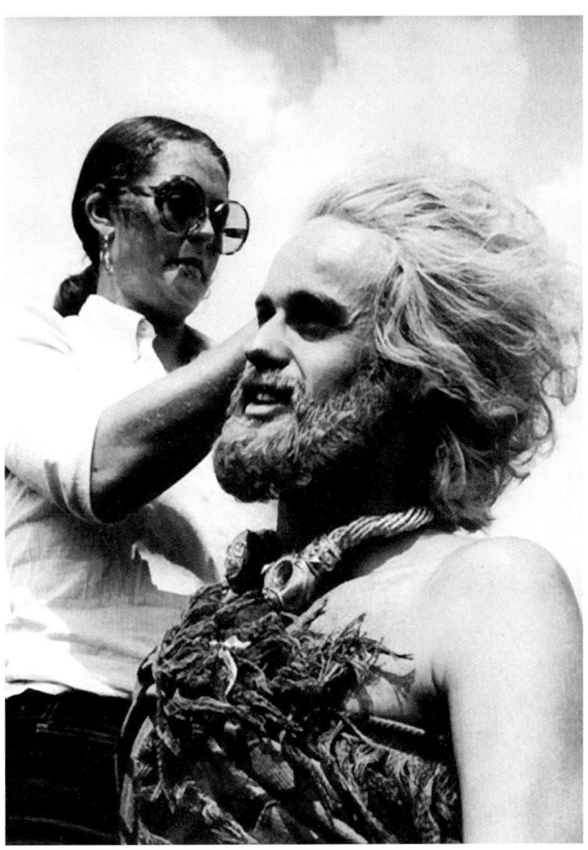

8. The BBC costume, wig and make-up transformation of Dave Buxton into Celtic warrior.
Photo: by Robin Fairweather

9. A practice session for Dave and Bill and the ponies on the first day of filming. Photo: Professor John Coles.

10. The padding that was added to the chariot floor was not enough to prevent jarring and further expletives! Photo: by Robin Fairweather.

11. Dave Buxton transformed into a Celtic warrior. Photo: by Robin Fairweather.

Once ready, the BBC began to film the chariot in action, but at the first attempt the ponies set off so sharply that the jerky start caused the standing warrior, Dave, *'to step ungraciously off the back of the chariot.'*

To film from the perspective of the chariot driver, the cameraman sat next to Bill who remembers:

> *'Sitting on the floor of the chariot going at speed with no suspension was very uncomfortable. The cameraman said something to the effect that it was ******* rough. At the end of the run the sound man, who had one of those furry microphones that can pick up a whisper "a mile away" asked him to refrain from the expletives!'*

Because the chariot was so difficult to drive without using traces, it wasn't possible to go fast enough safely. So a further day of filming took place a couple of weeks later, by which time Dave and Bill had left. A fellow student, Steve Smith was in charge at Snoot and helped out. This time a BBC stunt man took the reins and extra footage of the ponies going at speed was secured.

Sadly, there is no copy of the programme in the BBC archives and to date no other copies have come to light.

Postscript:

After filming was completed, the chariot was donated to the Museum of Antiquities in Edinburgh and displayed until the revamping of the building a few years ago. Dave and Bill think that they were paid £11 per week while training the ponies and the princely sum of about £11 pounds per day for the two days of filming. Trekking continued at Snoot until 1992, when the Youth Hostel was closed down. Since then the ponies have been kept in Edinburgh during term time and transported to Glendevon for summer trekking.

The Bolham Roman Fort Intaglio Ring

Might this be the first known depiction of an Exmoor pony?

In 2012 I visited Tiverton Museum and found myself looking at the exhibit about the excavations of a Roman fort at nearby Bolham. The model of the fort was very striking but a small dark object in the case in front caught my attention – or rather the photograph behind it.

The object was oval and very small, blackish in colour and the photograph showed what lay beneath the surface blackening – a pony. Carved stones such as this are known as intaglios and it would have been mounted on a ring.

The Devon Archaeological Society Proceedings No. 49, 1991 identified the gemstone as *'a heliotrope (bloodstone), a green jasper, flecked with red..... Its device is a horse in profile to the left. Its head is lowered as if the animal is about to graze.'*

Ian Marshman studied the Bolham Fort gems as a post-graduate student and he had told me:

> *'One of the things that makes the Tiverton gem so important is that it is thought to have been carved by an engraver at Bath. This is because the composition and engraving technique of the gem is similar to a group of gems which exhibit the hand of a single craftsman or workshop from Bath. They were found in a drain in the baths complex, which leads from both the sacred spring and the swimming bath. Thus debate still rages as to whether they were lost by bathers who had just bought them (they were fixed in rings with a natural resin that dissolved in water!) or if the engraver himself made an offering of a group of his gems. At any rate, it is very likely to have been engraved in Britain, most likely at Bath, and purchased by a soldier who was on leave at the spa. The Bath engraver is said to have been much more creative in his images of animals compared to those of humans or gods and goddesses, which are often almost mechanical reproductions of common images. So I think we can say that he clearly knew animals well and paid attention to getting their mannerisms and detail right.'*

12. *The intaglio ring found at the Roman Fort at Bolham near Tiverton.* Photo: Robert Wilkins, Institute of Archaeology, Oxford.

So, between AD 69 and AD 96, a soldier on leave buys himself a ring bearing an engraved gemstone intaglio from an engraver's workshop in Bath. He selects a design showing a horse; the proportions of the animal are such that this is actually what we today would call a pony. The image is a very natural representation which is unusual. This much we can be reasonably confident about.

However, this prompts many questions: did our soldier commission the engraving and ask for a pony design? What prompted the engraver to depict the pony so naturally? Had the engraver seen free-living ponies in Somerset or had the soldier and did he draw it for the engraver?

Of course, these are unanswerable questions. However, is it really that fanciful to imagine that the soldier or engraver had at some time seen wild ponies on the Somerset hills? If that informed the engraver's art, then perhaps this unknown craftsman from Roman Britain has given us the first ever pictorial record of an Exmoor pony.

The Withypool Miltons

In 1998, the passing of Fred Milton brought to an end the ownership of Exmoor ponies by the 'Withypool Miltons'. Fred left Herd 23 to Robin and Rex Milton of West Anstey: their great-grandfather and Fred's grandfather were brothers.

We'll start the story of Fred's family in 1807, when his great-great-grandfather Nicholas took on the tenancy of Landacre Farm which borders Withypool Common. This seems to be the first involvement with Exmoor ponies; Fred Milton wrote in the *Exmoor Review* 1968:

> *'He was interested in Exmoor ponies and kept a number on the Common. His sons also learned to look after them, especially young Nicholas II, who spent much of his time riding his pony, shepherding and looking after the stock of ponies.'*

Amidst many of our conversations about his family's ponies, Fred told me that his great-great-grandfather Nicholas had attended the stock dispersal sale when the Royal Forest was sold in 1818 and had purchased ponies.

'Young Nicholas' took over when his father retired in the early 1840s. Fred recorded that he wasn't popular with the other owners of ponies on the Common as he rigidly checked up on them.

Young Nicholas had three brothers, Samuel and John who were a little older and Robert, some years younger. John married Ann Steer in 1826 and they had two children, Mary Ann and another John, Fred's grandfather. In the *Exmoor Review* article Fred wrote:

> *'I met a dealer from Reading some years after he had retired from business, and he told me he had bought scores of Exmoor ponies from my*

13. Milton ponies with Landacre Farm in the distance.
Photo: John Keene.

14. Fred Milton in the 1980s.

grandfather and the family. "The pure-breds" he said, "with the well-known mealy muzzle, were outstanding, and surpassed all others in stamina."'

Fred's father Charles John Milton was born at Dadhayes Farm in 1870, the fifth of six children. Charles left school at the age of thirteen and went to work on Weatherslade Farm. The tenant, John Tucker, taught him about horses during the four years he was there. Next he worked in haulage at Exford and then worked at Newlands in Withypool, primarily working with horses. He returned to Dadhayes around 1890. Fred wrote:

'He took a very keen interest in Exmoor ponies and in 1890 played the responsible part in collecting, marking and selling for his father, uncles and brothers.'

John Milton of Partridge Arms, West Anstey (father of Robin and Rex) told me that Charles Milton supplied ponies to the surveyors of Withypool Parish, sometime in the 1800s.

In his *Exmoor Review* article, Fred tells of hard times selling ponies in the 1890s:

'During the 1880s the sales for Exmoor ponies were good, but early in the 1890s the prices at Bampton dropped considerably, although those at Bridgwater kept up.

The following year arrangements were made to rail the ponies from Dulverton to Bridgwater, but the overhead cost of transport and forage very nearly cancelled out the extra money made. The next year they drove the ponies on foot to Bridgwater, a two-day journey, lodging a night at Crowcombe, about half way. This also did not prove successful, the ponies being tired and sore-footed. So it was decided to revert to Bampton. Nevertheless contact had been made with dealers from the north, who promised to come to Bampton in future. So the sales improved again and stayed steady for several years. The colts of two to three years in age were in demand and sold for pit ponies. The fillies also went well for cross-breeding for riding ponies and light carthorses.'

Fred told me that the last of the ponies to be sold for pit work was in 1919.

In 1900, Charles Milton took on the tenancy of Knighton Farm and did well. He was married to Mary Bushen in 1905. On marrying, Charles bought Weatherslade Farm and Frederick Charles J. (Fred) was born there in 1907. He grew up in the midst of an extended family many of whom were involved with rearing and selling ponies. Naturally, he learned to ride when very young and like many local children, rode to school in Withypool at ten years old, leaving his pony at George Hooper's stable, behind the Royal Oak inn.

Fred regaled me once with memories of coming home from school in summer and

15. Fred Milton judging, at the Royal Bath & West Show, in 1973. Photo: Exmoor Pony Society Archive.

16. Part of the original farmhouse at Weatherslade, far left, adjoining one of the barns.

17. Foreground L-R: David Mansell, Fred Milton and Rex Milton at Weatherslade after the gathering in the late 1980s.

saddling up his pony to go shepherding out on Withypool Common. He said:

> *'My grandfather, father and uncles were very keen on keeping ponies and taught me all about conformation. On summer evenings we would ride out and look at the ponies. They would point out to me which were good suckers – even at two weeks old they would say "that'll be a prize winner."'*

Fred left school early, rather reluctantly, to work on the farm, primarily shepherding out on the moors. He also had to drive cattle to summer grazing, often miles away plus of course the annual gathering of the ponies and being one of the drovers to get them 'on the hoof' to Bampton.

He told me that the Milton family always undertook their own droving right up until the 1930s; presumably transporting animals by lorry put an end to this tradition. John Milton told of how he remembered, in the late 1930s, when he was seven or eight, the ponies being taken down to Bampton Fair. It involved starting at about six a.m. in the dark, with lanterns, and nine or ten riders would drive 50 - 60 ponies; it took about three hours for them to reach Bampton. After crossing some fields, they would drive the ponies through the streets to the auction field.

Fred explained that in years when yields from other stock were poor, the money from selling ponies was a very welcome addition to the hill farmer's income. In Martin Hesp's film, 'The Exmoor Pony', Fred explained *'My great-grandfather, grandfather and uncle reared ponies for their livelihood, not just as a hobby.'* However, when prices dropped in the depression of the '30s, Charles Milton wanted to get rid of the ponies but Fred wouldn't agree and selected the best of the mares and kept them living free.

There seems to have been no Milton involvement in the Exmoor Pony Society when it was formed in 1920 and Herd 23 registrations did not start until 1938. Fred used two stallions to found his registered herd, one from Herd 1, owned by the Hawkridge Westcotts, and the other was called Bradymoor, one of the Herd 48 stallions owned by the Williams family. Fred took an active role in the E.P.S., serving as President more than once and was both a judge and inspector.

I was told that Fred was so bonded with his ponies that he could go out onto Bradymoor and call them to him. Certainly I remember many gatherings when, once the ponies were trapped in the funnel near Kitridge Lane or back in the yard at Weatherslade, Fred, despite his years, would walk amongst them, obviously delighted to be with them.

Fred and Ena didn't have any children so when advancing years made running the farm and the pony herd too much to cope with alone, Robin and Rex Milton from West Anstey began helping. After at least five generations of the Miltons being pony breeders, Fred was anxious that his beloved Herd 23 should not leave the Milton family and so bequeathed it to the 'Milton boys'. Robin did not share his brother's interest in the ponies and it is Rex who runs the Milton Exmoor pony herd today.

18. Herd 23 at the end of the gathering in 2007.

Did an Exmoor Ever Meet Sir Walter Scott?

When I was researching in the Devon Record Office at Exeter, I came upon an intriguing letter to Sir Thomas Acland from his brother-in-law Matthew Fortescue. Writing from Cameron, in Fife, dated 24 February 1818, Matthew complained:

'I quite forgot when I was last with you to mention about the Exmoor pony. I find he is so wild that he will be useless to me, which is very unfortunate after all the trouble and expense I have had with him. First you see I can never put a child upon him. Second, I have no place where I can turn him to graze and he eats as much hay for me as a big horse without any hopes of him becoming useful as a shooting pony or a steady beast for [illegible name] *on a hot day instead of walking. It is therefore ridiculous my hanging on to him any longer tho I am very loth to part with him. What shall I do with him? I was thinking that as you want a pony for Walter Scott it would not cost you more money to have this one cut and sent to the riding school to be perfectly broken than what would be the expense and risk of sending down another. If you are determined on sending one I know the person at the Edinburgh Riding School and have no doubt but that I could get him to take the pony in hand and break him perfectly. It would be highly ridiculous for me to go to such expense for myself as I could buy a bigger pony for what he has already cost me. But if Walter Scott must have an Exmoor I do not know that, considering expense and risk, you could send him one cheaper.'*

19. Sir Thomas Dyke Acland, 10th Baronet from a drawing by G. Richmond.

20. Sir Walter Scott and his dogs by Henry Raeburn circa 1820s.

Upon reading this, my immediate question was whether this Walter Scott was in fact the famous Sir Walter Scott. Could it be that this literary giant had really received an Exmoor pony from the Acland family?

The Abbotsford Collection of Scott's papers includes a letter to Sir Walter Scott from Sir Thomas Acland about the proposed gift of an Exmoor pony. Sir Thomas's hand-writing is very difficult to read in several places (indicated by a question mark for each illegible word in the transcript that follows).

Killerton
Sep 27 1817

My Dear Sir,

You once did our Western Borders the honor to ? and me your acceptance of an Exmoor Pony, if I could find a ? opportunity of conveying him to your neighbourhood. I have lately received from the Forest a dark chestnut of great beauty with all his visible honors about him unharmed, and promising great strength, tho' his stature is small and his ? slight and not inelegant.

If you will do me the favour to fulfil your part of the engagement as I am now ready to fulfil mine. I shall have an excellent occasion to send him safely together with one of his fellows who is about to take his passage in a ? ? to my brother-in-law Mat Fortescue who is established in Fife, having married one of the Christies of Scoonie. His name is to be "Pixie" a class of beings who have not yet entirely deserted their favourite haunts on the skirts of our mountains and glens and who are pretty nearly allied to your "Brownies ". If you prefer the latter name as ? more intelligible for Scottish ears, for I believe ours is a provincial title, we have no objection and I am sure he will have none, to the translation.

I believe you know his race is perfectly wild, receiving neither benefit or injury at the hand of man till they are taken at their full growth for service and I observe ? Leach classes them as a distinct and indigenous species. It is astonishing how many hours these little animals will carry one of our large "hill-country fellows" in a day up hill and down hill at his own pace, without apparent fatigue. They are perfectly sure-footed and as for a ?, they will foot it from hag to hag, with the "? ?-? ? " ? ? ? - so that if you will accept my little Pixie's services - in the first place ? of my Foresters (soon alas to be so no more thanks to Acts of Parliament and ? Economy I will be highly flattered and ? I hope he will repay you by his fidelity to yourself as a Shooting Pony, by his agility and grace under one of your children.

I need not tell you, who are a Forester yourself, that not a hair of his head ?? of his ? must be ? ?

We are all anxious for Rob Roy's appearance in the ? If you should be able to ? the author do tell him that he is as ? to the good-humour of our fire-sides as the good Harvest and ? ? ? no longer.

Remember Lady A. and myself ? to Mrs Scott and ? " the Jocks Daughter" as well as to all Edinburgh friends who recollect us. I believe ? ? in you ? ? ? Sincere

T.D. Acland

21. Transcript of the letter from Sir Thomas Dyke Acland to Sir Walter Scott. (?=unreadable)

So, it was the famous Sir Walter Scott to whom Matthew Fortescue had referred in his letter. Sir Thomas Acland's letter to Scott confirms the intention to make this gift and it is obvious that Sir Thomas Acland viewed the acceptance of a pony as a considerable honour and that he admired Scott and his novels; but was that intention ever carried out?

In *Notes and Index to Sir Herbert Grierson's Edition of the Letters of Sir Walter Scott*, published in 1979, Dr James Clarkson Corson recorded that Sir Thomas Acland had presented Sir Walter Scott with a Dartmoor forest stallion, Cremona, in 1817.

So, did Sir Thomas send two ponies on separate occasions? Did Matthew Fortescue manage to rid himself of his wild Exmoor pony? Sadly, it is unlikely that we will ever know the answers. Once again, we have to rue the day that so many of the Acland papers were lost in a fire at Holnicote House on Exmoor. Perhaps within those records of the pony herd would have been some ledger that noted the transporting of Pixie to Scotland.

The Hawkridge Westcotts

The Hawkridge Westcotts originated from North Molton and we'll start their story with William Holcombe Westcott who was born in 1817 at Barton Farm. He married a Dulverton girl called Isabella Saunders in 1836 and at some point after 1851 the family moved to Rowe Farm at Hawkridge. They had eight children, the youngest of whom was Richard (Dick) Saunders born in 1854. William Holcombe Westcott was breeding Exmoor ponies in about 1891.

Dick Westcott married Mary Fry from Old Shute, Dulverton and they rented Zeal Farm, also in Hawkridge, from the Carnarvon Estate. He also bred Exmoor ponies and attended the meeting at the Red Lion in Dulverton in November 1920 that led to the formation of the Exmoor Pony Society; he was actively involved right from the start.

Dick and Mary had three children, Charles Maurice in 1879, Sydney John in 1881 and Geraldine Mary in 1882. Sydney eventually farmed Zeal and Geraldine married Tom Pring who farmed Champson at Molland. Neither Sydney nor Geraldine had any children. Maurice married Salome Bawden in 1902 and they moved to Woodlands Farm at East Anstey where they produced no fewer than eleven children!

Mary's diary for 1891-1892 has survived. Her October 1891 entries include:

'28th October Tuesday to North Molton Fair. Back home and marked the ponies ready for Bampton Fair and took them to Old Shute.
29th October Thursday morning Dick, Maurice, Sydney, Fred and Frank went to Bampton Fair.
30th October Friday – took the Rutherford ponies and Bessie's sucker to station and trucked them at Dulverton Station.
31st October Mr. Tapp and Mr. (space) *were here to see Exmoor ponies.*
3rd November Dick and Maurice went to Brushford Market and trucked the three ponies for Yorkshire.'

Mary died in 1894 and Dick Westcott married twice afterwards but with no further children.

Maurice began breeding ponies around 1915/16 when living at East Anstey. His registrations in the National Pony Stud Book show that he had stock from his father and from the Acland herd. Once the Exmoor Pony Society was formed, his herd numbers were 1 and 28; the fifth edition

Left: *22. Richard Saunders Westcott.* Photo: courtesy of Margaret Rawle née Westcott.

Below: *23. Sydney John Westcott with his pen of Herd 1 ponies, from Zeal, at Bampton Fair pre-1924.* Photo: courtesy of Margaret Rawle née Westcott.

Bottom: *24. Charles Maurice Westcott.* Photo: courtesy of Margaret Rawle née Westcott.

25. *Sid Westcott selling a sucker at Bampton Fair in the 1940s.* Photo: courtesy of Linda Westcott.

of the E.P.S. Stud Book records that he also purchased some foundation mares from James Milton of Withypool. Herd 1 was passed on to Sydney Junior (known as Sid) and Herd 28 passed first to Bob and later to Charlie.

In 1929, Sydney Senior bought Draydon Farm, Dulverton for his brother Maurice and his family. Not all the eleven children went to live at Draydon – Sid, Bob, Richard, Mabel, Winifred, Lucy and Muriel stayed with their father at Draydon whilst Charlie, Doris and Joyce went to live at Zeal with their uncle. At Draydon, Sid also registered ponies in Herd 10 (the number having been reallocated by the E. P. S. as the original herd 10 had closed); it later passed to Bob after Sid's death in 1978.

An article 'It's Fun for the Westcotts' in *The Illustrated London News* of 16 November 1946 featured the gathering of Herd 1. Maurice and sons Sid and Charlie are pictured catching their ponies back at one of the farms. The article tell us: *'Farmer Westcott is so proud of his herd that he grazes it on 400 acres of moorland which are fenced to prevent straying and to safeguard the stock from breeding with other ponies which are not up to Westcott standard.'*

Following Maurice's death in 1958, Sid was most definitely in charge at Draydon. He was also an inspector for the Exmoor Pony Society and advised on the management of the Acland herd. When Sid died in 1978, Herd 1 was closed, Draydon was sold and Bob and Lucy, with Joyce,

Far left: *26. Robert (Bob) Westcott probably at Exford Show in the 1970s.* Photo: John Keene.

Left: *27. Charlie Westcott.*
Photo: The Mary Etherington Archive.

moved to Tippacott Farm above Brendon where Bob continued with Herd 10 until retiring in 2001 and giving four foals and a yearling to his nephew Julian.

Charlie was the only one of the brothers to have a family of his own. He married Linda Tyndale-Powell in 1955 and they had sons Oliver, Peter and Julian. Linda later bred Exmoors in her own right (Herd 7) and became both an E.P.S. judge and inspector, like Charlie. During World War II, Charlie was a member of the Exmoor Mounted Home Guard. For shepherding at Zeal, Charlie rode an unregistered Exmoor pony called Rustle as it was low enough to reach down and turn a sheep that was on its back. He also hunted on Rustle. Mary Etherington had given Rustle to Charlie in payment for grazing her Exmoor ponies with the Westcott ponies on Halscombe Allotment. Lilo Lumb also had ponies running with Herd 1.

In 1947, Charlie and Stan Tucker took ponies to North Holland Zoo by boat from Dover (see page 104). The export of these ponies had been arranged by Mary Etherington.

A few years later, Charlie took the Herd 1 stallion Crackshot I up to Scotland and released him onto the Pentland Hills to join Mary Etherington's ponies. Mary later presented Charlie and Linda with a colour pastel picture of Crackshot by J. Baillie, as a wedding present. In 1972 Charlie and family left Zeal and bought some land and a barn that they converted at Higher Clitsom, Roadwater. Linda also had some land nearby at Hook Hill where she had her Exmoors. The family then moved to Hook Hill Farm in 1976 and on to nearby Mill Reef Farm in 1999.

Charlie died in 2013 aged 102. Julian and wife April, with daughters Abbie and Robyn, have enthusiastically carried on the family's long tradition of breeding and showing Exmoor ponies. In 2007, Julian and April re-started Herd 1 registrations after nearly fifty years of dormancy; Abbie is continuing Herd 10 and Robyn Herd 28.

28. Herd 1 at West Hollowcombe Farm, Hawkridge pre-1945, having been gathered from Halscombe Allotment and Lords. Photo: courtesy of Margaret Rawle née Westcott.

29. Gathering Herd 1. Photo: courtesy of Margaret Rawle née Westcott.

30. Sid Westcott with Heatherman.
Photo: courtesy of Margaret Rawle née Westcott.

31. Skyman. Photo: Exmoor Pony Society Archive.

32. Herd 1 ponies at Draydon. Photo: John Keene.

The Hawkridge Westcotts were hugely influential within the Exmoor pony breed both through their own ponies and because Sid Westcott was very much involved in the management of the Acland herd; he is often credited with restoring the Acland herd after the end of World War II when it was in disarray.

It was the stallion Heatherman, bred by Lilo Lumb (see page 103) that Sid Westcott considered near perfection. Heatherman was used in the 1950s to sire Herd 1 stallions Hawkridge Man and Skyman. He was the model for the Beswick Exmoor Pony (see page 129).

Fred Westcott, born in 1871, was the son of Thomas Westcott and cousin to Maurice Westcott. As a child he lived at Cockram, Hawkridge and then went to live at Zeal, helping his uncle Dick on the farm. By 1901, he had moved to Knaplock Farm on the edge of Winsford Hill, as a shepherd. In 1908, Fred married Polly Trebble and by 1911 they were farming Tarr Farm at Tarr Steps. Fred and Polly had five children, Irene, Herbert, Thomas, Sidney and Muriel. I met up with Muriel, aged 96, who told me about life at Tarr Farm:

> *'I went to school in Hawkridge which was about one and a half miles away and it meant crossing the bridge every day. Sometimes I had a lift from my brother and he would ride his motorbike over the bridge.'*

Muriel's father Fred owned some pure-bred Exmoor ponies, probably no more than ten she thought. They ran free on Bradley Hams with

some of the Acland herd. He also had one or two to ride at home. He kept the ponies just to sell one or two a year. When the Exmoor Pony Society formed, Fred Westcott's herd number was 58. The Historical section of the Exmoor Pony Society Stud Book shows that his foundation stock were homebred plus individual ponies from the Aclands, Daniel Evans and a stallion from Earl Fortescue.

Muriel recalled that Fred rode an Exmoor for farm work and gathered his own ponies back to the farm each year before Bampton Fair; she didn't think they were brought in along with the Acland herd.

Fred Westcott died in 1925 when Muriel was five. According to E.P.S. records, Polly continued the pony herd for a few years but there were no further registrations.

Left: 33. *Fred and Polly Westcott.*
Photo: courtesy of Muriel Mason née Westcott.

34. *This treasured photograph, taken by Alfred Vowles (a regular visitor to Tarr Farm) shows Fred Westcott riding one of his Exmoor ponies at Tarr Steps.* Photo: courtesy of Muriel Mason née Westcott.

John Leech 1817–1864

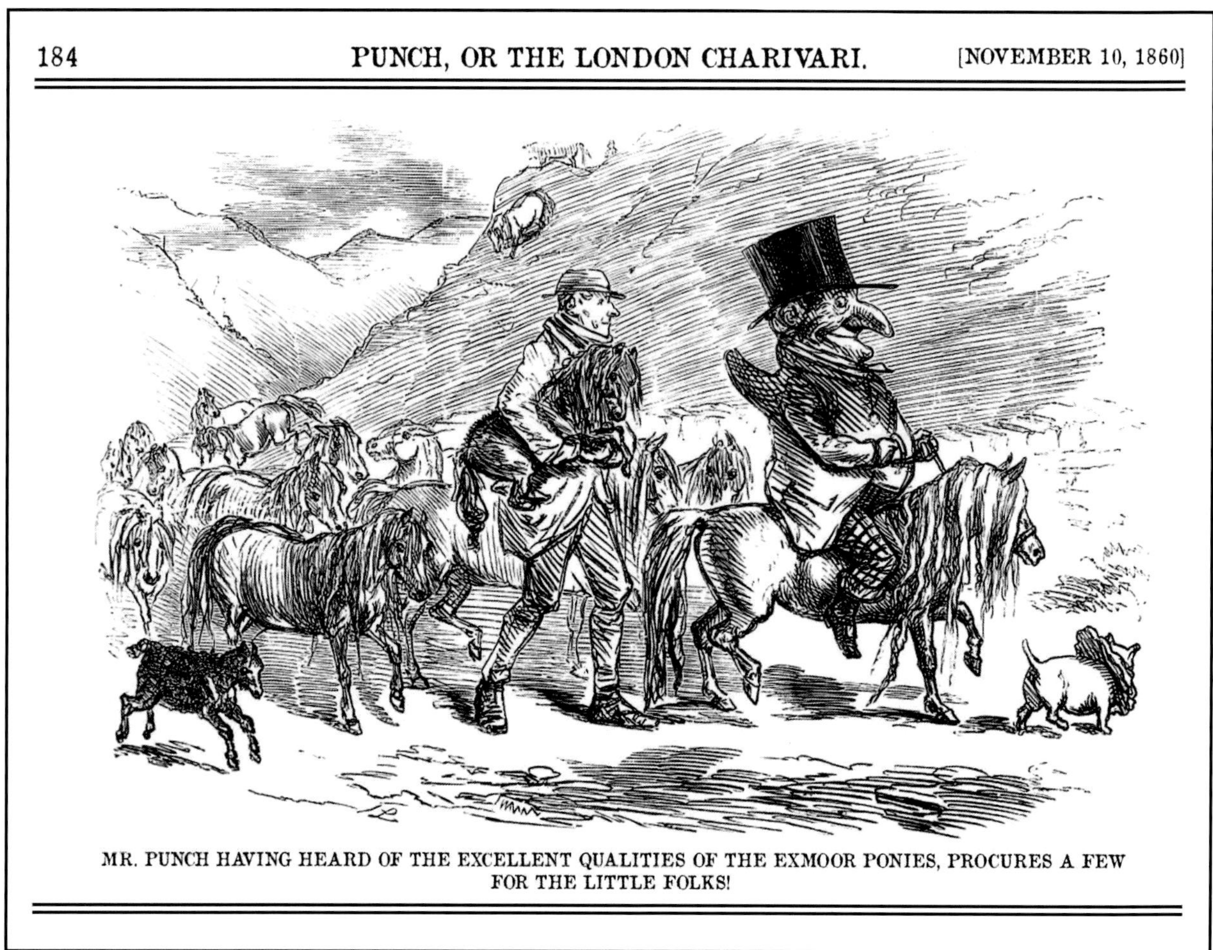

184 PUNCH, OR THE LONDON CHARIVARI. [NOVEMBER 10, 1860]

MR. PUNCH HAVING HEARD OF THE EXCELLENT QUALITIES OF THE EXMOOR PONIES, PROCURES A FEW FOR THE LITTLE FOLKS!

35. This cartoon seems to be John Leech's only depiction of Exmoor ponies.

The issue of *Punch* published on 10 November 1860 included a cartoon in which John Leech featured Exmoor Ponies in the illustrious company of Mr Punch.

John Leech was born in London in 1817 and educated at Charterhouse. At sixteen, he began training to be a doctor at St Bartholomew's Hospital. Whilst a student there, he produced excellent anatomical drawings and this led to portrait commissions. Art took over from medicine and he left to pursue a career as an artist. He published various pamphlets illustrated with his drawings of ordinary people in the streets of London and often humorous. He began providing illustrations for magazines such as *Bells Life* in London, the *London Magazine* and the *Illustrated London News*, during the 1840s.

However, he is best remembered for his illustrations and cartoons for the magazine *Punch* which was launched in 1841. Over a period of twenty-three years, around three thousand of his drawings and six hundred of his cartoons were published in *Punch*. It has been said that much of the success of the magazine, between the mid-1840s and mid 1860s, can be attributed to the impact of Leech's artwork.

He was a skilled social observer and gentle satirist, at times focusing readers' attention on social injustice; equally though, he could also be light-hearted, his drawings exposing the humour to be found in more well-to-do Victorian England. He was a close friend of Charles Dickens.

New Zealand

In an old Exmoor Pony Society Newsletter I came across a brief reference to Exmoor ponies having been exported to Hawkes Bay in North Island, New Zealand in the 1800s. I was intrigued. Would it be possible to find any trace of these ponies? The Hawkes Bay Museum is situated in the town of Napier and I contacted their archivist Gail Pope. She located an article *'Ponies in Hawkes Bay – as told by Mrs Olga Hudson, née Carlyon in 1950'* about the Carlyon ponies: *'Major George Gwavas Carlyon, who in his early years served with the British Army at the Crimea War, emigrated to New Zealand in 1856. With him came his wife and family, cattle for the property he intended to buy, and moorland ponies from which his famous strain were produced.'*

George Carlyon was born near Hartland on the North Devon coast; prior to emigrating, he lived at Tregrehan, near St Austell in Cornwall. So his 'moorland ponies' could have come from Bodmin Moor, Dartmoor or Exmoor. Shipping ponies to New Zealand in the mid-1800s was no easy task and the journey must have been a dreadful experience for the animals. The ponies would have been lowered into the ship's hold by winch and pulley, much as depicted by an early settler in New Zealand, William Webster Hawkins, who drew such a scene in his diary in 1867.

Olga Hudson's article also relates that George Carlyon made a visit to England during the 1860s in order to purchase more cattle, to improve his herd, and specifically to find a good stallion to take back to New Zealand: *'In London, he soon found a stallion belonging to an aristocrat who daily drove him around the streets and parks in his carriage. The horse was a cream Exmoor* with black mane and tail, just what he was looking for, but the owner would not sell at any price. Carlyon purchased cattle and other horses, for which he arranged accommodation on the ship that he was returning in. A few days before sailing, the Exmoor stallion became mysteriously lame in the hind quarters, and the owner offered him to Carlyon for breeding purposes only! On the day before sailing, the gypsy groom arrived at the ship offering to look after the cattle and horses, at no charge, during the journey. Carlyon signed him on, and he stayed at Gwavas for many years.*

Legend has it that the gypsy was responsible for the unsolved lameness. In Hawkes Bay the stallion quickly recovered from his lameness. He proved a great success in the breeding sphere, stamping his good quality and markings on all his progeny. The breed became famous in Hawkes Bay and beyond, and pony breeders kept the strain going for some years after the stud was sold.'

Note: * This was obviously not from one of the pure-bred herds.

36. 'Picton Wharf – shipping the horses to Wellington, Tommy going aloft' drawn by William Webster Hawkins in 1867. Picture from the William Hawkins Collection, Alexander Turnbull Library, Wellington, N.Z.

Unless George Carlyon's original shipment of 'moorland ponies' included any Acland Exmoors, it would seem unlikely that any pure-bred Exmoors were taken to New Zealand's North Island. Certainly, if any were, the genes were quickly diluted. Sources of information about the feral Kaimanawa horses of North Island frequently state that Exmoor ponies contributed to their genetic make-up (because Carlyon ponies, crossed with Welsh stallions imported by Sir Donald Mclean produced the Comet breed and during the 1870s, McLean released a Comet stallion and several mares on the Kaingaroa Plains – these animals contributed to the Kaimanawa population). Given that in all probability, all the imported 'Exmoors' were crossbred, this suggestion that the true Exmoor pony directly played a part in the creation of the Kaimanawa Horse is extremely doubtful.

This might not be the end of the story of Exmoors and New Zealand though. Amongst the many British emigrants to New Zealand was John Barton Arundel Acland, the sixth son of Sir Thomas Dyke Acland (the Sir Thomas who conserved the true Exmoor ponies when the Royal Forest of Exmoor was sold in 1818).

John Acland and his friend Charles Tripp set sail for South Island on the ship the Royal Stuart in 1854. They arrived in Lyttleton in January 1855 and started a sheep station at Mount Peel. This was 110,000 acres of high sheep country and their aim was to reproduce 'the best of England in the Antipodes'. Their partnership lasted until 1862 and once the station was solely John Acland's, he named the homestead 'Holnicote' after the Acland family's house on Exmoor.

No cargo list survives for that sailing of the *Royal Stuart* so we will never know whether John Acland took any of the family's ponies to New Zealand with him or had any sent out later. Perhaps though it is not completely fanciful to imagine him shepherding out on the hills of Mount Peel, on a true Exmoor.

India?

An item in the *Western Morning News*, 9 May 1930, tells us that the Exmoor Pony Society received an enquiry about sending Exmoor ponies to India. The Minute Books for the time are sadly lacking in any further information. However, amongst the photographs in the Exmoor Pony Society archive is the one reproduced here, with an Exmoor-like animal second from the right. Tibetan ponies can sometimes exhibit this primitive colouring but why is this picture in the archive?

37. Nothing is known as to where or when this photo was taken.
Photo: Exmoor Pony Society Archive.

The Thornes of Twitchen

James Thorne started his herd of Exmoor ponies in 1865 when living at Brightworthy Farm; Brightworthy had grazing rights on Withypool Common, which bordered the farm, so it is likely but not certain that his ponies roamed the Common.

James married Mary Milton in 1868 and they had seven children. One of their sons, William (born in 1872), gave a talk in 1945 and said:

> *'My father lived at Brightworthy, sixty-five years ago. He kept from 15 to 20 breeding mares and a stallion. He used sometimes to take as many as 50 ponies to Bampton Fair, by road all the way. He was a speculating kind of man. I daresay he would have bought in some to sell again. I've heard him say he attended Bampton Fair every single fair – without a break – for 50 years. His ponies were always pure bred. He used to ride out on the hill and come home at night and say to us: "I've seen a beautiful sucker to-day. I must see if I can't buy that."'*

38. James Thorne. Photo: courtesy of Mary Werner née Thorne.

In 1880, the family moved to Higher House Farm in Twitchen, a few miles away, and grazed their ponies on the moorland enclosure of Litton's Moor (also called Lyddons Common) a couple of miles from the farm.

William Thorne married Mary Annie Dufty Newton and they had a son Leo and a daughter Doris. William became a founder member of the Exmoor Pony Society in 1921 and was allocated herd number 44. He was also an active member of the Exmoor Horn Sheep Breeders' Society and became a Justice of the Peace. As well as farming Higher House, he bought and sold horses and ponies.

His son Leo wrote in the 1974 Exmoor Pony Society Newsletter:

> *'One of the best ponies that my father bred that I can remember quite well was a stallion called Jan Ridd. In 1913 the late Lord Poltimore, of Court Hall, started a herd of Exmoors and he persuaded my father to sell him Jan Ridd. Lord Poltimore died in 1917 when he looked like building up a fine herd and they were all sold: one can only say the pity of it all.'*

39. William and Mary Thorne with Leo. Photo: courtesy of Mary Werner née Thorne.

William and Mary's son Leo had been born in 1904 and he inherited the farm and the ponies when William died in 1946. He continued the pony herd, but with small numbers. He married Phyllis Mary Pugsley and they had two children,

Above: 41. *Mary Werner with two year-old Treasure Time Lass at Exford Show in 2011.*

Left: 40. *Leo Thorne at Exford Show in 1960.*
Photo: courtesy of Mary Werner née Thorne.

Below: 42. *Herd 44 on Littons Moor.*
Photo: courtesy of Mary Werner née Thorne.

Mary and Anthony.

Mary recalled that her father Leo had one particular old mare who in 1957, when she came in season, took herself off to Withypool Common and ran with Forest, one of the Milton stallions; subsequently, her foal Mountain Lass III ended up branded 23/52 in error.

Leo Thorne was very active in the Exmoor Pony Society; he was both an Inspector and a Judge and served as President in 1975. He both showed and judged ponies, sheep and cattle. He also rode in point to point races (needless to say, not on an Exmoor pony!)

Leo died in 1982 leaving just two mares, Mountain Lass VI and Mountain Lass VII, daughters of the misbranded Herd 44 mare; both were completely unhandled. Leo had been most concerned that Herd 44 wouldn't come to an end and so daughter Mary and her husband Rick Werner took on the responsibility for the ponies. Mary recalled that it took half a day to get a head collar on one mare and three weeks for the other! After a further three weeks work leading the mares, Mary and Rick walked them from Twitchen to Knighton Farm at Withypool to visit Creenagh Mitchell's stallion Dazzling Boy. The stallion First Time was one of the resulting foals.

Mary and Rick still run Herd 44 on Littons Moor at Sandyway.

Robert Smith of Simonsbath

This engraving illustrated an article 'Improved Exmoors – Bred by Mr. Robert Smith of Emmett's Grange, South Molton' in *The Sporting Review* in 1867. The writer says:

'Lunette, the bay mare pony on the right, foaled in 1860, is by Bobby out of Brunette, a picked Exmoor pony mare, with some of the oldest blood of the Hills in her veins, and a dash of the Katerfelto. Lunette. who stands 13 hands high, was sold by private contract to Mr. Milward, and exhibited by him at the Salisbury Meeting of the Bath and West of England Society in 1866 ... The other pony in the plate is The Chieftain, also foaled in 1860, and by Bobby out of Nellie by Greyling ... The Chieftain was only exhibited on one occasion—viz., at the Royal Society's Meeting at Plymouth, in 1865, in the Exmoor Pony Stallion Class, where he was not noticed ... Bobby, the sire of both those ponies, and hence the improvement traced in their title, was bred by that capital sportsman, the late Mr. Ramsay, of Barnton.'

Robert Smith was a well-known, progressive agriculturalist of his time; he farmed at Burleigh-on-the-Hill, near Oakham, Leicestershire, where he was famous for his Shorthorn herd of cattle and Leicester flock of sheep. In 1848 he moved to Exmoor to take up the post of Agent and Steward, working for Frederic Knight. John Knight, father of Frederic, had purchased the Royal Forest of Exmoor from the Crown in 1818 and handed control of his estate to his son in 1841. In *The Heritage of Exmoor*, Roger Burton says: *'On his arrival, Smith moved into and took the tenancy of Emmetts Grange, one of the new farms, together with 674 acres; combining his duties as Agent with the equally demanding challenge to become a hill farmer.'* By 1851, Robert Smith had 120 horses; at his final stock sale though, only 40 cobs, Exmoor ponies and galloways were auctioned. Robert Smith was

43. *An engraving, by Edward Hacker from a painting by Edward Corbet, of 'improved Exmoors'. An illustration from* The Sporting Review, *1867, edited by 'Craven', John William Carleton. Edward Hacker (1813 - 1905) was a line engraver who specialised in animal and sporting prints. He produced a number of engravings of pictures drawn by artist Edward Corbet (1815 - 1890) who was known for his naive paintings of farm animals published in the* Farmer's Magazine *and for paintings of horses in the* Sporting Magazine.

Agent and Steward until dismissed or resigned in March 1861 but continued to farm Emmetts Grange until 1868.

The 1867 *Sporting Review* article relates:

'Mr. Smith, who has now been for twenty years on the Moor, began with Mr. Knight's ponies, for whom he was the agent; but he subsequently established a stud on his own farm, and the two herds or drives are now entirely distinct. His notion from the first was a nick with the short-legged thoroughbred horse, so as to bring cobs and galloways ranging from thirteen-three to fourteen-three inches high. The first result of this experiment was tested by a sale at Simonsbath, a village in the centre of the Hills, where many a wrestling match has come off, many a keg been tapped, and many a haunch done justice to, with all the keen enjoyment for which stolen pleasures are proverbial. Bampton Fair, the autumn pony fair of the Hills, was the next place of sale, and then to suit more distant customers the lots were brought up to Taunton. Here, however, the interests of Mr. Knight and Mr. Smith were divided, the latter eventually making Bristol the mart for his galloways, where they are still sold, and Mr. Knight bringing up his ponies to Reading, until last season, when they were put up at Edgbaston, near Birmingham.

At starting, Mr. Smith made use of anything that was handy, and he began on the way to better things with Old Port as a sire. This horse was beautifully bred, being by Sir Hercules out of Beeswing; but he was nothing more than a cast-off, and, from what we remember of his tall, narrow frame when he ran for the Derby, anything but a suitable cross for the Exmoor pony mares. He was followed by his son, the little steeplechase horse, Exmoor; but the produce of both these was too high and light, and, though now and then one would make thirty, or even occasionally fifty guineas, too many stopped at the tens and 'teens. Then came Bobby .... but the subsequent services of an Arabian led to no very profitable results, and the experiment was soon abandoned. Small thoroughbred horses, with short joints and smart action, have since been settled down to, and at the recent sale, Nutshell by Nutwith took the top figures.

When we saw Bobby in the North of Devon, some eight or nine years since, we thus wrote of his value as a cross: "Certainly, as far as looks can go, his use is well warranted. But Bobby's character is even better still. He is the sire of many famous hacks in Nottinghamshire, and some of the best of those clever cobs Mr. Milward annually brings up have been got by him ... The only question is, whether the cross with bigger animals may not gradually destroy the true character of the pony? But, as it is, the Exmoor has been 'improved' to the picture we now see. The original moor or mountain pony was a very different animal, with neither the size, power, nor handsome appearance of the present representative of the race."'

Mr. Robert Smith has a very plenteous crop of "Bobby" foals this year from the Exmoor pony mares, which he purchased from the stock of Mr. Knight, M.P. Nearly the whole of them are bays, and generally with a small star on the forehead. He has not hired St. Michael, but Rangoon, an Arab charger, who was ridden in the Crimea, and intends to try a second edition of that Eastern cross to which the Knight Exmoors owe so much of their celebrity. Magnet, a grandson of Lanercost, has also been used, and thus the place of the renowned "Bobby", who has been at his old quarters near Newark-upon-Trent this season, bids fair to be filled up. Mr. Smith's Exmoor cobs will be sold at Taunton this year on the last Saturday in September, and Mr. Knight's Exmoor ponies which are being broke to the saddle (a great boon to purchasers) will, we believe, be sold about the same time, either there or at Bridgwater.

44. Extract from The Illustrated London News, *29 June* 1861

Australia

In the Exmoor Pony Society Newsletter 1981, Penelope Power wrote about two Exmoor stallions having been imported into Australia in the mid 1800s by a James Yeo. I was lucky enough to locate one of the Australian branch of the Yeo family, Ann Gugler, and learn more about these ponies.

In August 1855, James and Elizabeth Yeo and seven children, together with James's brother George Shapland Yeo and nephew James Yeo, left Swimbridge in Devon and boarded the ship *James Baines* in Liverpool to emigrate to Australia. When they arrived in Melbourne, after a voyage of 79 days, they transferred to a steamship, the Hellespont, and continued to Sydney. From there they travelled by train to Morpeth, near Maitland, in New South Wales, where they settled.

Horses and ponies were vital for settlers in those days and the Yeos were all accomplished horsemen and women. The family brought horses into Australia at various times, particularly George Shapland Yeo.

In the period 1880 – 1882, James senior imported a stallion 'Sir Thomas' from the Acland herd. This was the first of two known true Exmoors to enter Australia: A.C. Mardon recorded the second in the *Journal of the Royal Agricultural Society of England 1912* writing that in 1911 one of Sir Thomas Acland's ponies was sold for export to Australia.

Early in the 1900s, James Yeo senior imported another Exmoor stallion 'Dennington Court' but nothing is recorded of its origin or whether it was from a pure or crossed herd. However, the Yeo's ancestral home was Dennington Court, which might suggest that this animal had been bred by the family. James senior's father and mother in Swimbridge (also James and Elizabeth – very confusing) were in the business of exporting ponies.

The Acland stallion Sir Thomas sired Tam o' Shanter, a pony stallion that had a significant influence upon the development of the Australian Stud Pony.

Penelope Power visited Australia in 1981 and reported that she had seen a herd of 'part-bred Exmoors' in New South Wales at about 13.2hh, very uniform in type with mealy nose, toad eye and a white star but she had no information on their breeding. Settlers' horses and ponies that escaped or were released or abandoned were the ancestors of the feral herds of 'brumbies' so perhaps some of those Acland genes persist in the free-living horses of the mountains of New South Wales.

45. *Probably George Shapland Yeo.* Photo: courtesy of Ann Gugler.

Bampton Fair 1881

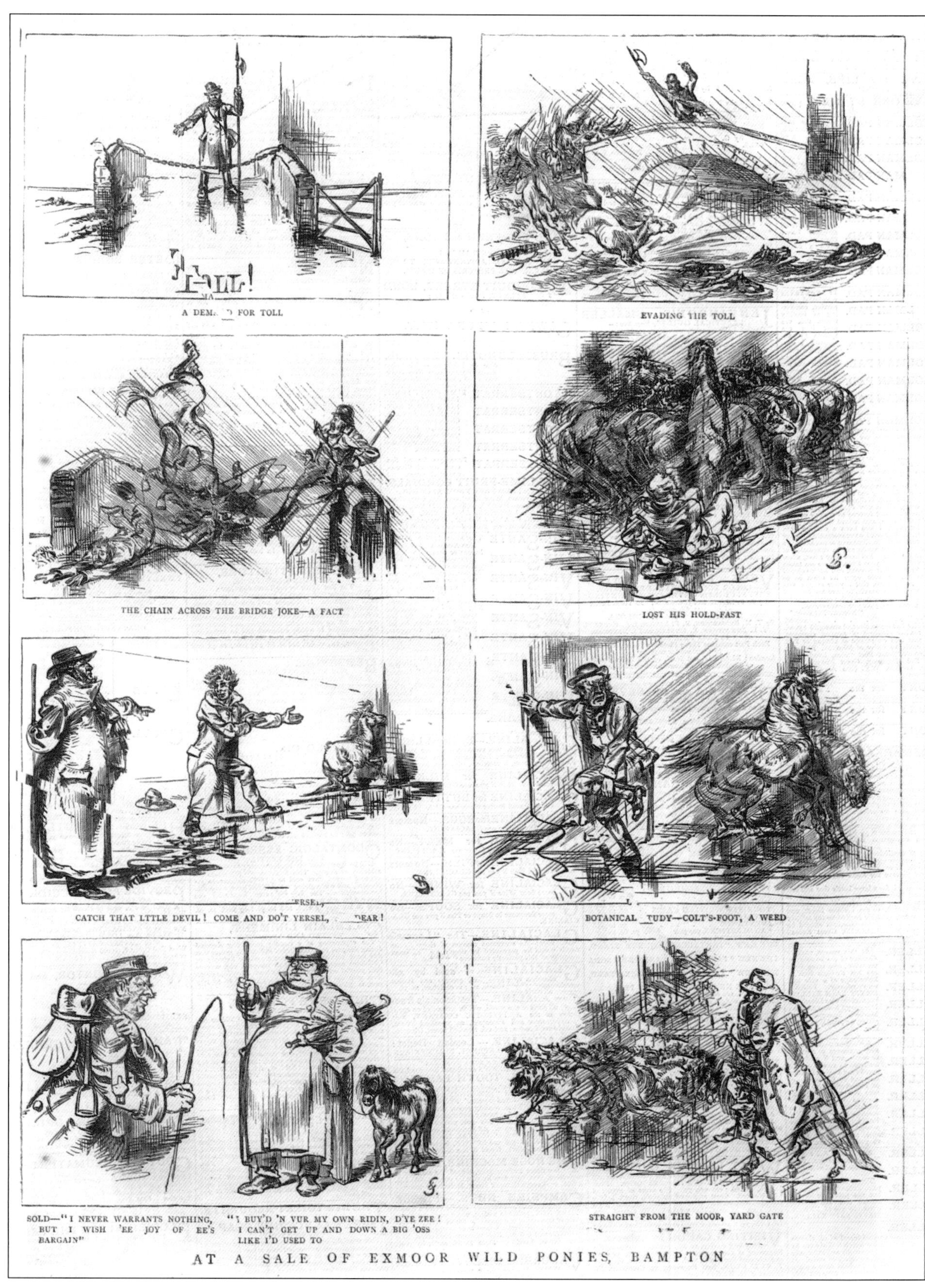

46. *'At a sale of Exmoor Wild Ponies Bampton' from* The Graphic, *30 July 1881.* The Graphic *was a British weekly illustrated newspaper published between 1869 and 1932.*

The Excavations of General Pitt Rivers

Augustus Pitt Rivers has been called 'the father of scientific archaeology'. He was born in 1827 and commissioned into the Grenadier Guards at the age of eighteen. He served in the Crimea but was soon invalided home.

He developed a growing interest in scientific subjects and was inspired by Darwin's theory of evolution to formulate his own theory on the evolution of culture. The latter led to his amassing a huge private collection of ethnographic and anthropological objects that now reside in the Pitt Rivers Museum in Oxford.

His interest in archaeology began in the mid-1860s and in 1868 he undertook his first independent excavation at a hill fort on the South Downs in Sussex. His military training and a meticulous approach made him stand out from his contemporaries. He recognised that recording the finds in great detail, including position, made it possible to deduce information about the people who had lived there.

47. General Augustus Pitt Rivers.
Photo: Dorset County Museum.

In 1880, he inherited the Rivers estate on the Wiltshire/Dorset border at Cranborne Chase. This made him a wealthy man so he could fund further archaeological digs. Also, the estate itself had great potential for archaeological investigation. The results of all his excavations in Cranborne Chase are contained in four volumes that were privately printed in 1888. Volume II includes the digs at Rotherley and Woodcuts, both Romano-British sites. Here he discovered many horse bones. He concluded:

> *'They were a pastoral and agricultural tribe, and very probably they devoted some attention to the rearing of horses, but they fed upon domesticated rather than wild animals.'*

Pitt Rivers was keen to understand what sort of animals they had kept. He wrote:

> *'An almost new branch of enquiry has been added to this volume by the careful measurement of all the bones of domesticated animals, of which a large number have been found in the Romano-British villages; 15 animals have been killed for comparison as test animals after external measurement, and by this means, the size of all the animals whose bones have been found in the villages has been ascertained.'*

In the case of horses, the unfortunate reference animals were a part-bred horse, a brown carthorse with a Roman nose, a chestnut New Forest pony and a dark brown Exmoor pony. The Exmoor pony was sixteen years old and 11-2½hh. There is no record of where it came from.

From his analysis of the comparative measurements he concluded:

> *'The Exmoor pony is probably the nearest approach that can be found at the present time to the horse of the Romanised Britons in this district.'*

Whilst a sample size of one reference animal would not meet today's standards, Pitt Rivers must be hailed as the person who seems to have made the first scientific observation as to the Exmoor pony being little changed from ancient British ponies.

Molland Pony Sale

48. This might possibly be ponies on their way to Molland pony sale, probably from the 1930s. Leading the procession is Sidney Westcott in the centre. Photo: courtesy of Margaret Rawle née Westcott.

The Molland pony sale took place on the Monday before Bampton Fair (held on the last Thursday of October). The sale was held at the Black Cock Inn beside Molland railway station; the auction field is now the pub's caravan site. The earliest record of it seems to be for 1893 and the sale ceased in the early 1950s. Apparently, some dealers would attend the Molland sale, where prices were generally lower than at Bampton, and then drive the ponies they bought down to Bampton in the hope of making a quick profit.

Bill Rashley of Molland, who I interviewed in 2000, told me that he lived in Twitchen between 1935 and 1944 and worked for Leo Thorne (see pages 25 - 26). They had about 14 or 15 Exmoor pony mares. They would gather them, brand them and sell some. Bill never went to Bampton Fair because he took their ponies to Molland pony sale. (Note: the Thornes certainly sold ponies at Bampton too). All sorts of horses and ponies were sold at Molland. He also recalled Leo Thorne once buying a bull in Exeter and he, Bill, had to walk it 37 miles back to Twitchen! Bill said that Fred Milton also used to sell ponies at the Molland sale.

Sales by Auction.

MOLLAND PONY AND HORSE SALE
MONDAY NEXT.

BLACKFORD AND SON (at the request of several well-known breeders of the district) will Sell by Auction at their Mart (close to Molland Station, G.W.R.), on Monday next, 16th October, at 1 o'clock to the minu'e, about

85

First-class Exmoor Ponies, Cobs, Hacks and Hunters.

The Auctioneers have much pleasure in calling particular attention of Gentlemen, Horse Dealers and others to this important announcement, as it is an unrefutable fact that the district around Molland is justly celebrated for its breed of the above-named animals.

MOLLAND GREAT PONY SALE.
(Close to the Railway Station.)

BLACKFORD AND SON will conduct their ANNUAL PONY SALE on Monday next, 22nd October, at 12 noon, when they will have on offer about 130 First-Class EXMOOR PONIES, COBS, AND COLTS from the Best Breeders in the District.

Advertisements from the North Devon Journal.
Left: *49. 12 October 1893.*
Above: *50. 18 October 1906.*

South Hill

South Hill was an Exmoor stallion, bred by Sir Thomas Acland, and named after the small moorland enclosure that was once part of an open expanse including Winsford Hill. South Hill figures in some pedigrees of ponies registered in the Polo & Riding Pony Stud Book, where it specifically states that he was a pure Exmoor. The registration of one of his progeny, Royal Jubilee, notes, regarding South Hill, that this stallion was sold to the Duchess of Hamilton. This was Mary, wife of William, the twelfth Duke of Hamilton. How intriguing! Why would the wife of a Scottish peer be buying a wild pony stallion from Exmoor?

We know that the Duchess visited Exmoor and actually saw South Hill in the flesh – this is recorded in the wonderful article by Evelyn March Phillips in the *Pall Mall Magazine* of 1896:

> *'They jump like deer, and make nothing of a five-barred gate. "South Hill" – a beautiful pony now in the possession of the Duchess of Hamilton – was seen by that lady to clear two five-barred gates and a hurdle; and she vowed to have him, cost what he might ... An amusing piece of politeness on the part of "South Hill" is vouched for by the pony-herd* and other eye-witnesses. When he ran with the mares in the little paddocks around Ashway, he was often to be seen rising on his hind legs and holding back the gate leading to the moor with his fore feet, while the ladies of his harem passed through.'*

* 'pony-herd' was the herd manager for the Aclands.

The Duke and Duchess lived at their Easton Estate in Suffolk. They had many stables and a Stud. In 1875, they had followed the fashion of the day and built a Farm Park. Was South Hill taken to Easton or did he perhaps stay on Exmoor?

51. The Duchess and Lady Mary circa 1895.
Photo: courtesy of Brian Boon.

The Duchess was passionate about hunting and may well have visited Exmoor many times. Perhaps she used South Hill to breed hunters either on Exmoor or back in Suffolk. Perhaps he was broken to saddle and her daughter Mary rode him out hunting when she was old enough. Alas, we will probably never know.

52. The Perfect Gentleman by Alma Swan.

Daniel Evans

NOVEMBER 26, 1897 THE WESTMINSTER BUDGET 13

EXMOOR PONIES.

A CHAT WITH AN EXMOOR AUCTIONEER.

Mr. "Dan" Evans, a good-looking, well-built man, about sixty, is at once auctioneer to Sir Thomas Dyke Acland and landlord of the Royal Oak, Winsford, Somerset. Having seen him many times at Bampton Fair, and wanting to know something about Exmoor

A GIPSY DEALER.
(From a Photograph by Scott and Sons, Exeter.)

ponies, I called on him at his home, when the following colloquy ensued.

"Now, Mr. Evans, please tell me all you know about Exmoor ponies."

"I'm afraid I can't tell you anything new. There are lots of animals on the moor claiming to be Exmoor ponies, and sold as such, but a distinguishing mark of the true Exmoor strain is a whole colour. I mean by that the absence of a white star on the forehead or any white about the feet and legs. The only exception, if you call it an exception, is a mottled grey, which may be genuine enough. The right colour is bay or brown, with mealy mouth; sometimes a very dark brown, but neither black nor chestnut. The Exmoor pony has small ears, a broad forehead, and open nostrils."

"What would you consider the average size of these ponies?"

"I should say about twelve hands. Thirteen hands would certainly be a tall pony. The strength and endurance of the breed are proverbial; if you want size, it must be got by crossing. The

JUST ARRIVED FROM THE MOOR.
(From a Photograph by Scott and Sons, Exeter.)

best plan is to cross with the sires—say, a pure-bred sire and a little Devonshire cob or pack mare. The blood or quality should be in the sire, and the size in the mare. A foal got by Royal Oak, an Exmoor stallion, out of a mare with white streaks exhibited all the points of a pure Exmoor pony. On the other hand, about eight or nine years ago Sir Thomas Acland tried some experiments with the mares: first with a Russian stallion, a bigger and coarser breed than the Exmoor pony, and, secondly, with "Varmint," a Knowstone roadster. In each case the result was unsatisfactory. I am informed that in the late Sir Frederick Knight's (now Lord Ebrington's) herd the ponies have been crossed with Arabs, but with that we have nothing to do."

"I believe these ponies live longer and thrive better than larger animals?"

"Yes, the mare on which Mr. Charles Acland learned to ride bred a foal after she was thirty. Up on the hills they drop their foals like deer, and run quite wild. In the winter they may get a little hay, but never oats."

"Is anyone specially employed to look after them?"

"Rawle, of Ashway, near Tarr Steps; his father was herdsman before him. One of his duties is to collect the ponies and drive them into Bampton Fair, which, as you know, is held on the last Thursday in October."

"What is your opinion of the Fair?"

"That it is steadily growing in popularity. The cutting of the Devon and Somerset and Exe Valley Lines has rendered the place easily accessible, and facilitated the removal of the ponies. I have been selling for nearly thirty years, and usually dispose of from seventy to eighty animals."

"Thanks"; and, guided by the telegraph wires, I wended my way through a white Exmoor mist back to Dulverton.

F. J. S.

53. *From* The Westminster Budget, *26 November 1897.*

My first encounter with Daniel Evans was in a newspaper called *The Westminster Budget* in an article written by F.J. Snell 'Exmoor Ponies – a chat with an Exmoor Auctioneer'. *The Westminster Budget* was a British national newspaper from 1893 to 1904.

Daniel Evans was also mentioned in another short article on Exmoor ponies in 1897, this time in a publication called *The Ludgate*:

> *'About the inbred courtesy of the pony on his native heath, Mr. Evans repeats some delectable stories which, if they came from other lips, would be challenged and characterised as "tall". Thus he is acquainted with an Exmoor stallion who, "on the hills," will stand and open the gates with his forepaws to let the mares pass. Evidently that stallion was well-versed in his duties.'*

> ***"All you have to do is treat 'em kindly, like you would your wife or your sweetheart, and not beat 'em or blackguard 'em."***
>
> Daniel Evans, on how to ensure a good temper in an Exmoor pony, in *The Ludgate*, 1897.

54. Daniel Evans (centre, with beard) conducting the auction behind the Tiverton Hotel on Bampton Fair Day circa 1900. Photo: Tiverton Museum.

The following description of Daniel Evans comes from an article entitled 'The Wild Ponies of Exmoor' published in 1909 in a magazine called *The Wide World:*

> *'Wend your way down to the auction rings where in stout pens in the orchards these caged atoms of wildness are huddled together, and from a safe distance hear Mr. D. Evans, a leading auctioneer, air his original quips on the qualities and action of his "goods." For over half a century this gentleman has been knocking these bundles of trouble down to speculative buyers, and what he does not know about a native Exmoor pony is not worth burning candle light to find out.'*

Daniel Evans died on 4 September 1913 aged 87 and is buried in Winsford Churchyard.

Note: *The Wide World Magazine* was a British magazine published monthly between April 1898 and December 1965.

'Goose fairs, mop fairs, feather fairs are all alike – the objects of their existence have ceased to be; but Bampton Pony Fair still flourishes, for it is like nothing else in the world – it exists as the sole method of transferring the wild little mountain steeds to the slavery of the outside world.'

From the article in the *Wide World*, 1909.

55. Photograph of the pens at Bampton in about 1900. Photo: from the Reg Kingdon collection.

The Acland Herd after 1818

In 1818, Sir Thomas Acland, 10th Baronet, failed in his bid to purchase the Royal Forest of Exmoor. He had been Warden of the Royal Forest and as such owned Exmoor ponies that had grazed the open moorlands. Various sources record that he took twenty (some say thirty) of his 'best' ponies to Old Ashway Farm close to Winsford Hill; according to an 1896 account, these included four stallions and the rest were mares.

Old Ashway Farm adjoined an enclosed area of about 150 acres of open moorland known as Ashway Side. In addition, the Aclands owned a larger moorland area that encompassed the now separated areas of South Hill, Winsford Hill and Bradley Moor; Varle Hill, lying between Ashway Side and this large 'open range' was also theirs.

In 2016 Penny Beattie was sorting through family papers; her grandmother was Mabel (Maimie) Acland. She found some type-written pages that were an analysis of registrations in the Polo Pony Stud Books with additional notes. Under Volume VIII (1905) is written:

> *'Mrs. Froude Bawden (née Parkman) whose father had charge of the Acland ponies for many years, tells me that Sir Thomas Acland maintained four separate herds, each with its own stallions; that on Ashway Side (which was the only enclosed area) had three stallions. Tenant farmers owning pure Exmoor mares were allowed to run them on the open hills with the Acland stallions.'*

So although writers refer to 'the Acland Herd', it is important to understand that there were actually two Acland pony populations, segregated from each other. The fact that one area, Ashway Side was identified as enclosed is crucial in explaining how the Aclands were able to preserve the 'old strain' of ponies as a pure-bred population whilst also experimenting to a small extent with crossing. The Tithe Map of about 1840 shows that Ashway Side and Varle Hill were separate enclosures, so Varle Hill provided additional protection against contact between the ponies on the two areas.

The first Acland registrations other than in their own records (lost in a fire at Holnicote in the 1940s) were in the Polo Pony Stud Book of 1905: entries show that the mares were all named after the area they were from: *'Ashway Side 1,2 and 3; Bradley Moors 1 and 2; South Hill 1,2 and 3; Winsford Hill 1,2,3,4,5 and 6.'*

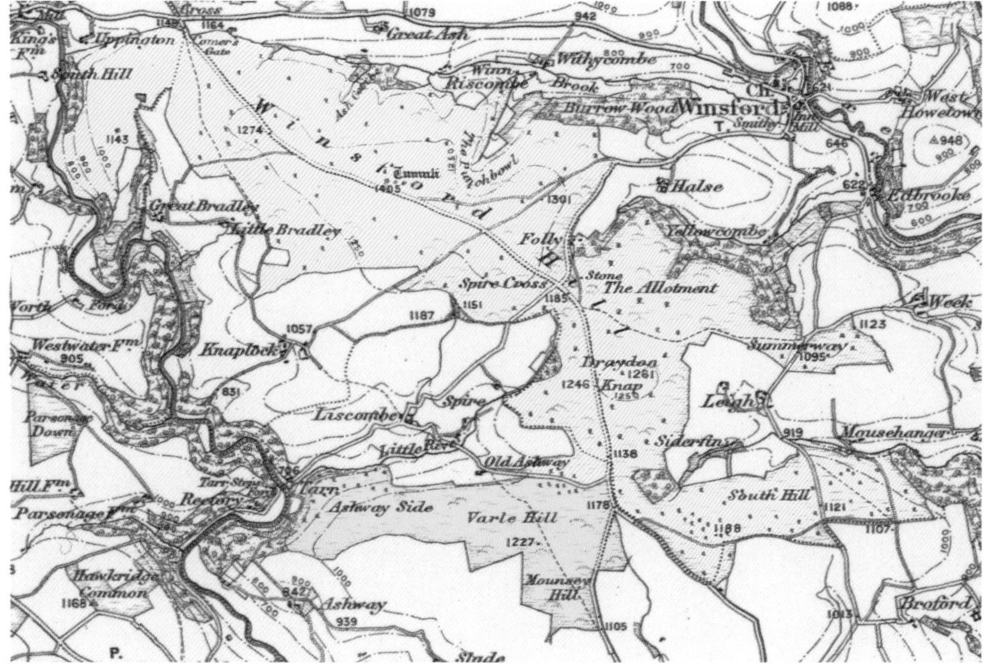

56. Extract from the 1898 Ordnance Survey map of the area. The open 'range' of Bradley Moor, Winsford Hill and South Hill is in pink and the enclosures of Ashway Side/Varle Hill in green (separate in 1840 and within living memory).

57. *Old Ashway Farm in 1896 (an engraving from* Pall Mall Magazine*).*

58. *Old Ashway in 2016.*

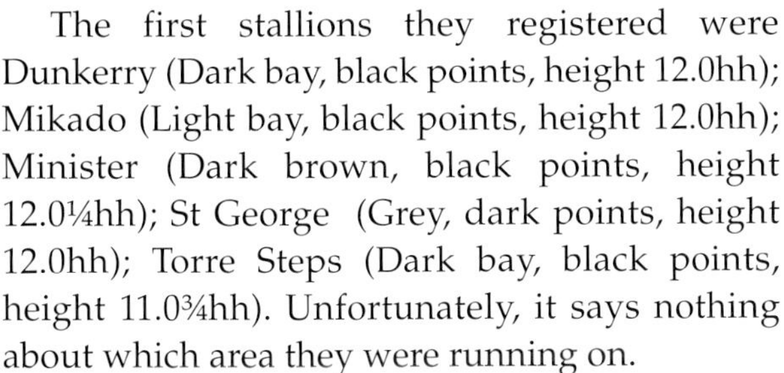

The first stallions they registered were Dunkerry (Dark bay, black points, height 12.0hh); Mikado (Light bay, black points, height 12.0hh); Minister (Dark brown, black points, height 12.0¼hh); St George (Grey, dark points, height 12.0hh); Torre Steps (Dark bay, black points, height 11.0¾hh). Unfortunately, it says nothing about which area they were running on.

With regard to other owners running their pure-bred mares on the Bradley Moor/Winsford Hill/ South Hill grazings, we hear more of this from Colonel F.H. Reeks, who was agent for the Killerton and Holnicote estates from 1929 to 1939. In 'The Acland Herd of Exmoor Ponies' (*Exmoor Review*, 1970), Reeks says that his information came from Tom Parkman (who managed the Acland pony herds) and Parkman's daughter Gladys Bawden. He wrote:

> *'Sir Thomas decided to take 20 of the best of his ponies, and in this he was joined by a number of farmers, and segregated them on his own hill grazings in order to retain the stamp and character of the original breed. I do not know how many of the local farmers adopted the same line, but there is little doubt two of them were Mr. Thorne of Great Bradley and Mr. Crick of Great Ash.'*

In addition, Mr Daniel Evans, publican at the Royal Oak in Winsford, was allowed to graze his mares on Winsford Hill as 'payment' for his services as auctioneer of the Acland ponies at Bampton Fair (see page 34).

The Acland Greys

What are we to make of the Aclands' grey stallion, St George in those first registrations? Given the Acland commitment to breeding 'pure' and conserving the original type of pony, then if St George carried non-Exmoor genes, they would surely not have allowed him to run on Ashway Side; but they could have run him on the Bradley Moor/Winsford Hill/ South Hill expanse without compromising their conservation aims. In fact we can be sure that St George did run on the 'open range' as the Cricks of Great Ash registered a pony by him.

Understanding the system of two segregated populations within the Acland 'herd' means that the existence of St George and other greys does not undermine the many statements regarding the Aclands protecting the old strain from introduced outside genes.

In *Exmoor Ponies – Survival of the Fittest*, I speculated that the grey ponies in this photograph might have been a rare, and lost, natural variant of the true Exmoor. The clarification of how the Aclands organised their pony breeding means that we can now set that idea aside.

59. *Acland ponies around 1900 including two greys.*
Photo: the Mary Etherington Archive.

Dr Watney's Arab-Exmoor Crosses

On 19 July 1899, the following article appeared in *The Sketch*, a weekly newspaper that focused upon matters related to the aristocracy and landed gentry.

Exmoor Ponies in Berkshire

'The Exmoor pony may not impress you favourably at first sight, particularly if you be of orderly mind, with a prejudice in favour of smooth coat and kempt mane and tail. Life on the Berkshire Downs, free as that on Exmoor, does not make for the superficial graces; but brief acquaintance with this transplanted herd shows that, while richer grazing and milder climate have contributed to add a hand or more to the pony's stature, the little beast has lost nothing of his sagacity and sure-footedness. Nothing will induce the pony to set hoof on bog or quagmire; no ground is sufficiently rough to bring him down; and when the loose stone wall of Exmoor divides him from a field of oats, this acrobat among equines puts his toe in a convenient crevice and gets over – somehow; he may arrive on his head or his back, but he arrives; he eats all he can, which is much, and tumbles cheerfully over the wall again without waiting for the despoiled farmer to encourage his return with well-aimed stones.

There is no opportunity for this feat of agility on the Buckhold lands, for the great paddocks are fenced with wire which the Exmoor pony has not yet learned to negotiate; there are no bogs on these flinty wolds to exercise his sense of unsound ground, but there are hills nearly perpendicular down which the drove thunders under flying mane and tail, and ranges gaily away, leaving you to reconcile with the laws of gravitation the failure of the whole crowd to break their necks. Shy as these Exmoors are at large, when once caught, handled and broken, they are charmingly docile, and make perfect children's ponies. The Welsh pony has an ugly habit of kicking, born of much harrying by sheep-dogs; the Shetland pony's manners sometimes leave much to be desired; but the Exmoor neither kicks or bites: it is blessed with a singularly even temper.

Like other wild, or half-wild, British ponies, it has an extraordinary constitution, seemingly affected by neither heat nor cold. When the snow lies deep, a daily ration of hay is served out to the ponies, but from wind and rain they find shelter only under the lee of the plantations. Until taken up to be broken they are never under a roof.

Dr. Herbert Watney, to whom the Buckhold droves belong, has tried the experiment of crossing the purest obtainable Exmoor mares with an Arab. From Mr. Wilfrid Blunt he procured a perfect picture of an Arab pony, bred at Crabbet Park, and turned him out to run with the mares.

EXMOOR MARE AND FOAL.

AN ARAB-EXMOOR MARE.

60. and 61. Illustrations from the article in The Sketch *1899. Note that the Exmoor mare has a high-set tail – was this perhaps itself an Exmoor cross?*

One need know little of horseflesh to be able to distinguish the Arab-Exmoor mare from the pure Exmoor. All the distinctive Arab character is there: she has the beautiful, lean head, the proudly carried tail set high, the long pasterns; and, oddly enough, her Arab blood has done nothing to qualify the sure-footedness of her mother's family. The Arab is not generally a pleasant hack, for those long, sloping pasterns make him often a stumbler on the smooth road; the Arab-Exmoor, despite the long pasterns, has the goat-like agility of the moorland pony on the worst ground, his iron constitution, and adds thereto increased size and good looks.'

Sir Walter Gilbey also wrote in *Ponies Past and Present* published in 1900:

'Dr. Watney laid the foundations of his herd by the purchase of about a dozen mares of the Knight and Ackland strains, and to serve them he acquired the 13.2 Exmoor stallion Katerfelto, winner of the first prize in his class at the "Royal" in 1890.

The stallion runs with the mares, and the herd lead on the Berkshire Downs exactly the same free life they led on Exmoor; they are never brought under cover, and only when the snow buries the herbage in severe winters do they receive a daily ration of hay. The richer grazing and their exclusive service by Katerfelto has resulted in a distinct increase in size, the ponies ranging from 11.3 to 13.3 in height, yet retaining all the characteristics of the Exmoor native stock.

Dr Watney drafted off a number of the best mares to form a herd for service by the Arab pony stallion Nejram, a bay standing 14.2 bred by Mr. Wilford Blunt at Crabbet Park. Nejram's stock show in marked degree the distinctive character of their sire in the high set and carriage of the tail, full barrel, blood-like head and the long pastern; but at the same time they inherit from their dams the wonderful sure-footedness of the Exmoor pony. These ponies run from about 13 hands to 13.3. Half a dozen of these Arab-Exmoors were sold in the year 1898 at an average price of over £14.14s each. Twelve pure Exmoors by Katerfelto, also handled but unbroken, 3 years old, brought an average of over £16.16s.'

LEADING AWAY PONIES FROM EXMOOR.

62. *From* The Illustrated London News, *22 October 1853.*

On Exmoor, John Knight had become renowned for crossing Exmoor mares with Arab stallions after he bought The Royal Forest in 1818. This is one of two illustrations accompanying an article *'The Ponies of Exmoor'* in 1853 on the subject of visiting the Knight pony sale in Simonsbath.

Wild Ass and Zebra – Exmoor Crosses

This photograph is of an Exmoor mare with her foal sired by a Kiang. The Kiang is the largest of the species of wild asses and inhabits the high plateau of Tibet. This hybrid foal was the result of James Cossar Ewart's 'Penycuik Experiments'. Cossar Ewart was professor of natural history at Edinburgh University and conducted many breeding experiments involving zebra, wild asses and ponies. I found the story of the Kiang – Exmoor pony cross in his paper 'The Wild Horse' (*Proc. Royal Soc. of Edinburgh, 1903*).

63. *The Kiang-Exmoor hybrid foal with its Exmoor dam, one of the illustrations in Cossar Ewart's paper 'The Wild Horse'.* Photo: Darwin-Wilmot.

'With the help of Lord Arthur Cecil I succeeded early in 1902 in securing a male wild Asiatic ass ... 'Jacob', the wild ass, was mated with the dun Mongol mare, with a brownish-yellow Exmoor pony, and with a bay Shetland-Welsh pony ... The Exmoor having foaled first, her hybrid may be first considered. It may be mentioned that the Exmoor pony had in 1900 and again in 1901 a zebra hybrid, the sire being the Burchell zebra 'Matopo' used in my telegony experiments. In the case of her Kiang hybrid the period of gestation was 335 days (one day short of what is regarded as the normal time), but she carried her 1900 zebra hybrid 357 days, three weeks beyond the normal time. The Exmoor zebra hybrids are as nearly as possible intermediate between a zebra and a pony; the Kiang hybrid on the other hand, might almost pass for a pure-bred wild ass. In Mendelian terms the Exmoor pony proved recessive, the wild ass dominant. In zebra hybrids the ground colour has invariably been darker than in the zebra parent; but the Kiang hybrid is decidedly lighter in colour than her wild sire, while in make she strongly suggests an Onager – the wild ass so often associated with the Runn of Crutch. Alike in make and colour the Kiang hybrid differs from a young Prejvalsky foal.

I have never seen a new-born wild horse; but if one may judge from the conformation of the hocks, from the coarse legs, big joints and large head of the yearlings – to their close resemblance to dwarf cart-horse foals – it may be assumed they are neither characterized by unusual agility nor fleetness. The Kiang hybrid, on the other hand, looks as if built for speed, and almost from the moment of its birth has by its energy and vivacity been a source of considerable anxiety to its by no means placid Exmoor dam. When four days old it walked over twenty miles; on the fifth day instead of resting it was unusually active, as if anxious to make up for the enforced idleness of the previous evening.'

Far left: 64. *James Cossar Ewart with a zebra.* Photo: Flatters & Garnett Ltd./Special Collections, University of Edinburgh Library.

Left: 65. *The Kiang-Exmoor hybrid foal – one of the illustrations in Cossar Ewart's 'The Wild Horse'.* Photo: Adderley

'There Goes Old Tom'

This is an old Somerset folk song that Ruth L. Tongue included in her book *The Chime Child* published in 1967. It had been sung to her by William Webber in 1906 when he was seventy. William Webber was a groom at the stableyard in Tangier, Taunton. Ruth Tongue wrote,

> *'He was a small, quick man with a bright eye. He was a wonderful hand with horses – they loved him nearly as much as I did; he had a clear, fluty voice for a good song. His only grievance was that there were so few songs about horses – hunting, yes, but actual horses – no.'*
>
> She recalled *'his perpetual tuneful whistling of airs dear to my soul.'*

There was an old pony just twelve hands high.
Hard away, hark away, there goes old Tom.
His muzzle was mealy with a nice toad-eye.
Over, hup over!
Over, hup over!
He'd hunt all out over but never in vain.
Hard away, hark away, there goes old Tom.
And bring farmer home in the fog and the rain.
Over, out over!
Over, out over!
At wall or water when hounds did run on,
Over or under or through went Old Tom.
Over, hup over!
Hard away, hark away, there goes old Tom.

He'd trot on to market and think it was play,
And bring missus safe to the end of the day.
He'd carry the baby so sweet as a song,
But he hadn't a minute for them as was wrong.
For his heels went up and his head it went down,
And he'd kick 'en so nicely right down to the town.

They both of 'en died the same day it was said,
And farmer's in churchyard among his dear dead.
They laid the old pony in Ten Acre Mow,
'Twas kind in old Tommy to help it to grow.
With his mealy nose and his titupping toes,
The ponies still follow wherever he goes.
His ghost leads 'en on with cunning and care,
Out away over from Bampton Fair.

66. The music for 'There Goes Old Tom' as collected by Ruth Tongue.

Note: There is a tradition that 'Old Tom' the pony ghost takes the herds away before the round-ups. He is sometimes heard above Chetsford Bridge calling a warning and ponies scatter at once. 'Old' is a term of affection but is also used politely with reference to the 'Other World'.

In 2005, the Pennymoor Singaround from near Tiverton recorded the song for me to hear at last. It was great to hear it brought to life after so long. This is, as far as I know, the only song about an Exmoor pony. When I asked them to do this, no-one within the group had heard of it but Bob and Jacqueline Patten, folk song archivists were able to supply it. Jon Shapley was the soloist and the MP3 recording was made at the Cruwys Arms in Pennymoor. Jon subsequently made a professional recording at Newcastle University whilst studying for a degree in music.

The Need for an Exmoor Pony Society

The earliest suggestion I have found, that an Exmoor Pony Society should be formed, was in 1908. So concern as to the future of the breed pre-dates the actual creation of a breed society by some twelve years.

The Exmoor Pony Show, held annually at Lynton, was started in connection with the working-men's movement in aid of the Hospital and other Lynton charities, but quite apart from the substantial assistance it has been the means of giving in this direction the Show has rendered an invaluable service in the interests of the finest breed of ponies in the Kingdom. The Lynton Show has served to bring into prominence the striking merits of the hardy Exmoor pony, and has at the same time greatly widened the circle of the admirers of the unrivalled breed—with the incidental result that it has benefited the breeders and sellers of the famous ponies by extending the sale market. But it has done more. The Show has been the means of directing attention to the fact that there is a danger of the breed being, through carelessness, allowed to deteriorate. In the course of the speech-making at the Exhibition held last Thursday Mr. E. J. Soares, M.P., expressed regret that the entries included fewer pure-breed Exmoors than he was accustomed to see at Lynton and Mr. E.A.V. Stanley (Master of the Devon and Somerset Staghounds) and Major Pen-Curzon, both experts, followed up this allusion by some strong remarks which every farmer in the Exmoor country and all others interested in the breeding of Exmoor ponies will do wisely to take to heart. The Exmoor type is strongly marked, and the pure-blooded Exmoor pony is without a rival in the world for sturdiness and stamina. This grand type of pony is, as Mr. Soares put it, a most valuable asset to Devon and Somerset, and it would be a grave misfortune if through laxity the breed were allowed to deteriorate. We have no doubt the warnings uttered at Lynton on Thursday will bear fruit. But having regard to the importance of the issues involved, is it prudent to leave precautionary measures to individual exertion? Is it not a case for organised effort? The establishment of the Devon Herd Book, coupled with the work of the Devon Cattle Breeders' Society, has rendered incalculable service in the preservation of the purity of the breed of the world-famous Devon Cattle, and in the interests of Devon Longwool sheep and Exmoor sheep similar organisations have been founded in recent years. Has not the time come when, with a view to preserving the true type of the moorland pony, an Exmoor Pony Society should be started? We commend the suggestion to all admirers of the breed, and in particular to the farmers and others who stand to lose so much if the fears expressed freely at Lynton Show become realised.

67. From the North Devon Journal, *13 August 1908.*

The West Somerset Yeomanry

Amongst the many anecdotes told to me by John Milton was one about the West Somerset Yeomanry.:

> *'When I was a young boy, before the Second World War, the West Somerset Yeomanry came to Exmoor for training and set up their camp near Four Fields, on the edge of Withypool Common. They were a voluntary cavalry unit.*
>
> *They hired ponies from my father to use as pack ponies for the transport of their supplies.'*

John remembered lying on the hillside above the camp, watching their training activities.

The West Somerset Yeomanry held manoeuvres on Exmoor annually and, fortunately, two postcards survive in the Somerset Heritage Centre that show the camp when it was held at Highercombe, between Dulverton and Winsford Hill, in 1909.

Dulverton resident Mr Kemp, who ran the newsagents until the early 1980s remembered the August Bank Holiday in 1914 when he watched the West Somerset Yeomanry pass through Dulverton with their horses and gun carriages.

It was important for the West Somerset Yeomanry manoeuvres to include practise with pack animals as these were relied upon, in both World War I and II, to transport supplies to the front line and cope with terrain where use of vehicles was impossible.

68. Left *and* 69. below:
The West Somerset Yeomanry camp in 1909.
Photos: Somerset Archives and Local Studies Service (South West Heritage Trust) DD/SLI/15/16/15 and 16.

Charles Reid

These photographs of Exmoor Ponies are almost certainly all of Acland ponies; they were taken in the early 1900s when they had a small number of greys amongst them (see page 37).

The photographer is credited as 'Chas Reid', 'C. Reid, Wishaw' and just 'Reid'. Charles Reid (senior, 1837 - 1929) was one of the first Scottish commercial photographers. He was based firstly in Turriff and, after 1876, in Wishaw, 15 miles from Glasgow. He was a pioneer of livestock and wildlife photography – a difficult art in those days of very long exposures. He travelled all over the British Isles in a career that lasted fifty years, photographing prize-winning livestock of notable landowners and also race horses. For many years he was the official photographer to the Highland and Agricultural Society of Scotland and to the Royal Agricultural Society of England.

One of his sons was also called Charles and by the age of fourteen was his assistant; he eventually took over the business when his father died. So, it could have been either Charles Senior or Charles Junior who visited Exmoor and photographed the Acland ponies. We don't know the date of the top image but it would seem likely, given their base was in Scotland, that they made just the one visit.

Purchased from a well known auction site, unfortunately the images 70. above *and 71.* below *arrived with no information as to the books from which they had been extracted. The one above is credited to Chas Reid and the one below to C. Reid, Wishaw.*

72. Charles Reid Senior. Reproduced with acknowledgement to the Hamilton Town House Reference Library and to the Hamilton Natural History Society.

73. A plate from Livestock of the Farm Volume 3 Horses *by Professor C. Bryner Jones, 1915. Credit states 'Reid'.*

The Crockfords and Westerns of Luckwell Bridge

The Exmoor Pony Society Stud Book records that the Crockford family's involvement with Exmoor ponies started with Joseph Crockford who founded Herd 12. His father James was farming Great Hawkwell Farm in 1841 and the family is known to have rented fields in the area before that.

William Crockford was born in 1879, the youngest child of Joseph and Mary Crockford; he had a brother James and three sisters. James eventually left the area and farmed in Hampshire and so it was William who took over at Hawkwell. William married Ethel May Melhuish around 1913 and they had a daughter, Betty, in 1918.

William wrote about their pony herd in *The Little Horses of Exmoor* in 1947:

> *'My father always had pure-bred Exmoor ponies, and so have I. They run on an allotment called Codsend Moors all the year round. That moor adjoins Dunkery and it is very cold and rough there in winter.'*

(the full text is included in *Exmoor Ponies – Survival of the Fittest*, 2008).

74. William and Ethel on their wedding day in about 1913. Photo: courtesy of Gay Seguro.

The earliest registrations in the name of Crockford, in the National Pony Stud Book of 1924, relate to ponies bred by the Aclands but listed under the name of William Crockford. Of

75. William Crockford (right) with Bill Western at Dunster Show, probably in the late 1920s or early 1930s. Photo courtesy of Gay Seguro.

76. Bill Western outside the farmhouse at Hawkwell. Photo: courtesy of John and Anne Western.

these, the first pony was foaled in 1915.

In 1919, the first Herd 12 pony was registered and this won an N.P.S. 1922-23 silver medal at Exford Show.

William Charles Western (Bill), great-great-nephew of William Crockford, was born in Cutcombe in 1910. He helped William Crockford at Hawkwell Farm after school and at weekends. He left school at fourteen and went to live and work at Hawkwell full-time.

Bill was a good rider and hunted with both the Devon and Somerset Staghounds and the Exmoor Foxhounds, riding an Exmoor pony. He helped William Crockford with all aspects of the pony herd including accompanying him to local shows and to some further afield, taking ponies by rail – see page 74.

Bill's diary for 1939 relates: *'Tuesday 8th August – went out (walked) to the moor after the ponies for Exford Show in the morning but failed to get them. We got two of them back in the evening. Wednesday 9th August – Tommy and the two year old both won 2nd prizes.'* Interestingly, Bill made no mention at all of the war in his diary entries for that year.

When William Crockford died in 1964, Hawkwell Farm passed to his daughter Betty: she decided to sell the farm and offered Bill Western first refusal. By this time, Bill had married Nora Dixon who he had met when she was sent to Somerset from Yorkshire during the war as a Land Girl. Bill and his brother Wilf had served in the Home Guard. So, Bill and Wilf bought the farm, although Wilf had no interest in the ponies.

Herd 12 passed into very capable hands, as Bill was recognised locally as a good stockman. He was always willing to part with good ponies to help found new herds. He was an active member of the Exmoor Pony Society, serving on Committee a number of times and acting as both Society inspector and judge: he judged all over the country, Nora accompanying him on such trips. Bill was always keen to encourage younger people to become interested in the ponies: Gill Langdon remembers him as her main 'mentor'.

Bill and Nora Western had two children, John and Rosalind. John married Anne Painter in 1973 and with their young family of Michael and Cathy, they joined Bill and Nora at Hawkwell. Bill never really retired but after Nora died in 1985, his health deteriorated and he became less actively involved. His love for the ponies never waned and he never missed a gathering day, when the herd was brought in to await inspection.

Bill died in December 1997 after a long illness. John and Anne continue to farm at Hawkwell and of course inherited the pony herd too. They are both E.P.S. inspectors and judges, as is son Michael.

77. Hawkwell Staghunter, born in 1959 and sired by Herd 12's stallion Aclander. Photo: courtesy of John and Anne Western.

The Founding of the Exmoor Pony Society

After 1908, the next mention of an Exmoor Pony Society in the local papers seems to be a notice advertising that a meeting was to be held in Dulverton in 1920.

- A MEETING -
Will be held on
Friday, November 26th Next,
At the
LION HOTEL, DULVERTON,
At 2.45 p.m., to FORM an "EXMOOR PONY SOCIETY."
Earl Fortescue in the Chair.
D. J. TAPP, Convener.

78. *From the* West Somerset Free Press, *20 November 1920.*

The following edition on 4 December 1920 carried the report of the meeting, which began:

'THE PURE-BRED EXMOOR PONY SOCIETY FOR ITS MAINTENANCE FORMED AT DULVERTON'

The report went on to say:

'It was proposed, if they at that meeting agreed, that an Exmoor Pony Society should be formed on the same lines generally speaking as the Exmoor Horn Sheep Flock Book and Society. This proposal was accepted, with the issue of pony identification by brand marks and individual pony numbers being deferred for in-depth consideration at a later date. A second proposal was also passed – That up to 31st December 1923, ponies shall be admitted to the register if recommended by not less than two inspectors and approved by the committee, but that after that date no ponies shall be admitted to the register unless they are the offspring of ponies registered in the society's stud book.'

79. *David Tapp.* Photo: courtesy of Diana Wilson and Martin Tapp.

D.J. Tapp (1862 - 1949)

David James Tapp was born at Knaplock Farm, Winsford; his family had lived in the district for generations. Having learnt farming from his father, David farmed at Broford, near Dulverton, and then became tenant of Highercombe Farm between Dulverton and Winsford Hill around 1899; he eventually purchased Highercombe. (Note: Highercombe had once been a hunting lodge for the Acland family). He started his flock of Exmoor Horn Sheep in 1900 and farmed Highercombe until 1937.

He was very active in public service, representing Dulverton district on the Somerset County Council up to the First World War. During the war years he was chairman of the Dulverton Area Farmers and, for some years after the war, chairman of the Dulverton branch of the National Farmers Union. He was also a Justice of the Peace. He married twice and had three children by his first wife, who died in 1900, and two by his second wife who he married in 1919.

(continued overleaf)

The meeting went on to unanimously elect Lord Fortescue as President. Reginald Le Bas had offered to become Secretary and he was elected. David Tapp insisted that the meeting should appoint a provisional executive committee, their task to consider the appointment of inspectors who would be passing ponies for registration; the executive committee would then report their recommendations to a general meeting of the newly formed E.P.S. within three months. The members of that committee were: R.S. Westcott, T. Parkman, W. Pring, Mr. Perkins, A.G. Westcott, G. Molland, F.G. Heal and David Tapp himself.

There was also debate around setting the basics of a breed standard with regards to height and permitted colours. Defining the maximum permitted height brought forth differing opinions but the majority supported 12.3 hands for stallions and 12.2 hands for mares. With regard to a rule about permitted colours, it was agreed to allow 'bays, browns, blacks and greys but not chestnuts.'

Dr Collyns had asked the Chairman earlier in the meeting whether rules passed at this inaugural meeting would be binding on the society if one was formed. Lord Fortescue had answered that this would not necessarily be the case but they might be put to a future meeting for confirmation.

Date of Birth - 1920 or 1921?

The received wisdom has always been that the Exmoor Pony Society was founded at the Red Lion Hotel in Dulverton and in 1921; this was the year quoted in Reginald Le Bas' obituary, *The Pure Bred Exmoor Pony* by Anthony Dent in 1970, the EPS breed leaflet in the early 1980's, *The Exmoor Pony* by Elizabeth Polling in 1986 and my book in 1993 and 2008. We can now see that the conception/birth of the Society was that night in November 1920; the first actual meeting of the Society was on 10 March 1921.

(D.J. Tapp continued)

David Tapp was renowned for his work for the Exmoor Horn Sheep Breeders' Society. He became the first secretary when it was formed in 1906. The society's first annual report referred to : *'the success and rapidity with which all the necessary steps for its formation were carried out, were mainly due to the energy, tact, and urbanity with which he devoted himself to the initiation and development of the Society.'* The Sheep Breeders' Society made him a Life Member and later, in 1940, President, in recognition of all his service to the society.

With his experience of founding and progressing the Sheep Breeders' Society, it is not surprising that David Tapp was the convenor of the meeting to consider the creation of an equivalent society to look after the interests of the Exmoor pony breed. His obituary in the *West Somerset Free Press* in September 1949 stated:

'In the Exmoor Pony Society, after its formation, Mr. Tapp also found a channel through which his services and his influence were turned to help secure the preservation, in its pure form, of another habitant of the West-Country, the Exmoor pony. For many years he was a member of the Council of the Society and one of its appointed inspectors of ponies.'

80. David Tapp with an Exmoor Horn ram.
Photo: courtesy of Diana Wilson and Martin Tapp.

E.P.S. Honorary Secretaries

81. List of Honorary Secretaries.

82. Reginald Le Bas heading through Winsford to the Meet of the Devon & Somerset Staghounds.
Photo: courtesy of Ann Le Bas.

Reginald Le Bas
Secretary 1920 – 1935

Reginald Vincent Le Bas (1856 -1938) was the first Secretary of the Exmoor Pony Society and undertook this role from its foundation until 1935.

His grand-daughter, artist Ann Le Bas of Winsford, told me that prior to the first meeting where the Society was officially formed, there had been a meeting between him, Lord Fortescue and Sir Francis Acland, probably at his home Exe Vale House; she presumed that this led to the founding meeting at the Red Lion in Dulverton. She remembers that as a child at Exe Vale House she used to sit on the floor during Exmoor Pony Society committee meetings. Once business was concluded she would then sit on committee members' laps.

Reginald Le Bas first came to know and love Exmoor as a boy, spending holidays with his uncle, the Reverend W. Thompson, at Simonsbath. According to Ann, his journey to Exmoor back then involved the train from Paddington to Bristol; paddle-steamer from Bristol to Lynmouth; and finally, a horse-drawn coach from Lynmouth to Simonsbath.

Reginald's father was also a vicar, preaching at Charterhouse in London, where Reginald was at school. However, Reginald opted for the Law and was called to the Bar in 1894; he specialised in divorce law and became well-known for this in the legal profession. During the years of World War I, while living in London, he enrolled as a special constable and he was among those who had the privilege of patrolling Buckingham Palace.

> The farmers of Exmoor – at any rate, those who still breed Exmoor ponies – will have grateful memories of the keen interest Mr Le Bas took in the preservation of the breed and the efforts which he made, through the Exmoor Pony Society, to encourage and ensure their continuity.
>
> *Extract from Reginald Le Bas' obituary from the* West Somerset Free Press.

When Reginald retired, in about 1920, he and his wife settled in Winsford. His obituary tells us:

> *'The interests of his leisure years were numerous. Almost immediately after settling down at Winsford he gave his attention with energy and enthusiasm to the formation of the Exmoor Pony Society, the objects of which were to determine the type and to improve and encourage the breeding of ponies of the right type, to form a stud-book for the breed, and to institute shows or classes at existing shows of Exmoor ponies. From the time of the founding of the society, in 1921, until about three years ago when his health necessitated retirement, Mr. Le Bas acted as honorary secretary and it was an interest very dear to his heart.'*

For many years Reginald was a member of the Exford Horse Show committee and also a member of the Devon and Somerset Staghounds' committee. In addition to those leisure interests, he served as a Justice of the Peace for Somerset, sitting on the Dulverton Bench for about fifteen years.

When Reginald Le Bas retired from being Secretary of the Exmoor Pony Society, his son, Captain Rainald Stephen Le Bas, Ann's father, decided not to take over from him as his father would probably not have liked it if he had changed anything.

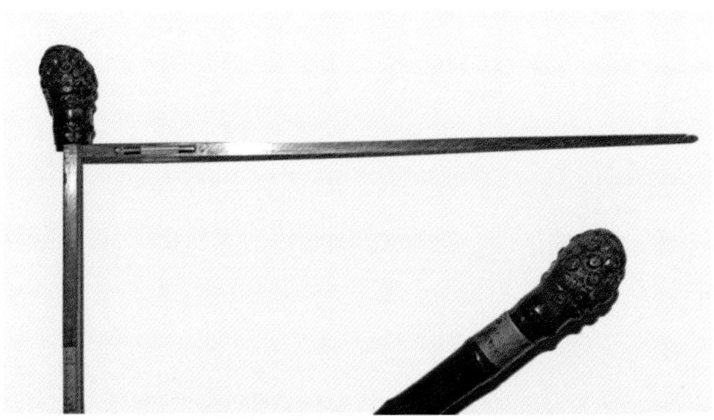

84. This was Reginald Le Bas' equine measuring stick that he used to measure the heights of the Exmoor Pony foundation stock when inspected for the Stud Book.

John Follett Pugsley
Secretary 1935 – 1947

John Follett Pugsley became Exmoor Pony Society Secretary when Reginald Le Bas retired in 1935. His tenure as Secretary lasted twelve years; his resignation was reported in the write-up of the Society's AGM in 1947.

83. John Follett Pugsley (in the bowler hat), probably at Exford Show. Photo: The Mary Etherington Archive.

Like his predecessor, John Follett Pugsley was also a solicitor. As well as serving the Exmoor Pony Society, he was Tiverton Town Clerk for twenty years and became a Governor of Blundell's School in Tiverton, where he had been educated. He was also treasurer of a number of charities. The report of his funeral in the *West Somerset Free Press* of 3 November 1956 described his 'long career of public service' and the sense of deep loss felt in Tiverton and also in Wiveliscombe, where he died, aged 86.

John Follett Pugsley would have been well-known to many in the Exmoor Pony Society prior to becoming Secretary as he was a keen supporter of many of the local hunts; he was also Secretary of the Tiverton Staghounds between 1928 and 1945.

Dick Hern
Secretary 1947 – 1949

When talking to Ann Le Bas about her grandfather, she mentioned that John Follett Pugsley took over from him and then he handed the reins to Dick Hern, who became famous as a horse trainer. This surprised me as I had found no mention of Dick Hern; it was generally understood that John Follett Pugsley was Secretary until 1949.

However, the archives of the *West Somerset Free Press* confirmed that John Follett Pugsley's resignation had been in 1947. Also in the National Pony Stud Book for 1948, the Hon. Secretary is listed as 'Major W. Hern, Porlock Vale, Minehead, Somerset.'

William Richard Hern was born on 20 January 1921 at Holford, near Bridgwater in Somerset. Dick was sent to Monmouth School and then Millfield in Somerset. From a young boy, he competed successfully in horse shows and he also hunted with the West Somerset Foxhounds. He was an amateur jockey and rode in point-to-points. Of his long relationship with horses he said '*I cannot remember being unable to ride*'.

In 1939, he was commissioned into the North Irish Horse before seeing active service in North Africa and Italy. After the war, Dick Hern worked at the Porlock Vale Riding School in Somerset, and in 1952 was the chief instructor and coach to the gold medal winning British show-jumping team at the Helsinki Olympic Games.

Subsequently, he took up racehorse training with considerable success, winning the St Leger six times and becoming trainer for the Queen. Then, in 1984, after a hunting accident, he was partially paralysed but continued as a trainer. Four years later, he was controversially sacked by the Queen's Racing Manager.

There is no record of his tenure as E.P.S. Secretary, as the Minute Books for 1947 to 1955 have not survived. His authorised biography makes no mention of his time serving the cause of the Exmoor pony.

Lt.-Colonel Victor Munckton
Secretary 1949 – 1971

When Dick Hern resigned, the post of Secretary was taken up by Lt-Colonel Victor Charles Alexander Munckton. Victor was born in March 1886 at Colehill in Dorset. Nothing is known of his early life but he was married in 1910 in London. He served in the First World War in the Royal Field Artillery, attaining the rank of Lieutenant by the end of the war and Captain six months later.

In July 1921 Victor Munckton and his wife sailed from London to Bombay, India. There he served in the Rajput Regiment of the Indian Army, retiring in 1946.

During his time as E.P.S. Secretary, Victor

85. Colonel Munckton on his chestnut charger, Monmouth, taken in 1937 at Fort Sandiman, on the North West Frontier, India.
Photo: Exmoor Pony Society Newsletter 1972.

Munckton produced the Society's first printed stud book and, later, a second edition. The 1972 E.P.S. Newsletter referring to his retirement in 1971, stated:

> *'So that we should not lose his invaluable advice, Mr. Milton suggested that Colonel Munckton should be made an Honorary Life-Consultant. This he has accepted, and in so doing will remain in touch with problems, ponies and owners.'*

Jeanne Watts (née Head)
Secretary from 1971 – 1981

In 1966, the Exmoor Pony Society decided to recruit an assistant to help Colonel Munckton and in October Miss Jeanne Head was selected. After two years she became Joint Secretary and then took over from Colonel Munckton when he retired in 1971. In December of that year she married local farrier John Watts.

Jeanne was born in Surrey in 1923. During World War II she worked for a year at the Army Remount Depot at Melton Mowbray. Subsequently, she spent two years as a riding instructor with Messrs. Holden Brothers (location unknown). Her training had been at Captain Younghusband's Little Stanmore Riding Stables where horses were trained for appearances in

86. Jeanne Watts at her home in Sampford Brett near Williton.
Photo: Exmoor Pony Society archive.

films. There she gained the British Horse Society's Preliminary Certificate.

It is not clear when Jeanne moved to Somerset. When she applied for the post of Assistant Secretary, she was living at Rodhuish. She hunted with the West Somerset Foxhounds.

Jeanne believed whole-heartedly that the Society should proactively promote the Exmoor breed. Once she became Secretary, she began giving slide talks, starting with a further education group in Minehead. She wrote articles for various publications and, on meeting photographer John Keene at Bampton Fair, sparked his interest in taking photographs for the Society. Jeanne undertook the production of the third edition of the Stud Book and produced a Breed Handbook, based on her talks.

Another of her initiatives was encouraging vets who had trained at the Royal (Dick) Veterinary College in Edinburgh and had experience with the Exmoor pony trekking herd, to become actively involved in the E.P.S.

Jeanne and others worked to establish herds away from Exmoor that duplicated the family lines in the three main herds, Anchor, 12 and 23, as insurance against disease or catastrophe devastating the moorland herds.

In 1975 Mr G. Gibbons was appointed as Joint Secretary, in preparation for him becoming Secretary in early 1976 on Jeanne's retirement. However, when he resigned in May 1976, Jeanne returned and finally retired in 1981. Ann Morgan was her Assistant Secretary 1978 -1979 and Joint Secretary between 1980 and 1981. Between 1967 and 1981, the workload had increased significantly, with the membership roughly tripling.

Jeanne was passionate about both the ponies and the Society. She died in 2004 and is remembered for both her dedication and determination.

Ken Walker
Secretary from 1981 – 1985

Ken Walker became Secretary when Jeanne and Ann retired in August 1981. He had left Brighton College, where he was Bursar, and moved to Exmoor, near Parracombe, bringing his hunters with him. The 1981 newsletter described him as 'a hunting man of West Country stock'. For most of his career he had worked for Shell overseas. He died in 2014.

As Ken's successors David Mansell, and Sue McGeever, are happily still with us, I will leave their stories to be told by a future chronicler.

The Williams Family of Great Ash

Great Ash is one of the farms that borders the open moorland of Winsford Hill close to Comers Cross on the road down to Winsford. In the early 1900s, it was farmed by Thomas & R. Crick, who came from Exford. The tenants of Great Ash were allowed to graze pure-bred Exmoor mares on the open moorland area that spanned Bradley Moor, Winsford Hill and South Hill, where only the land-owners, the Aclands, ran stallions.

By the time the Exmoor Pony Society was formed in 1920/21, Harry Williams had bought Great Ash from the Aclands and he immediately began registering with the Exmoor Pony Society. His herd number was 48. His Exmoor ponies were never grazed on the open moorland; they were always kept on the farm.

His grandson Robert told me:

'Grandfather had about 20 mares and won lots of prizes in the early 1950s. The two main show mares were Sally and Willows. He also had the stallion Ashill; it was named after a small clump of trees – if you come over Winsford Hill and look down towards Little Ash, you can see the trees in a field. Grandfather didn't smoke or drink much and the Exmoor ponies were his hobby. He once hired a lorry for £100 for a week to take ponies to show them at Roehampton and Ascot.'

When Harry Williams died, in 1950, Robert's father Bob took over and kept the herd going for a few years until 1957. Like Harry, Bob was involved with the Exmoor Pony Society as both a judge and an inspector. Bob often spent his holidays away judging but his interest in the Exmoors waned. He became more interested in trying to breed a racehorse: he put one of the Exmoor mares to to a Highland stallion and then the resulting cross to a Thoroughbred stallion. However, the end result was not successful as a racehorse.

The Williams family had considerable showing successes with home-bred ponies. At Exford Show in 1951, 1952 and 1953, herd 48 foals were placed first in the class for the best sucker, for which Lady Munnings had presented the A.J. Munnings trophy; on the third successive win, the trophy was awarded to Bob Williams for perpetuity.

87. Harry Williams with 1st and 2nd prize-winners at Dunster Show in 1954. Photo: courtesy of Robert Williams.

88. Bob Williams at Great Ash.
Photo: courtesy of Robert Williams.

89. Robert at home with the A.J. Munnings Cup and the medals won by Willows (a Bath & West and South Counties Society medal) and by Ashill (a National Pony Society medal at Exford in 1951).

Harry Williams had help with showing his ponies: Robert told me:

'Stan Blake used to live at Nethercott below Great Ash and his brother decided to sell up which meant that Stan would be homeless. Stan worked for the Williams family and so they invited him to live at Great Ash for a while. He stayed 17 years. He showed the Exmoor ponies and had a memorable outfit for shows – black and white check britches, brown boots and leggings and a red waistcoat. He would get the ponies calm for a class by simply walking them round and round in circles. He went on the week's trip to Roehampton and Ascot. Fred Rawle was involved too.'

Herd 48 was very important in the breeding of Herd 23 owned by Fred Milton; he used their stallions Bradymoor and Ashill in the 1940s. Ashill was one of only six stallions that existed by the end of World War II and the sire of Herd 23's stallion Forest. The Herd 48 ponies were kept in a 31 acre field just a few hundred yards along the road from Great Ash. Not much further along is the top entrance across the fields to Weatherslade Farm which was home to Fred Milton, who must have either walked his mares to the Great Ash field to run with their stallion or perhaps had stallions on loan to run on Withypool Common.

Robert remembers that Herd 48 foals were usually sold at Bampton Fair:

'It was my job to go into the pen and catch the foal to be auctioned. Ken Govier would catch hold of one end and me the other. Our ponies were taken to Bampton by lorry or trailer, never driven on the hoof. Sometimes they were sold privately too. Ernest Hawkins from Withypool sold a lot at Bampton too.'

Above left: *90. Robert with Willows and foal.*
Photo: courtesy of Robert Williams.

Above right: *91. Harry's wife with Stan Blake at Great Ash.* Photo: The Mary Etherington Archive.

Right: *92. Robert, aged three, riding the Highland/ Exmoor cross, with father Bob in the field where Herd 48 lived at Great Ash.*
Photo: courtesy of Robert Williams.

The Porlock Westcotts

93. Robert Westcott (far left in the cart) and fellow pony gatherers during their welcome lunch break.
Photo: Alfred Vowles.

Robert Westcott was born in 1843 and became a miller in Wootton Courtenay, as was his father John. In 1869, he married Sarah Clatworthy and they had eleven children. Robert continued to be a miller until 1873, when he moved the family to Eastcott Farm, near Porlock.

The eldest of the eleven children was Arthur George, born in 1870 and he enters the story of Exmoor ponies when the Exmoor Pony Society was formed, attending the founding meeting at the Red Lion Hotel in Dulverton in 1920. He became a member of the first Society committee and was a pony breeder. The Historical Supplement to the Exmoor Pony Society Stud Book shows that his herd number was 10 but he only ever registered seven ponies – five foundation stock and two of their progeny. His foundation stallion was bred by Charlie Westcott from Hawkridge (no relation as far as I can determine).

I met David Westcott, Arthur's nephew, in 2000 and he told me that not long after Arthur's father Robert had moved to Eastcott Farm, he became involved in organising the gathering of ponies from Porlock Common. He also explained that the ponies that ran on Porlock Common back in the 1920s were a mixture of true but unregistered Exmoors and also cross-bred ponies. He explained that the week of the gathering and the sales was looked upon as a week's holiday for those on the farms.

Alfred Vowles (see page 59) featured the Porlock pony gathering in the *West Somerset Free Press* in October 1921, highlighting how much the day was enjoyed by those involved:

> *'Exmoor Pony Gather Preparatory to Bampton Fair – This took place on Wednesday last in beautiful weather, Alderman's Barrow being the rendezvous, as in former years. A fine lot of ponies were galloped in by the various groups of horsemen, and by 1 p.m. all had arrived. Mr. Robert Westcott, of Eastcott, was again the host of the day, and everyone present was warmly invited to assemble round his spring-cart and help himself to hunks of bread and cheese and cake, cups of tea and mugs of Eastcott home-brew. All did justice to Mr. Westcott's kindness, and during this happy open-air luncheon, he gave a short but impressive lecture on the great qualities of the Exmoor pony, his pointed and humorous*

94. One of the postcards published by photographer Alfred Vowles showing predominantly cross-bred Porlock ponies either ready to depart for Bampton or possibly at Exford on the way. Robert Westcott is 7th from the left .

remarks being particularly directed to the younger generation present and to those who may not yet have become members of the Exmoor Pony Society. With admirable enthusiasm he exclaimed that it was folly not to join such an excellent institution.'

David Westcott, when interviewed by David Ramsey for his book *Unforgotten Exmoor,* said that the day after the gathering, the ponies would be driven to Brendon pony sale and the unsold animals and their drovers stayed that night in Brendon. The next day, the pony drovers began the journey to Bampton Fair, staying Tuesday night at Stone Farm, Exford and reaching Bampton on the Wednesday for the sale the following day.

A wonderful account of the drovers taking the ponies to Bampton survives in *The Somerset Yearbook* of 1920, written by Alfred Vowles, who participated, 'seated on a shaggy little Exmoor' – see next page for the full article.

Despite Robert Westcott's passionate advocacy for the Exmoor Pony Society, and his son Arthur's active service on the first committee, registrations by Arthur (Herd 10) ceased in 1924 and by brother Ernest (Herd 11) in 1950. There seems to be no record as to whether they stopped breeding ponies at all or simply did not register them with the Society or changed wholly to cross-breeding.

However, today, two great-great-grandsons of Robert Westcott, Malcolm and Nick, are once again registering ponies in Herds 4 and 11 respectively; Herd 4 was originally assigned to John Follett Pugsley who was E.P.S. Secretary between 1935 and 1947 (see page 50).

95. L-R Jim Moffat, Lilian Moffat (David Westcott's cousin), Jack Woolacott and Margaret Moffat at Birchanger Farm near Porlock in the mid 1940s.
Photo: the Mary Etherington Archive.

The Porlock to Bampton Pony Expedition 1920

The Porlock to Bampton Pony Expedition, 1920.

By ALFRED VOWLES, F.R.G.S.

THE PONY PENS AT BAMPTON FAIR.

BEAUTIFUL weather favoured the proceedings this year, and the enjoyment of the " outing," and the results from a financial point of view, are considered by those best able to judge to have eclipsed all former years.

The drive to Bampton Fair is a red-letter experience for many an Exmoor farmer. The little adventures, exciting experiences (minor and harmless in their way), the meeting of many old friends, and the general good cheer, are incentives to join such an expedition. The meet of the Porlock men took place at 10 a.m. on Wednesday, the 28th October, at Bucket Hole, where 42 of the prettiest and liveliest ponies had been collected and were awaiting the long journey to Bampton.

A dense fog enveloped the country, so that the start was delayed, and minds became anxious lest this adverse, but temporary, climatic condition should prove dangerous to the proceedings. To loosen a herd of wild ponies on to the moors in a thick fog and drive them to a given point is a very ticklish enterprise indeed. Mr. George Westcott, of Bromham Farm, fathered the drive as in former years, he being assisted by such able thrusters as Messrs. Ernest, Cecil, Harold, and Freddie Westcott, John, Will, and Sam Rawle, Jack Harding, and Sid Braddick. Major Vere Foster came over from Cloutsham to help across the first stretch of open country, while your humble contributor, seated on a shaggy little Exmoor, acted as a reserve and an admirer of the proceedings. As no signs of the fog clearing were visible at 10.30, the order was given to move off, and in a few moments the drive swept out of the enclosures on to the open heather. Two riders preceded the party as guides, three charged along in single file on each flank and three brought up the rear. The ponies were thus hemmed in on all sides, and made to gallop along with a good deal if thrust, lusty shouting, and whip cracking. Such boisterous tactics kept the ponies interested and helped to divert their attentions from their free and happy homeland outside the human cordon! The fog still lay thick upon the moor, and necessitated a very close formation, so much so that few opportunities were given the ponies to escape, but at one point

34

96. Recreated from The Somerset Year Book Vol. XVIII - XIX (1919 - 1920) published by The Society of Somerset Folk.

looked as though many of them would break away and become lost in the fog. When skirting the boggy ground of Exford Common the leaders on the left flank suddenly broke past the leading horseman, but thanks to the splendid lungs and fine horsemanship of Farmer Will Rawle, they were headed back to the herd without loss or casualty.

The expedition got into Exford at 11.30, the galloping and shouting horsemen and general pandemonium bringing the inhabitants (including the school children) to their doors. In the village a general mix-up was narrowly averted with the pony herd of the Culbone men, who were just departing for Bampton. With lusty cries of the chase and the winding of a hunting horn they

Barle, with its glorious and romantic woodlands, looking gorgeous in their autumnal colours. At 2.30 the column was winding its way at a steady trot into the sporting town of Dulverton, where it was to rest during the night. In a cloud of vapour and dust the ponies and riders thundered through the narrow winding streets, causing no end of consternation and excitement among the inhabitants! The ponies were driven to a field, and well they deserved their rest and feed of luscious green grass. The men and horses adjourned to stables and billets, and during the evening the former were able to see the sights of the town, look up old staghunting friends, and wile away the time in pleasant country fashion.

CROSSING EXMOOR FROM PORLOCK TO BAMPTON.

moved off at the gallop, thus allowing a free road to the Crown Hotel for the men of Porlock. In the yard of this sporting hostelry the ponies were given an hour's "breather," while those in charge refreshed themselves with the good things supplied by Host and Hostess Baker. Before leaving, the fog lifted, so the party and the ponies were photographed, and a very pretty picture they make!

By one o'clock the expedition was well on its way again, passing Gibbet Post (where wicked men in less refined times were hanged by the neck), and Comer's Gate (where Exmoor pixies play on moonlight nights), and on, on, on, over the four miles of heather of Winsford Hill; then down, down, down to the valley of the

Up again next morning long before the sun, and to stables and breakfasts. Before many a Dulverton man bad forsaken his pillow the ponies had been rounded up and counted and galloped through the town *en route* to Bampton. They crossed Exe Bridge (over the parapet of which jumped Tom Faggus and his strawberry mare to escape their captors) into Devon, and the remaining four miles to Bampton Fair were covered in quick time. Great care had to be exercised in passing through the crooked old town, owing to the early crowds of people, herds of bullocks, and horses, and other cumbersome obstacles. By thrusting forward at the gallop and sweeping aside everybody and everything, the ponies were driven to the

35

97. Recreated from The Somerset Year Book Vol. XVIII - XIX (1919 - 1920) published by The Society of Somerset Folk.

auction pens without mishap. The last burst, boisterous and lively to a degree, ended the journey of 24 miles – a journey full of interest, excitement and good fellowship.

Keen competition ensued at the auction, Stallions ranging in price up to £25 and £80, Mares nearly as much, and Suckers up to £10. A good average price before the War for the last-names one was one guinea. Times have changed, even on Exmoor!

When the Ponies have been sold and safely handed over to their new owners, the Farmer is free to enjoy the fun of the Fair, and the cheap-jacks, quacks, jugglers and round-abouts, &c., fascinate him until late in the day. Then with pockets bulging with delicacies of the Fair (for the Missus and Kiddies at home or the Sweetheart as the case may be!), a substantial cheque folded away in his wallet and a contentment to be envied, he starts on the long ride home by the light of the Hunter's Moon.

98. Recreated from The Somerset Year Book Vol. XVIII - XIX (1919 - 1920) published by The Society of Somerset Folk.

Note: This account of cross-bred ponies being taken to Bampton, portrays the experiences of pony drovers that held true whichever herds were involved. However, for the pure-bred herds, being located further south on Exmoor, the journey was shorter and did not necessitate overnight stops.

Alfred Vowles

Alfred Charles Vowles was born in 1882 near Cheddar in Somerset. Four years later, his father James died and the family was left almost penniless. He left the village school at fourteen to go to the Royal Navy College at Greenwich. After a time living with his brother near London and working in an office, and a period of ill-health spent back in Somerset, Alfred went to work for the Eastman Kodak Company in London. He borrowed a camera from Kodak and during a period working in Germany, travelled in Russia, taking many photographs. Returning to England, he found it hard to settle back into office work and resigned in 1905, returning to Somerset.

Alfred's next job was as a photographer, travelling all over Somerset and Devon. In her biographical article, held in the Somerset Heritage Centre, Margaret Jordan wrote:

> *'He travelled scores of miles on his bicycle controlling the machine with his right hand only and carrying in his left hand his camera and tripod and over his shoulder a canvas bag with half plates, finding lodgings in the towns and villages as he went. He photographed people, businesses, farms and livestock doing all his own printing, finishing and mounting working in sheds or stables aided by lots of blackout material and water from a nearby well or pump.'*

In 1911 Alfred Vowles bought himself a horse-drawn caravan (without a horse) which became both home and photographic laboratory in Minehead. He also bought a 3A Folding Pocket Kodak, the camera he used for four decades . He photographed landscapes, animals and people, documenting some twenty-five years of Exmoor life, travelling either on foot or on his motorcycle. He also wrote for local newspapers and magazines and produced many of his photographs as postcards (now highly collectable).

By 1920, he was living in a house in Minehead, with his photographic business doing well. A decade later, he married Lilian Bowerman and they had a son Roland in 1932; Roland emigrated to New Zealand when he was twenty. However, by the end of WWII, the marriage had ended. Alfred sold up and left Exmoor, leaving all his negatives behind. Fortunately, they came to light in the 1970s.

Alfred Vowles married for a second time in 1947; his second wife was poet Dorothy McGriger Phillips. She refused to take the name of Vowles and so he changed his name to Phillips. They lived in North Berwick in Scotland, where he died on 24 February 1965.

The Green Family and the Acland Herd

In 1927, Frank Green bought Old Ashway Farm and the adjoining land of Ashway Side and Varle Hill from Tom Parkman (the Acland herd manager). Part of the purchase agreement was that each pony within the Acland herd kept on Ashway Side would be owned jointly by Sir Francis Acland and Frank Green. In 1939, Sir Francis died and his son Richard inherited the half-share in the pony herd. Frank Green's great nephew, Colonel Simon Lycett-Green recorded in the herd Stud Book in 1952:

> *'Frank Green was very zealous in guarding the rights of the herd, so much so that he eventually bought Sir Richard Acland's share and they became wholly his property, except that he always maintained that they were part of the estate and could not be separated from it. He regarded himself as keeper of the herd rather than owner.'*

This brought to an end the involvement of the Acland family with the fate of the true Exmoor ponies that had started in 1767.

So, who was Frank Green and what brought him to Exmoor? Francis William Green was the second son of Sir Edward Green, M.P. for Wakefield in Yorkshire, and his wife Mary Lycett. He was educated at Eton and Oxford and in 1860 entered the family's engineering firm in Wakefield. His grandfather's invention of a fuel economiser for steam boilers had made the family very wealthy. The Greens moved in high social circles too, largely because of their enthusiasm for fox-hunting and shooting.

It was stag-hunting that first brought Frank Green to Exmoor. His obituary in the *West Somerset Free Press* in 1954 stated:

> *'A keen follower and generous supporter of the Devon and Somerset Staghounds, Mr. Green had been in the habit of coming to this part of the country during the hunting season before he*

99. Frank Green. Photo: A.H. Poole/National Library of Ireland.

settled here. For many years he was a guaranteeing member of the Hunt committee; he was also on the committee of the Exmoor Foxhounds for several years and at point-to-point meetings in the district, Exford Horse Show, and other such events he was a familiar figure. He was a member also of the Exmoor Horn Sheep Breeders' Society.'

Undoubtedly, then, Frank Green mixed in the same social circle as the Aclands and so would have come to know first hand all about the famous Acland herd of Exmoor ponies.

Being the second son, Frank's destiny was to be running the family's engineering works, whilst his elder brother devoted his energies to hunting. Frank described himself as *'the industrious apprentice, who slaved in the muck and grime so that the rest of the family could enjoy their lives of leisure.'* However, he was also a cultured man who had artistic interests in York. Between 1897 and 1914, he lived in, and fully restored, The Treasurer's House in York and assembled a huge collection of antiques. In July 1930, he gave the house and its contents to the National Trust and moved to Dulverton.

As well as Old Ashway, Frank Green purchased other property in and around Dulverton, including Ashwick and The Green Hotel. He was known locally for his generosity but also for eccentricity and extravagance.

It seems that Frank Green managed the pony herd on the basis of minimal interference with their natural life. Tom Parkman's daughter, Gladys Bawden, wrote in a letter:

> *'After father moved to Winsford when Mr. Frank Green bought Old Ashway and Ashway Side from him, occasionally father, on Mr. Green's request went over and looked at the ponies … No-one was on the spot to see them every day, no-one in charge!'*

Things came to a head during World War II, with the theft of all but a dozen of the ponies. Simon Lycett-Green wrote:

> *'The dark days of the 1939-45 war brought dark days, too, for the Acland Herd. They remained living on the hill and at the time of meat rationing and shortage some criminal butchers visited Exmoor and trapped the majority of the herd in one of the narrow lanes and stole them away. They must have employed some local aid but the criminals were never caught. Frank Green spent several hundreds of pounds in trying to trace the ponies and it was ascertained that they were taken as far as Cumberland.'*

100. Rose Green with Exmoor mare Greengage in 1956.
Photo: Wallace Ashwick Estate Archives.

The loss of most of the herd had a profound effect on Frank Green and he hid the remaining ponies away on the farm, as far away from the lanes as possible. He would not return them to the moor after the war ended and didn't even trust officials of the Exmoor Pony Society; in 1948, he refused to allow E.P.S. inspectors access to the foals.

Not long after, Simon Lycett-Green bought Old Ashway Farm and Ashway Side and Frank Green gave Ashwick to Simon's daughter, Rose (who married Captain Ronnie Wallace in 1964). Frank, in his late eighties, was no longer up to managing the farming and so Simon and Rose took on the pony herd. A combination of old age and fear of outsiders had resulted in Frank Green being less than diligent in maintaining segregation of the herd and some of the animals were of doubtful purity; so, with help from Sid Westcott, they reduced the herd back down to twelve mares and a stallion and reinstated inspection and registration.

Frank Green died on Saturday 27 March 1954 aged 93. He was buried in Wakefield but a memorial service was held in Dulverton. After her father Simon's death in 2003, Rose Wallace became sole owner of the herd and, in turn, after her passing in 2005, son David and his wife Emma inherited the ponies. Whilst locally, and within the Exmoor Pony Society, the herd is usually referred to as the 'Anchor Herd' (after the anchor brand-mark), within the family it has always been known as the 'Acland Herd' and Frank Green's principle of guardianship has been handed down alongside the ponies.

Eleanor Helme

Eleanor Helme (1887 - 1967) was a highly talented golfer who represented England internationally on four occasions. Perhaps unsurprisingly, her career in writing began as a golfing correspondent beginning at the *Yorkshire Post* in 1910 and later for the *Daily Telegraph* and *The Tatler*, amongst others.

Eleanor also became a writer of fiction and non-fiction books. She wrote on themes of golf, wildlife, Christian subjects and children's adventures with ponies; the pony books are set on Exmoor, a favoured holiday destination for her.

In 1933, whilst staying at Cloutsham, Eleanor bought a plot of land on the outskirts of the village of Luccombe. At the end of World War II, she stayed in Porlock whilst she had a house built on the plot. So it was that, together with her sister Vera, she came to live permanently at *Three Gates* in Luccombe where they stayed until 1964, then moving to Minehead.

Her first children's story about ponies was a joint project with writer Nance Paul. *Jerry – the story of an Exmoor Pony* was illustrated by Cecil Aldin and published in 1930. A sequel followed in 1932, *The Joker and Jerry Again,* with the same collaborator. Her Exmoor pony hero, Jerry, was undoubtedly not a pure-bred Exmoor, being described as having a white patch on his face, as did his mother, plus a white star.

After that, she wrote on her own and *Mayfly – The Grey Pony* was published in 1935, followed by *Runaway Mike* the following year, again featuring cross-bred ponies as their main characters. In 1946, Eyre & Spottiswoode published *Shank's Pony,* the first in a series of three stories about a Cockney lad called Davy and his various exploits on Exmoor. The second and third books, *Suitable Owners* and *White Winter* featured a pure-bred Exmoor pony called Adam. *White Winter* tells the story of the incredibly harsh winter of 1947. Eleanor had met the artist Lionel Edwards sometime before 1935 and he illustrated the trilogy.

101. Eleanor Helme outside 'Three Gates', Luccombe riding Sarah in May 1954. Photo: courtesy of Freda James and Eric Rowlands.

The Real Adam

In 1999, Mrs Gill Lyon from Bicester visited the Exmoor Pony Society stand at the Christmas Equine Fair at Westpoint, Exeter. She told me that Eleanor Helme used to visit their farm at Cloutsham and had based the pony hero of her stories *Suitable Owners* and *White Winter* on their pony Adam.

Gill later wrote, telling me more:

'Adam was bred by Mr. French (of Malmsmead I believe) and was sold to Tony Collins, unbroken, who trained him to saddle. My grandfather, G.F. Jackson, bought him for me when I was ten and Adam was six. Adam had a brand F just below and behind his saddle. It is entirely due to this little fellow that I am so besotted with our equine friends!

With me, Adam won Exmoor classes (and I still have the clock that was his prize at one). Handy Pony, gymkhana events (particularly bending races), hunting, jumping – he tried his hand at everything. During the war my mother worked for Bob Nancekivell at Cloud as a land

girl. Adam was her means of getting there and, if it was wet, she carried a large, brilliantly coloured golf umbrella – the picture was wonderful.

I only knew Adam to behave badly once and that was at Brendon Show. We were doing well until the judge Tommy Hancock M.S.H. decided to ride them all. Adam took exception and took Tommy straight out of the ring! Needless to say, we weren't placed. By the time Adam died in 1960, he was a venerable gentleman who had certainly done his bit to foster many small children's love of ponies.'

Left: *102. Adam at a meet at Cloutsham in 1936.*
Photo: Gill Lyon

Below: *103. Adam, in summer 1960, the year he died, aged over forty with the last child he taught to ride.*

Note: Adam's F brand tells us that he had not been registered in the Exmoor Pony Society Stud Book. Using a single letter in the saddle area seems to have been widely used for non-registered Exmoor ponies. Here, F was breeder Mr French's mark and there are photos in the Mary Etherington Archive showing an E brand (Etherington?) and an H brand (possibly Hawkins).

Joan Wanklyn

Above: *104. The booklet's cover and,* right: *105. enlargement of the Exmoor panel.*

In the 1930s the gentlemen's outfitters Moss Bros., situated in Covent Garden, London, produced their first story booklet for customers – *All at Sea* about cruising. Subsequently, they looked to their market for riding clothing and commissioned R.S. Summerhays to write the text for a booklet called *Ponies*. Joan Wanklyn provided the illustrations, some of which were reproduced by permission of the Ponies of Britain Club.

Joan Wanklyn (1924 - 1999) was born near Stevenage in Hertfordshire into a family 'mad on horses'. She studied at the Royal Drawing Society Studios and Chelsea Polytechnic and at the Central School of Art. In the 1950s, she wrote and illustrated several children's books on animal subjects; one of these was about a pony. She also illustrated three of the Punchbowl Farm pony books by Monica Edwards, as well as many other children's books, mostly on animal and equestrian subjects. She was a regular contributor to the early Pony Club annuals and books, as well as regularly contributing illustrations to *Pony* magazine and judging the magazine's annual Harry Hall Drawing Competition.

106. *The inside illustration for Exmoor ponies.*

Exmoor Ponies

by Gefa Gay

from the *Western Morning News*, Friday 17 April 1931

If you journey'd over Exmoor in the happy
days of old,
Be it silver in the moonlight or ablaze with
liquid gold,
There was stir of life about you … tossing
mane and flying tail:
If you journey'd over Exmoor ere the herds
began to fail.

If you journey over Exmoor scarce a pony
will you see;
All about you in the sunlight birds are
wheeling silently.
Maybe you'll glimpse a shadow … catch
the echo of a neigh …
But the pony-herds of Exmoor, they will
soon have passed away.

If you journey over Exmoor in the days that
are to be,
You will find it lone and empty from Dunkery
to the sea;
Not a pony-herd will scatter; not a red deer
leap or start:
Only jagged rocks to tell you of old Exmoor's
broken heart.

107. The Anchor Herd near Mounsey Gate.

Richard Kingsley Tayler

Little is known about photographer Richard Kingsley Tayler other than his production of this set of postcards – presumed to be from the late 1930s. The photographs feature the Westcott family's ponies at Hawkridge (see pages 17 - 21).

He was born in 1905 in Redruth, Cornwall and

Pure Bred Exmoor Suckers leaving Hawkridge for New Homes R. KINGSLEY TAYLER

THREE TYPICAL PURE BRED EXMOOR SUCKERS R. KINGSLEY TAYLER

Left: *108. Charlie Westcott with suckers.*

Above: *109. Suckers belonging to the Hawkridge Westcotts.*

Right: *110. Portrait of a Herd 1 pony.*

Exmoor Ponies claim direct descent from pre-historic horses R. KINGSLEY TAYLER

PURE BRED EXMOOR PONIES GATHERED FOR BAMPTON FAIR R. KINGSLEY TAYLER

Above: *111. Westcott ponies, probably at Zeal Farm, Hawkridge.*

Right: *112. Herd 1 stallion Caractacus, born in 1935.*

"CARACTACUS," PURE BRED EXMOOR STALLION R. KINGSLEY TAYLER

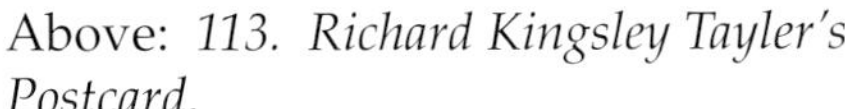
Above: *113. Richard Kingsley Tayler's Postcard.*

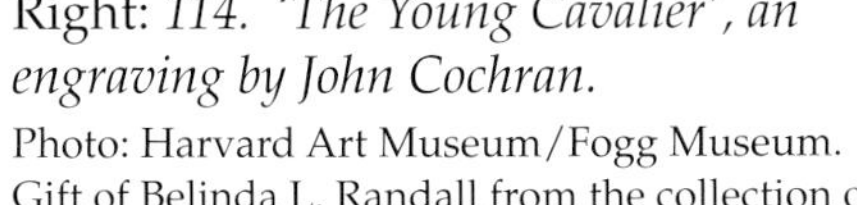
Right: *114. 'The Young Cavalier', an engraving by John Cochran.*
Photo: Harvard Art Museum/Fogg Museum. Gift of Belinda L. Randall from the collection of John Witt Randall, R10181.

in 1935 opened his photographic business in The Avenue, Minehead. He married Barbara P. Ponter in September 1943 and died in March 1979.

There is a strange card included in the series depicting Exmoor ponies, somewhat at odds with the other pictures. This postcard was entitled 'Staffordshire Pottery Model – over 100 years old of Exmoor Pony'.

The Potteries Museum in Stoke-on-Trent identified the model as one of a pair depicting the Prince and Princess of Wales; the figure in the postcard is the Prince of Wales (later to become Edward VII). The original figures (probably dated in the late 1840s) are rare but copies were made from the original moulds as late as the 1950s. As many different companies produced such figures and seldom marked them in any way, it is not possible to identify which factory was responsible for the one photographed by Kingsley Tayler.

The model was based on an undated engraving by John Cochran entitled 'The Young Cavalier' and Cochran himself had based his engraving on a painting by William Salter (1804-1875) who has some 83 paintings in the National Portrait Gallery.

Unsurprisingly, none of the references to this Staffordshire figure give any information as to the type of pony the Prince of Wales is riding. To my eyes, the pony in Cochran's engraving looks rather more like a Shetland pony than an Exmoor. The painter of the pottery figures seems to have highlighted the eyes and accentuated the lighter muzzle compared to the engraving.

So, whilst the postcard, itself a rarity now, has a place in a collection of Exmoor pony memorabilia, the Staffordshire figure itself is a very doubtful contender.

Allen W. Seaby (1867 - 1953)

Allen William Seaby, Professor of Fine Art at Reading University from 1920 to 1933 was well-known for his wildlife illustrations, particularly of birds; he illustrated two of the Ladybird children's books. He was also author and illustrator of children's stories about British native ponies (including *Exmoor Lass* in 1928) and also two non-fiction books on the same subject – *British Ponies: Running Wild and Ridden* (1936) and *Our Ponies* (1949).

Allen Seaby was interested in the conservation of the native breeds and took a great interest in the natural life of the free-living animals. In *British Ponies Running Wild and Ridden* he wrote:

> *'Although I know it is an unpractical, uneconomic attitude, I myself am more interested in the pony on his native heath, untrammelled and free to go where he pleases.'*

In the introduction to *Our Ponies*, Allen Seaby refers to:

> *'The eleven to twelve hand Exmoor, used for so long in the mines'* and *'While in the cramped galleries of the coal mines small ponies were needed and no attempt was made to increase the size of the Exmoor.'*

Our Ponies was a paperback in the Puffin Picture Book series (number 78) and priced at one shilling and sixpence (which equates to 7.5 pence today).

In this publication, Allen Seaby depicted and described New Forest, Exmoor, Dartmoor, Wesh, Fells and Dales, Highland and Shetland ponies as well as briefly considering history, management and uses of native ponies.

Left: *115. Front cover of* Our Ponies.
Reproduced by kind permission of Robert Gillmor.

Below: *117. and 118. From* Our Ponies.
Reproduced by kind permission of Robert Gillmor.

116. Allen Seaby in 1947.
Photo: courtesy of Robert Gillmor.

EXMOOR PONIES

So many carelessly or cross-bred Dartmoor and Exmoor ponies are to be met with that it is often difficult to distinguish between them, but the correct types are quite unmistakable. The Exmoor, averaging twelve hands, should be mousey-brown in colour and under the belly and inside the fore-

Exmoor ponies above Weir-water coombe. In the distance is the old pack-pony trail which crossed Exmoor.

14

The hired pony. The path to the Doone Valley is on the right. The Badgworthy where John Ridd caught the loaches is below on the left.

arms and thighs the brown should merge into a lighter mealy colour, which should also surround the eye, the eye itself being particularly large and prominent - on Exmoor it is called the Toad eye. It is particularly important that the muzzle should be mealy-white and the nose and nostrils black : an Exmoor without a mealy nose is definitely not pure bred.

15

Allen Seaby's love of nature and art was certainly bequeathed to his grandson, Robert Gillmor. He is an ornithologist, print-maker, artist and illustrator of over 100 books. He is a past President of the Society of Wildlife Artists. In 2001 he was awarded the R.S.P.B. Medal, given for outstanding contribution to nature conservation; the medal bears the avocet, familiar from the R.S.P.B.'s logo, which was Robert's work.

119. *From* Our Ponies. Reproduced by kind permission of Robert Gillmor.

Disturbed. Above the Badgworthy.

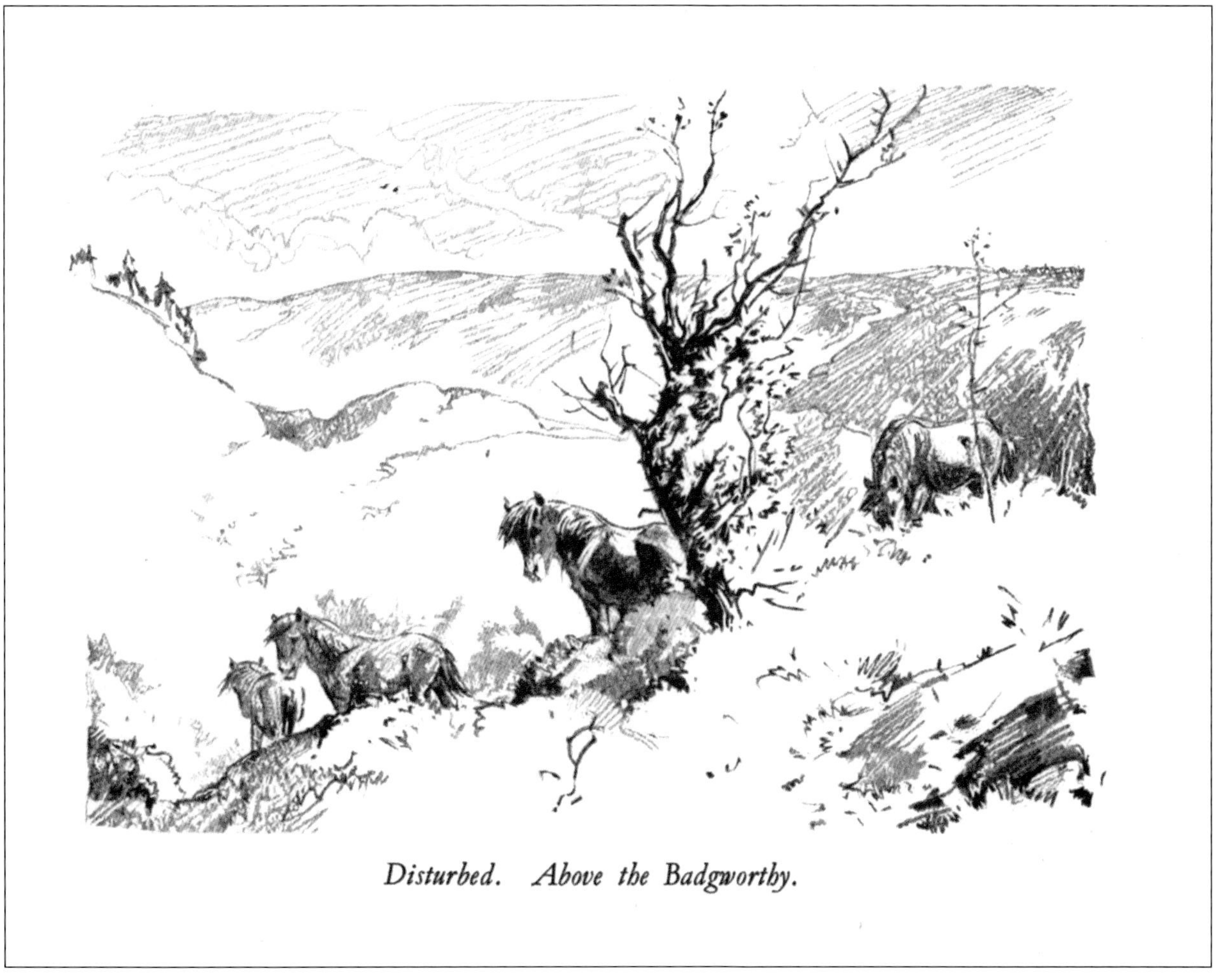

120. *One of the Exmoor illustrations from* British Ponies: Running Wild and Ridden. Reproduced by kind permission of Robert Gillmor.

Sophia Best

Mary Gertrude Sophia Best is certainly not a well-known name in the Exmoor pony world – but it should be. I first encountered Sophia, as she was known to friends, in a booklet *The Little Horses of Exmoor* which she and Mary Etherington published in 1947. In it Mary Etherington wrote:

> *'Miss M. G. S. Best, who has made a life-time study of the native pony breeds from the naturalist's point of view, has tracked the little horses in their wanderings from prehistoric times down to the present-day and has shown us what a rich inheritance we have in this rather desolate corner of moorland.'*

This suggests that it was Sophia Best who actually inspired Mary Etherington with the idea that the Exmoor pony was little altered from the original wild ponies of Britain. Yet it is Mary Etherington and her husband James Speed who are usually credited with originating the theory. Undoubtedly, their research considerably developed the theory but it is time, at last, to recognise this unsung heroine of Exmoor pony conservation. But who was she and how did she come to know Mary Etherington, Exmoor and the Exmoor ponies? Was it this lady who originated the idea that they were an ancient breed?

Sophia Best was born in Upper Clatford, Hampshire in November 1868. Her father was the Reverend Thomas Best and her mother's name was Louisa. She had several siblings. Sophia was christened in the church at nearby Abbot's Ann where her uncle, Samuel Best, was the rector. Her uncle was a highly educated man with a keen interest in geology, so perhaps he was influential in developing in her a love and knowledge of the natural world, particularly ornithology.

In 1911 Sophia appears on the list of Fellows of the Zoological Society of London and there are a number of letters in the Z.S.L. archives from her, all on the subject of birds. She was also a Fellow of the Royal Society for the Protection of Birds in 1912. In 1914, a letter in the archives of *The Spectator*, from 'Miss Best', reveals that she was at that time a member of the Selborne Society and the Photographic Society as well as a member of

THE

LITTLE HORSES of EXMOOR

by M. G. S. BEST & M. G. ETHERINGTON

Price 5/- net.

121. The 1947 booklet Sophia and Mary Etherington published jointly. The publication also includes contributions from William Crockford, David Tapp, Tom Pring and William Thorne.

the Ladies Athenaeum Club in London. Between 1914 and 1929, she had bird photographs and observations published in several magazines.

It was in the 1930s that she apparently first wrote about native ponies: in September 1937, *Riding & Driving – the Horselovers' Magazine* published an article by her about Bampton Fair (see page 88). Exmoor Pony Society Minutes of February 1939 record receiving a letter from her about obtaining good photographs for inclusion in a 'Moorland Pony Book proposed to be published by Country Life. She was elected as a member of the EPS that year.

She was also a contributor to *The Field* in the

1940s, with articles on Welsh ponies (April 1945) and Dartmoor and Exmoor ponies (September 1945). She wrote breed profiles for the National Pony Society's book *Mountain and Moorland Ponies of Great Britain* published in 1946; a number of her own photographs were included in the book.

We have Sophia's own words from 1947 in *The Little Horses of Exmoor* to tell us how she felt after spending time on Exmoor:

> *'It became more and more clear to me that the red deer and the ponies had histories dating back also to these very early days. The chief interest being that these animals are now living their own lives free and wild on the moor in just the same way that their ancestors had done for some thousands of years, forming an unbroken chain with the prehistoric "Little Horses" which lived there so long ago.'*

Sophia was not the first though to make a link between Exmoor ponies and ancient British ponies. That accolade, seemingly, must be given to archaeologist General Augustus Pitt Rivers (see page 31). Sophia would probably have known about Pitt Rivers' work, as the excavations were at Cranborne in Dorset and they lived less than 35 miles away.

She certainly knew about the breeding experiments of Professor James Cossar Ewart (see page 40) and his theory of *The Multiple Origin of Horses and Ponies*. Professor Cossar Ewart wrote:

> *'The origin of the dark-brown variety of the Celtic pony is also wrapped in mystery. These dark-brown ponies may represent another old variety from which the Exmoors have sprung – a variety which has contributed the tan-coloured muzzle and the ring around the eye so characteristic of many of the best Highland and Island garrons.'*

Sophia referred to his work in *The Little Horses of Exmoor*.

So it would seem that when Sophia encountered Exmoor ponies, she was already primed with the idea of their possible antiquity. She remains an 'unsung heroine' though because without her inspiring Mary Etherington, it is doubtful that the conservation of the pure bred moorland herds would have been taken up so ardently by Mary after their decimation during WWII; nor would Mary and James Speed have perhaps ever met and pursued their interest in Exmoor pony origins.

122. Sophia's last home, Broadwindsor, in the village of Amport near Andover.

In the course of researching Sophia Best, I visited the church at Abbot's Ann where she is buried. I also visited her final home, Broadwindsor, in the village of Amport, where she lived with her sister Eleanor for some years before she died in 1953. A local resident told me that they well remembered the sisters who used to sit and paint on the village green and the place was still known as 'Best Corner'.

Given Sophia's significance in the Exmoor pony story, surely she deserves more of a commemoration than just a local place name.

I have asked many elderly people on Exmoor if they remember Sophia, but no-one knew anything about her. We do know that she attended gatherings and Bampton Fair – were these simply a writer's research visits or did she have other links to Exmoor?

As described, she was a Fellow of the Zoological Society of London and a member of the Ladies Athenaeum Club in Dover Street, London, founded for ladies with interests in arts, literature, music and politics. Eleanor Helme (see pages 62 - 63), was also a Z.S.L. Fellow. It is reasonable to speculate that they might have met; maybe she was a member of the same ladies' club. Eleanor lived at Luccombe on Exmoor, so perhaps it was through visiting Eleanor Helme that Sophia was able to explore her interest in Exmoor ponies.

Old Farmer Mole

This wonderful tale comes from *Somerset Folklore* by Ruth Tongue. She noted 'I heard many versions of this tale as a child, but my favourite was this, told me by an old farm labourer at Kinsford in 1905.'

They'll tell 'ee three things 'bout an Exmoor Pony 'can climb a cleeve, carry a drunky, and zee a pixy'. And that's what old Varmer Mole's pony do.

Old Varmer Mole were a drunken old toad as lived out over to Hangley Cleave way and he gived his poor dear wife and liddle children a shocking life of it. He never come back from the market till his pockets were empty and he was zo vull of zider he'd zit on pony 'hind-zide afore' a zingin' and zwearin' till her rolled into ditch and slept the night there – but if his poor missus didn't zit up all night vor'n he'd baste her and the children wicked.

Now the pixies they did mind'n and they went to mend his ways.

'Twad'n no manner of use to try to frighten pony – he were that foot-sure and way-wise he'd brought Varmer safe whoame drunk or asleep vor years, wheresoever the vule tried to ride'n tew.

This foggy night the old veller were wicked drunk and a-waving his gad and reckoning how he'd drub his Missus when he gets to whoame when her zee a light in the mist. 'Whoa, that vule!' Says he. 'Us be to whoame. Dang'n vor lighting a girt candle like thic. I'll warm her zides for it!' But the pony he wouldn' stop. He could a-zee the pixy holdin' thic light and 'twere over the blackest, deepest bog this zide of the Chains – zuck a pony down in a minute 'twould, rider and all. But the old man keeps on shouting, 'Whoa, fule, us be to whoame!' And rode straight for the bog – but pony digged in his vour liddle veet 'n her stood!

Varmer gets off'n and catches 'n a crack on the head and walks on to light. He hadn' goed two steps when the bog took and swallowed 'n!

Zo old pony trots whoame. And when they zee'd 'n come alone with peat-muck on his legs they knowed what did come to Varmer – and they did light every candle in the house and dancey!

After that Missus left a pail of clean water out at night vor pixy babies to wash in, pretty dears, and swept hearth vor pixies to dancey on and varm propsered wondervul, and old pony grew zo fat as a pig.

Ruth Tongue also included the possible inspiration for the tale as told to her eldest brother by the farmer at Kinsford in 1906:

'A farmer went to Lynmouth with his pack-horse for a load of lime to put heart in his poor fields. Returning in the mist he lost the way to Kinsford, and man and horse were swallowed in the quagmire. When it was drained years later, man and horse were found preserved by the lime.'

123. The bog took and swallowed 'n! by Alma Swan.

Making Merry

These stories were told to me by an elderly gentleman in the White Horse Inn in Exford in the mid-1970s.

Three young men had ponies to sell at Bampton Fair. They drove them down from Exmoor, put them in the auction field in Bampton and then booked two rooms at a local house for the night. They went to one of the pubs and got very drunk. When the pub closed, they emerged in a somewhat 'confused' state but by some means found their way to their lodging house. 'The Lord looks after drunks and little children.'

One of them went into one room whilst Sidney and Walter shared the other. Walter got into bed with his boots and spurs still on and Sidney, presumably beyond coherent thought, laid down under the bed. Well, in the night, Sidney awoke and said 'Ere, Walter, it must be cold, it be snowin': sure enough, white flakes were drifting down on him. For every time Walter turned over, his spurs ripped the sheet and mattress, sending down clouds of feathers!

After the pony sale the next day, they set off for home at a wild pace and, galloping out of Dulverton (after a session at the Red Lion), Sidney went right through the Fire Station doors and broke his pony's neck. The other two, still inebriated, never missed him and on Winsford Hill split up. One got home safely to Riscombe but Walter was found in the yard of his farm fast asleep on his horse!

Another time, the three were travelling over the moor late in the evening and reached the pub (Gallon House?) after it was shut. They wanted a drink and so threw gravel up at the Landlord's bedroom window several times. Eventually, he opened the window and very crossly asked them what they wanted. 'Come down and give us a drink will you?'. He refused and told them to go home. 'Oh come on Landlord, we just want an half 'n half and then we'll be on our way'. Suddenly, they were soaked by the contents of the publican's chamber pot. 'There,' he said, 'that's half mine and half the missus's.' (Note: half 'n half = half beer, half cider)

124. Passing Through by Alma Swan.

Travelling to Bampton

Fred Radley's earliest memory of Dulverton was of Exmoor ponies being driven through the town towards Bampton for the Fair. He stood at the door (they had a board across the door to stop him going out on the road) and there were all the ponies galloping through down Lady Street.

> *'It seemed to go on for ever, there must have been hundreds. They were just rushing by, little ponies. It was a wonderful sight. There was one in front and a horseman behind, on Exmoors.'*

They were small horses but they looked big to him as a child.

Note: Fred Radley was born in 1929. Source: The Exmoor Oral History Archive/Birdie Johnson.

By Train to Islington

125. One of the West Somerset Railway's steam engines at Dunster Station in recent times.

In 1900, the Polo Pony and Riding Pony Society (which became the National Pony Society in 1913) held its first annual show, including classes for Mountain and Moorland breeds, at the Royal Agricultural Hall, Islington in London. Understandably, the Exmoor breeders wanted to participate and show their ponies to the wider world. It is uncertain as to exactly when Exmoors were first shown at Islington but it is thought to have been in the early 1920s.

In practical terms this required considerable effort. I was told that William Crockford was one of the first to make the trip to London. This meant bringing the chosen pony/ponies from the moor back to West Hawkwell Farm at Luckwell Bridge and then walking them to Dunster Station, about eleven miles away. At the station, the animals would be loaded into a railway wagon and transported by steam train to Paddington Station in London. Once there, handlers and ponies walked a further five miles to Islington.

The story goes that usually the Exmoors were put at the bottom of the line because, unlike other breeds, they were shown in 'natural condition'; presumably too, the ponies (and perhaps handlers) would have received little training in show etiquette. Certainly, looking through the lists of prize-winners up to 1947, I found no Exmoors amongst them. At the end of the show the Exmoor contingent then had to retrace their journey on foot and by train.

How tempting it must have been to adopt more lenient showing rules that would have improved their chances competitively; it is to their great credit that they maintained the policy of not interfering with the natural appearance of the ponies.

126. Thought to be William Crockford with some of his Herd 12 ponies at the Breed Show on Exmoor.

School Days

'I was born at Higher Sherdon and we later moved to Brendon. I had an Exmoor pony called Topsy – my father broke him in for me to ride. I remember that once he got stuck in a bog on the farm and mother and father pulled him out. He was quite headstrong and would run off with me. I went to Countisbury School and walked all the way from Brendon; the moor was our school playground. On Sundays I rode my pony to Sunday School. Topsy was tied up to a fence whilst I was there.'

From Mrs Brook
(this probably relates to the 1930s).

Jean Campbell's transport to school in the late 1920s was provided by her pony. She started school at six and a half because her family lived 3 miles outside Dulverton at Hinam; the Local Education Authority decreed that this was the earliest age she could travel like this. Jean's earliest memory of her mother was being seen off to school. Jean would ride into Dulverton and stable the pony at the Blacksmith's shop. Her sister went part of the way with her.

Source: Exmoor Oral History Archive, Birdie Johnson.

John Milton, who lived at West Anstey, walked to school, a little way out of the village, but he recalled how children from the outlying farms rode to school on their ponies. There was a small farmstead, Woods Farm, near to West Anstey school that provided stabling specifically for the children's ponies whilst they were at their lessons.

Source: Exmoor Oral History Archive, Birdie Johnson.

127. School Transport by Alma Swan.

The Rabbit-Catcher

Bill Adams told me the story of his Exmoor pony at the Christmas Fatstock Show in South Molton in 2013.

His pony was called Nimble and had been born on Molland Moor into Herd 99 owned by the Dart family. Nimble had quite a party trick: you could put a pipe into his mouth and he would smoke! He was stolen at one point but Bill had got him back because he could prove the Exmoor pony found by the police was Nimble by offering him the pipe, which Nimble duly took.

Nimble had originally belonged to Les Hutchings who was a local rabbit-catcher. Les had a saddle that was specially adapted with prongs coming out from it on which he hung his traps and the rabbits he caught. He also rode Nimble all over Molland moor checking the sheep.

128. The Rabbit-Catcher by Alma Swan.

Exmoor Versatility

As told to Creenagh Mitchell by Muriel Bilkey (née Hooper).

'Our Exmoor pony, I remember, was named John Gay. He was a devil to catch but a great horse to ride. He was used for hunting, shepherding and family friends used to ride him. He loved hunting and was raring to go if he heard a hound.

He used to carry Dad to Home Guard points. My dad was John Hooper who lived at South Hill Farm, Withypool until 1947. My Uncle Clifford did the post round on John Gay and used him for ploughing. He was a young horse when Dad got him. He was very old when he died in 1950 (in his twenties).

I remember Dad and his father Arthur Hooper going to Exford Auction on him. One would start riding; half an hour before that the other would have started to walk. Then the one riding would catch up with the one walking and change over. Dad and Granddad called it 'hitching'.

My Granddad told me that when he was young he had an Exmoor pony. He told me they were hardy. He also told me he had a girl friend in Cardiff so he rode his pony to Porlock Weir, put the pony in the stable with hay and water and caught a boat to Cardiff to see his girlfriend and back, then to ride his awaiting pony home. So your pony was good transport and your best friend.

My Dad told me that in his teens he had an Exmoor pony. The girl he took to the dance would ride and Dad would lead the pony. They would dance every dance and then go home the same way. I don't know the names of the horses.

I learnt to ride on John Gay. My Granddad taught me. I also remember sitting in front of Granddad bare back, two on a horse gathering sheep on Withypool Common to take to Brightworthy for dipping. Mr. Dave Rawle lived there then. John Gay would sometimes not want to move very fast – he would then be called John Poke for, as they used to say, "poking" along.'

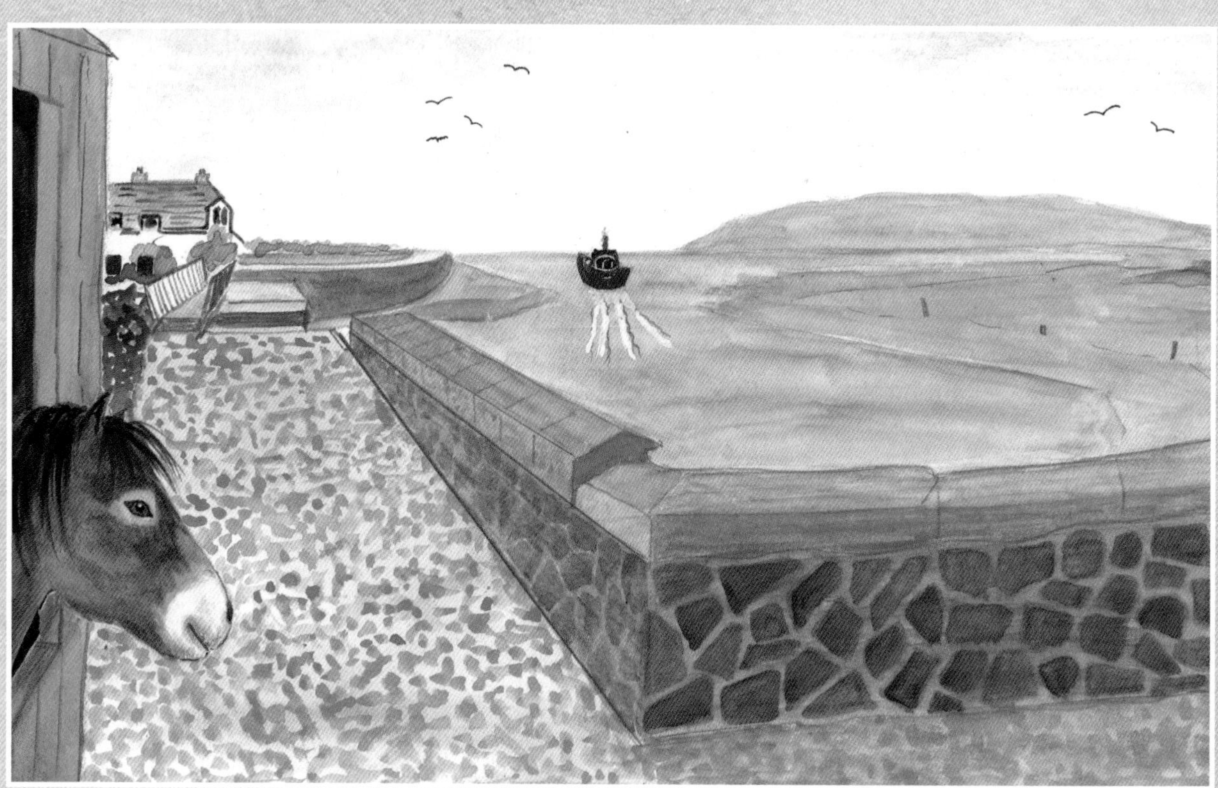

129. Long-stay pony parking by Alma Swan.

The Winter of 1947 – Survival Instinct

As told to Creenagh Mitchell by Muriel Bilkey (née Hooper).

'John Gay didn't like being indoors too long, summer or winter. 1947 was a bad winter. Someone staying at Worth Farm wanted him to ride for a day. It started to snow before they brought him back. In the meantime he stood under a hedge for shelter. He got snowed in like a sheep in a drift. The horse kept turning around and eating snow for a drink – it shows how hardy they are. It was days before we could get him out; me, a nine year old, went each day with Dad in the snow and ice to carry hay and straw to throw down to him in the room the horse had made for himself by keeping on turning round and eating away at the sides for a drink. He had worked this out for himself and was lovely and warm. We couldn't get out of South Hill by road and we went to the horse by going down the Barle and up by Batsom Farm onto Well and up to Worth Farm. It was a few outings with hay and straw with Dad I will never forget. John Gay was loving it. I remember he grew a longer coat. A pure Exmoor pony can cope with anything they have to. They are beautiful, tough and alert.'

130. *Natural wisdom by Alma Swan.*

Frozen to Death

Birdie Johnson interviewed Brian Windsor for her wonderful Exmoor Oral History Archive project and he told of ponies that were not as fortunate as John Gay.

In 1947, Brian Windsor was working for his father who ran the butcher's shop in Dulverton; Brian drove the van, delivering orders within a 20 mile radius. On the 29th of January, Brian's father told him to get the van loaded up and go to Withypool before the village became snowed in. He got as far as Folly Cross but the snow was already too deep to get through and he had to return to Dulverton, picking up the grocer whose van was already stuck. On his return, his father said that they would have to walk to Withypool the next morning. So the following day they borrowed a 'big, swish sledge' from Mrs Herbert at Pixton. They parcelled up meat and bread and loaded the sledge. They walked from Dulverton up past Highercombe and onto Winsford Hill, dragging the sledge behind them and eventually made it down into Withypool and delivered the supplies to Mrs Blackmore at Withypool Post Office.

The following week they were able to drive to Winsford so from there they pulled the sledge up the lane past Great Ash, heading for snow-bound Withypool. Brian recalled in his interview for the Exmoor Oral History Archive:

> *'On our first journey, at Comers Cross there was an old Exmoor thorn bush, a big type, with two Exmoor ponies under it; nose to tail; frozen solid. That's how cold it was. Absolutely rigid they were ... I walked over, couldn't believe it. They were as hard as nails.'*

Considering the legendary hardiness of Exmoor ponies, this story, perhaps above all, brings home just how extreme the conditions were in the winter of 1947.

Bampton Fair - the Annual Outing

Some years ago, Peter Hayward from Tamworth, Warwickshire visited the Exmoor Pony Society exhibition unit at a show in the Midlands and told of his Exmoor Pony during the 1940s. In 2016, I finally spoke directly with him, now aged ninety, and heard the stories in full.

In the early 1930s, Heard's garage in Torrington laid on a charabanc each October to take people to Bampton Fair for the day. They had quite a few regulars who would go every year including Peter's uncle, Tommy Reddaway. Each year he would buy an unhandled Exmoor foal for about five shillings and then had to manhandle the foal up into the charabanc to take it home to Torrington; the foal would stand in the aisle with the people in the seats around it hanging on!

Tommy Reddaway's grand-daughter Christine Reddaway recalled that her father Warwick told her that every year Tommy said he would buy him an Exmoor pony foal at Bampton Fair. However, every year, Tommy had sold it for a profit to a fellow passenger by the time they reached Torrington; her father never did get his Exmoor pony.

131. Hold on Tight by Alma Swan.

Tommy the Pony

Peter Hayward also told me how his first business relied on his pony Tommy.

'Originally, I kept a few chickens and sold the eggs for 10 old pence a dozen. I saved all the money and eventually I bought a pure-bred Exmoor pony called Tommy, together with a trap, cart and harness for £8. Tommy had originally been bought as a foal from Bampton Fair. I bought him from a man in Northam who had a small-holding but no longer needed him.

When I was 16, in 1942, I would drive the pony and cart into Torrington from our village St Giles, to do the shopping for my mother. There was only one bus a week in those days and very few people had cars in Torrington and petrol was rationed. I would see all the village ladies weighed down with lots of shopping, waiting for the bus. "I'll take shopping," I said. Because I didn't have a carrier's licence, I couldn't charge but could accept a tip and so the ladies would give me threepence or sixpence. I couldn't carry passengers because you needed a proper licence to do that.

Eventually, again saving my money, I was able to afford to buy a lorry for £25. I used to deliver things all over and that included Dulverton. In time I was able to buy a second lorry and had a transport business in the Midlands that my son still runs. So all of that was thanks to the chickens and to Tommy. Tommy was an easy pony to drive. Mind you, he'd make his way home quicker than how he went out.'

Good Companions

Many years ago, I took an elderly friend to visit the family she had once worked for when in service. They had moved to Sussex and were running a Thoroughbred Stud. Whilst there, I met their partner Miss Bunting and she told me the following fascinating story.

In the 1950s, Miss Bunting and her partner were going to sell a very good Thoroughbred filly. The horse was to be auctioned at a top London hotel, organised by The Sportsman's Club. The mare was quite highly strung but they had discovered that she was a much calmer animal when she was with Curly, their Exmoor pony gelding. So they decided that he would have to accompany the mare if she were to be able to deal with the stress of the occasion.

On the day, Curly was taken straight from the field, given a quick brush and then they loaded both animals without much difficulty and set off for the capital in a new nine-horse Commodore. When they reached the hotel, they had difficulty in backing the large vehicle to the tradesman's entrance and, on succeeding, discovered that the loading bay was too high off the ground. Eventually, the two animals walked out of the transporter onto two trestle tables and into the hotel.

However, their problems didn't stop there: the auction was being held on the 8th Floor! There was a large service lift but it was open-sided. Unsurprisingly, by this time, the filly was very unsettled but they led Curly onto the lift first and she followed him. She buried her head in his side so she could not see the 'moving walls'.

The filly sold very well and Miss Bunting recalled that the assembled company of bidders were very taken with Curly, who behaved impeccably throughout. She thought that he had been included in the purchase price as a necessary accessory but she could not remember for sure. Let's hope so.

132. Just Relax! by Alma Swan.

Shipping Exmoors to Canada

This was one of many stories Fred Milton told me during my visits to Weatherslade Farm.

In the 1950s, some Exmoor ponies were to be exported by sea to Canada, leaving from Bristol docks. The Exmoor Pony Society was worried, as an in-foal mare had been sent from Dartmoor and had arrived in Quebec in a bad state: so they wanted to check the conditions on the ship the Exmoors would travel on. Amongst the ponies being exported was a Herd 23 stallion and so Fred Milton undertook the task of travelling to Bristol and inspecting the vessel, accompanied by Bob Williams from Great Ash.

Fred, Bob and the ponies arrived at the Bristol docks at about 9.00 a.m. He saw the vet but was advised to wait whilst cars were being loaded. He had breakfast and then the R.S.P.C.A. inspector talked to him about how they would load the Exmoor ponies – Fred kept quiet. He heard how each pony would be put into a crate which would then be raised in a net and swung over to the ship.

With the help of six dock workers, the R.S.P.C.A. inspector got one of the suckers to its crate which was lifted up in the cargo net and taken aboard. This was repeated with another sucker.

Next came an unhandled three-year-old stallion (note: this may well have been Fred's pony, 23/49 which was going to Mr R. Hoggart of Clinton, Ontario). The inspector looked at the stallion and the stallion stared back intimidatingly. The inspector then asked Fred how they were going to get the stallion into a crate; Fred told him to get out of the way, at which the dock workers laughed. With a *'Go on boy'* from Fred, his unnamed stallion walked into the crate! Then, concerned at how the stallion might react to being hoisted across, Fred climbed onto the net and together they were swung out to the ship.

Fred inspected the conditions on board and reported back to the E.P.S. Committee that all was fine.

I remember Fred chuckling as he regaled me with another anecdote about ponies he sent to Canada:

> *'We had a bit of a laugh with those Canadians – one of them ordered a mare and we sent him a gelding!'*

Not the wisest of marketing strategies! This tale may have also related to Mr R. Hoggart as one of the Milton ponies listed as being sold to him in the 1950s was named English Joker!

133. Stay Calm by Alma Swan.

'Let the Train take the Strain'

134. Loading a mare and foal into a railway wagon. Breed of pony, location and date are not recorded but this is probably 1930s or '40s, somewhere in the West Country.

Photo © British Transport Films/National Railway Museum/Science and Society Picture Library.

In the late 1940s, Mary Etherington from Withypool was campaigning to raise awareness of the population crash Exmoor ponies had suffered during World War II and their resulting rarity. She felt that it was vital to their future to explore and confirm the views of her zoologist friend Sophia Best (see pages 70 - 71) that the Exmoor pony should be considered as a surviving representative of the original wild ponies of Britain. She contacted the Natural History Museum in London but little interest was shown. However, they suggested she should contact the Royal Scottish Museum. They, in turn, suggested she visit James Speed, a comparative anatomist at the Royal (Dick) Veterinary College in Edinburgh; he was studying the origins of British horses. This changed Mary's life dramatically as she moved to Edinburgh in 1950, worked alongside James Speed and eventually married him.

As part of moving from Withypool to Edinburgh, Mary had to organise transporting her own Exmoor ponies. In those days, movement of animals on the railways was commonplace and so the actual transport was not difficult to arrange. However, Mary had nowhere for them to go on arrival in Scotland. So, with great presence of mind, she booked herself a ticket to Edinburgh but the ponies had a much longer journey: she booked them to Edinburgh and then Edinburgh to Edinburgh, taking the animals in a huge loop back around the country. By the time they reached Edinburgh for the second time, a few days later, she had rented grazing for them. She would have had no qualms about sending them on this long detour because the railway companies provided very good conditions and care for animals they transported.

Outsmarted

In the early 1950s, Herbie Taylor, Roy Westcott and Sid Westcott gathered ponies off Dunkery and Wilmersham Common and drove them down to Wilmersham Farm, near Porlock. On reaching the farm, they drove the ponies into a large old barn and went into the farmhouse for some food and drink. After lunch the three men made their way back to the barn, opened the door and it was completely empty! The barn had a large opening but this had a twelve foot drop to the ground outside. The only explanation was that even with such a big drop, this had been the ponies' escape route. And where were the ponies? Back on the Common of course!

Source: Rob Taylor, son of Herbie Taylor.

135. The Great Escape by Alma Swan.

Assembly

Bill Adams of Brushford recalled that before the war, ponies destined for Bampton Fair had to be driven down from the moor. Pens were erected at Marsh Bridge and the owners of the herds first drove the ponies that were to be sold down to these holding pens where some stayed overnight. There were hundreds of ponies held there.

Student Days

When Barry Leek was a student at the Royal (Dick) Veterinary College in Edinburgh, he knew Mr and Mrs Speed well and rode their ponies. The photograph shows him riding Lorna Doone, who was a stable companion of Fisherman (see pages 119 - 120), on the lawn of the student hostel, Salisbury Green, with Arthur's Seat in the background. He recalled:

> *'After this photo was taken I rode the pony through french windows into and across the carpet of the lounge of the hostel relatively silently. Then we went into the hallway with its linoleum floor covering on top of a wooden floor. The sound of the hooves thundered up the stairwell and I heard the Housekeeper's door opening, so I quickened the pace, raced through the front door, and finally came to a mud scraper grid that ran the full width of the step beyond. The pony stopped dead. In desperation I dug my heels in and the pony made a great cat leap over the grid and we galloped along the gravel drive and out of sight.'*

136. Barry and Lorna Doone. Photo: courtesy of Barry Leek.

Tax Evasion

In days gone by, gipsies used to go to Bampton Fair to buy horses and ponies. Apparently, one in particular used to purchase a couple of wild Exmoor foals and then take them along the street to the White Horse Inn. He would hide them away in an upstairs room until after 6 p.m. to avoid the Fair toll that was payable up until then.

This story was told to me by an elderly visitor to the Exmoor Pony Society stand at Bampton Fair during the mid 1990s. One can only imagine the chaos of manhandling two wild foals up the stairs in the White Horse!

137. Engraving from The Illustrated London News, *10 November 1860.*

Inspecting Exmoor Ponies

In 1980, an unhandled two-year-old colt, Jeremy Stickles, was due to go to a new home at the Cardigan Wildlife Park in West Wales. The Park arranged to collect him from breeder Alec Copland and turned up with a trailer which already had one occupant – a bison! Apparently, the two animals travelled together without incident. On arrival, Jeremy Stickles was released into the bison enclosure, where he was to stay until some Exmoor mares arrived.

For some reason, Jeremy Stickles was still awaiting his Exmoor Pony Society inspection. Inspectors Wendy Vint and Charmian Ross-Thompson headed for Cardigan on the arranged date. However, when they arrived at the Park, it was deserted and they couldn't find any members of staff. They did though find Jeremy Stickles, still in the bison enclosure and they leant on the fence contemplating whether they would enter and do the inspection despite the absence of the owner. There was a wooden corral just inside the fence and they thought that if they could drive the colt into it, the inspection might just be possible.

At this point, one of the bison started walking determinedly towards them and, on reaching the corral, proceeded to attack and partly destroy it! At this, quite understandably, discretion proved the better part of valour and the two ladies abandoned the inspection and returned home.

Subsequently, Ruth and Dai Thomas undertook a second attempt and being vets proved to be very useful. This time, Jeremy was separated from his bison friends but he himself proved to be very uncooperative, biting poor Ruth's shoulder quite badly. So the rest of Jeremy Stickles' inspection was conducted with him horizontal, after some very necessary sedation.

138. The Better Part of Valour by Alma Swan.

Exmoor Pony Society

139. Sydney John Westcott.
Photo: courtesy of Margaret Rawle née Westcott.

Ann Le Bas, granddaughter of Reginald Le Bas, the first Secretary of the Exmoor Pony Society, recalled that as a small child she was often allowed the be present when her grandfather held meetings or dinners at home. She recalled one in particular as she was fascinated by one of the old farmers because he was cross-eyed. She also thought that Sydney Westcott's name was 'Sandy Waistcoat'!

Public Relations Ponies

From 1996 to 1999, our stallion Jeremy Stickles ran with the Exmoor National Park Authority's Herd H52 on the moorland beyond Warren Farm. Towards the end of his time there, one of the national park rangers took a party of visitors on a walk from Warren Farm to show them the herd. We met up at Exford Show some weeks afterwards and the ranger congratulated me on how well trained Jeremy was. This amazed me as he had never been handled, let alone trained! I sought more details and was told that as they had approached the herd, Jeremy had looked up, rounded up all his mares and paraded them in front of the delighted visitors – and then he did the same again and marched them back to where the herd had come from. Perhaps his early years at the Cardigan Wildlife Park had 'trained' him for public relations duties.

140. Jeremy Stickles in Seacombe Valley with the National Trust's herd of Exmoor ponies, Herd 201.

For many years the exhibition unit and pony corral were taken to the Royal Bath and West Show at Shepton Mallet. Various ponies undertook pen duty, some with more P.R. awareness than others. Undoubtedly, the greatest talent for attracting the public was demonstrated by stallion Waltersgay Grasshopper owned by Marion Williams and Irene Nash from Weston-super-Mare. Grasshopper, living at their riding school, was very people-orientated and loved the attention. He was very content when surrounded by admirers at the show but when things went quiet and he had no audience, he would let out an incredibly loud bellow; naturally, people turned and immediately came to see him.

Back in the 1990s, at Dunster Show, the Exmoor Pony Society had a pony on display in a corral beside the Society's exhibition unit. Experience had shown that a mare and foal always drew the most people. One year, David and Sandra Mansell took their mare Hock and her foal to undertake this public appearance. My husband Ian and I were helping: Ian took on the task of looking after the ponies whilst the rest of us talked to people. During the day, Ian refilled the ponies' water bucket and entered the pen to replace it. As he bent down to put the bucket in place, simultaneously the foal plugged into the milk bar rather enthusiastically. Unfortunately for Ian, Hock was standing right behind him and as the foal made her start, she sank her teeth into Ian's rear!

For some years, the Christmas Equine Fair at Westpoint, Exeter allowed breed societies to have a live pony on display indoors. One year, Cathy Wells provided her mare Cranbrookpaddocks Sanlucar for meeting the public. It was a tradition amongst the Exmoor Pony Society helpers at such events to indulge in a bag of freshly-made doughnuts. I was behind the sales table, with the pen and Sanlucar behind me, when the doughnuts arrived. Just as I had taken the offered doughnut, a large mouth appeared over my shoulder and tried to steal the sugary treat. She was most disgruntled at not being allowed to join in this ritual and, if a pony can, she sulked for some time.

Pony Racing on Exmoor

Harry Reed who lived at Knighton, Withypool had a brilliant mare called Speedwell. Horse and pony races were held at Comers Cross, above the village and, over a course of 3 miles, Speedwell beat everything! (Note: this was probably Speedwell 2/45 bred by Miss Etherington.)

Told to Creenagh Mitchell by Dave Rawle.

The pony races, formerly held at Hawkridge and Withypool, were given up during the war. It was said that the loss of visitors led to ponies being sold and the races ceased.

From The Somerset Home Guard *by J. Wilson.*

Racing 'Up-Country'

Many years ago I was told of a Thoroughbred racing stables on the island of Jersey where the 'Master of Horse' always rode an Exmoor gelding whilst the racehorses were being exercised. Although he couldn't keep up on the straights, he caught up on the bends and was always there at the end.

141. Keep Up by Alma Swan.

Did the Earth Move?

One summer, during the 1980s, three Knightoncombe ponies crossed the river from the farm and had to be retrieved. Bob Mitchell, with daughter Lindy and her friend Steve, set off with head-collars and caught them; they started the walk home. From Kitridge Lane they turned onto a rough track that zig-zags down the hill to a fording place across the River Barle. All was going steadily. Lindy takes up the story:

> *'The pony I was leading saw Steve and his pony coming to the zig-zag literally just above us on the steep track. This spooked my pony. We set off at great speed, with me 'skiing' alongside. Steve's pony then took off after us.'*

With the steepness of the track, the speed of descent increased and they parted Bob from his pony which then ran loose.

As Lindy and Steve approached the grassy area at the bottom of the hill it was quite evident that the ponies were going to jump and that they would have to hang on and jump with them. What they didn't expect was that as they took off, the two pairs sailed over an amorous couple on the ground under a blanket! It was quite a shock for all involved; imagine how the courting couple must have related the tale!

Shock gave way to hilarity all round. Eventually Bob, Lindy and Steve, with two ponies now under control and the third following behind, headed back to Knighton Farm with quite a story to tell. The moral of the tale is that there is probably no such thing as a truly safe place for an amorous adventure.

Call of the Wild

Some years ago I attended the inspection of the National Park's herd on Haddon Hill, above Wimbleball Lake. It was a crisp and sunny October afternoon and the ponies had been gathered into a fenced, wooded area the day before. The inspections, brandings and worming all went smoothly but there were quite a few foals that year and so it was late afternoon by the time the proceedings were completed.

Most of the foals were going to be used for conservation grazing and so had to be loaded into a horse lorry for their journey to the nature reserve. The driver reversed the lorry expertly so that the rear ramp was blocked either side by the bars of the race. The foals were herded into the pen that opened into the race and several of the helpers encouraged them forwards and up the ramp.

142. Awaiting inspection at Haddon Hill.

The herding instinct meant that the foals soon clattered up into the lorry – except one well-grown filly. She hung back and then stopped a few feet from the edge of the ramp. She looked at the other ponies inside the lorry and then turned and looked long and hard at the open moor beyond the pen. She repeated these gazes a couple of times and then, from a standing start, launched herself high and clean over the five foot barrier to her freedom.

The sun was close to setting and the sky rich in colour; her body gleamed in the last rays of the sun as she galloped for all she was worth away from captivity. It was a blessed nuisance for the rangers and all concerned but I am sure I can't have been the only one thinking, deep inside, 'Go girl!'

143. 'Freedom Lies in Being Bold' by Alma Swan.

Bampton Fair 1937

Sophia Best (see pages 70 - 71) visited Bampton Fair in 1937 and wrote an account of her experience:

THE PONIES OF BAMPTON FAIR

By M. G. S. Best

EXMOOR surely has more than its share of the wet, stormy weather for which the West of England is famous, and the day chosen to drive up the ponies on the moor was a good specimen of the worst of it.

A thick white mist rolled in from the Bristol Channel, at times blotting out everything to within a few yards, then drifting away on all sides, giving a temporary view of distant hills, to close down again in a few minutes.

From time to time a rider passed, one of the moorland farmers, mounted on a rough-coated cob, seeking for sight or sound of others bent on the same business.

The mist lifted again. Coming over the brow of the farther hill could be seen a herd of ponies galloping as hard as they could, heads up, manes and tails flying.

Behind them came a horseman, accompanied by a sheepdog or two, riding quietly along, occasionally cracking his whip to turn the ponies if they tried to break back.

From different points on the skyline many such groups of galloping ponies could be seen, all converging upon an open gateway leading into a lane, bordered by high banks, and gaining further shelter from the tall beech hedges growing on the top.

Across the lower end of the lane, to prevent escape in that direction, stood one or two farmers, their cobs tied to the hedge, under which they huddled, their tails to the bank, seeking such protection from the weather as they could find.

Quietly amongst the crowd of ponies moved two or three men, picking out a pony here, a mare and foal there, dividing them finally into two or three big herds. The ponies were passed on by a man stationed in the lane, who kept them where they were wanted by an outstretched arm.

It was no easy job to handle this mass of wild things, crowded together in the narrow lane, mostly strangers to each other, frightened and unhappy, each pushing its way into the densest part of the throng, trying to get as far as possible from the men who stood amongst them, and blocked their way to freedom.

Of all ages they were, from the fathers and mothers of the herds to foals only a few weeks old, and all colours too, though, wet as they were, they all looked the same dark brown, with here and there a chestnut. One there was almost white, but this was no Exmoor pony, neither was a young black cart horse, a stray from somewhere, who had joined up with a herd of ponies for company's sake. Most unwelcome he was, for even in the turmoil and alarms of the morning's work, angry squeals were heard as some one or other kicked him with right good will.

Every now and then a determined rush was made, then there was some shouting and an occasional crack of a whip, but for the most part the whole of the proceedings was carried out in almost silence, so much so, that the patter of the rain was very noticeable, a monotonous, depressing accompaniment to the scene.

Some of the farmers were there seeking ponies of their own which had strayed, as they will sometimes, through a gap in the hedge, or through an open gateway.

When the sorting was finished, the different herds were driven off to neighbouring farmyards where their owners could sort them out again, returning those for stock to the moor, and their usual carefree existence, keeping the "suckers" and the other saleable ponies for the fairs.

Exmoor Ponies in their pens at Bampton Fair. Waiting to be sorted out and dispatched to their various owners.

Once gathered in the yards, the ponies were quickly selected, such yearlings and "suckers" as were to be sold having their long tails trimmed up, not docked, for horse-hair fetches a good price nowadays. Then, after being marked with large numbers in white paint, the little fellows were turned out in a well-enclosed field.

The morning of the fair sees them on their way. Fifteen can pack into a cattle-lorry, by far the safest way to move them on these narrow Somerset lanes where such an unknown thing as a motor-car is a terror too alarming to face.

A small pony fair is held at Mollond, just before the big one at Bampton. There many ponies from outlying districts are sold, to be resold two days later, probably at a much higher price.

At Mollond, ponies were driven in in small drifts of half a dozen, or even less, only a few were dignified by conveyance in lorries. One small party, arriving after all the others had been sold, had been so scared on the roads that the little things had scrambled over every bank and hedge they could along the way. A very hot and bothered little herd finally arrived.

These small ponies can jump, too. One I saw rise gallantly at a five-barred gate out of the ring, smashing the top rail, to be sure, and landing on its head the other side; but it was a good effort for a yearling!

Bampton Fair, held on the last Thursday in October,

144. *From* Riding and Driving – The Horse Lovers Magazine, *September 1937.*

September, 1937 RIDING 117

has been an annual affair since Henry III granted them a charter.

An apple orchard seems a curious and unusual setting for a pony fair, there could be nothing like it elsewhere, but with so ancient a history, a choice and distinctive situation seems called for.

Fencing, high and very strong, is used for the pens, the drifts arriving from different districts being placed in the pen bearing the name of that district on it. Incidentally, the fencing affords excellent support from which to view the proceedings in the ring. The fencing, and the boughs of the apple-trees, providing stands for the onlookers.

The ring itself divides these arrival pens from others like them on the farther side. As the ponies are sold, they pass on to their respective pens beneath the apple trees, and there at the end of the sale they are picked out and dispatched by road or rail to their several destinations, no pony being considered sold until it is safely in the hands of the purchaser. To watch the picking out of these ponies is a liberal education as to how such a difficult job should, or should not, be done.

In one pen were 25 to 30 ponies, mostly yearlings, very wet and frightened. So wet were they that when still further alarmed such a cloud of steam rose from them that it looked like thick white smoke. Into this herd went several lads, with one man, not very sure of himself. Hustling them round the ring, the men endeavoured to catch the particular ones needed. The old man was soon knocked down and trampled on in the stampede, being rescued before he was quite smothered in the mud, lucky to have got off so lightly.

At a little distance along the row, more expert hands were dealing with the ponies. Very quietly two men with a halter went in amongst them, coaxing the one wanted into a corner. Holding him firmly by jaw and tail, slipping the halter over his head with wonderfully little fuss, and pushing him through the narrow gateway without alarming his companions in the enclosure.

Such handling is a joy to see, but one realises it is not learned in a day!

Moorland ponies are nowadays fetching good prices at the fairs. The demand for them for children's riding-ponies is an increasing one, being as they are so sure-footed, good-tempered and very hardy, and what appeals very strongly to the child, have a very good turn of speed!

Exmoor ponies on the moor below Dunkerry. The one with light mane and tail is an unusual colouring. (Left) Ponies brought off the moor to a farm.

A DRIFT OF EXMOOR PONIES: Typical of the breed with their "mealy" noses and small heads.

145. *From* Riding and Driving – The Horse Lovers Magazine, *September 1937.*

Sir Alfred James Munnings 1878 – 1959

Sir Alfred Munnings is considered to have been the foremost painter of horses of his time, producing many equine portraits as commissions and painting scenes of hunting and horse-racing. He held the post of President of the Royal Academy from 1944 to 1949 and was knighted in 1944. He was, however, a controversial figure also renowned for speaking his mind and upsetting people.

Violet, Lady Munnings, his second wife, frequently spent time on Exmoor, primarily to go hunting, and Sir Alfred would visit too. In his autobiography Munnings recalled:

'In a happy moment, when living in a rented house in Wootton Courtenay, my wife bought, for a song, a cottage adjoining the blacksmith's forge in that village below Dunkery Hill. For years this was her retreat in spring and autumn, and from there she went to meets, far and near, on Exmoor. She deserved those days, for not a week passed but she paid bills and sent the wages from 'Riverside' as it was called. For me there was nothing to do except paint or play about.'

However, when Castle House, their home in Essex, was commandeered during World War II, Sir Alfred moved to Exmoor. He and Violet lived in Withypool, renting a cottage next to the old Post Office behind the pub; he is also supposed to have had a studio in the loft of the Royal Oak Inn. The cottage also had to house the many paintings that he brought with him, deeming them not safe at Castle House.

Sir Alfred painted many landscapes around Withypool and some of the local people, such as Gladys Bawden and Mary Etherington. The free-living Exmoor Pony herds also captivated him and he wrote in *The Finish*, part 3 of his autobiography:

'Ponies on the moor – I always wanted to paint them. Wild ponies wandering free over thousands of acres of wide, undulating expanse. Herds of twenty or thirty, using their own territories – keeping to them, as birds do. If you want to find them, they have vanished. When least expecting them they appear on the skyline, or far below in a sheltered combe. Imagine an April day; the moors a patterned harmony of buff and brown, the gorse out in patches... A

146. Sir Alfred Munnings riding on Exmoor during the 1940s.
Photo: Richard Kingsley Tayler.

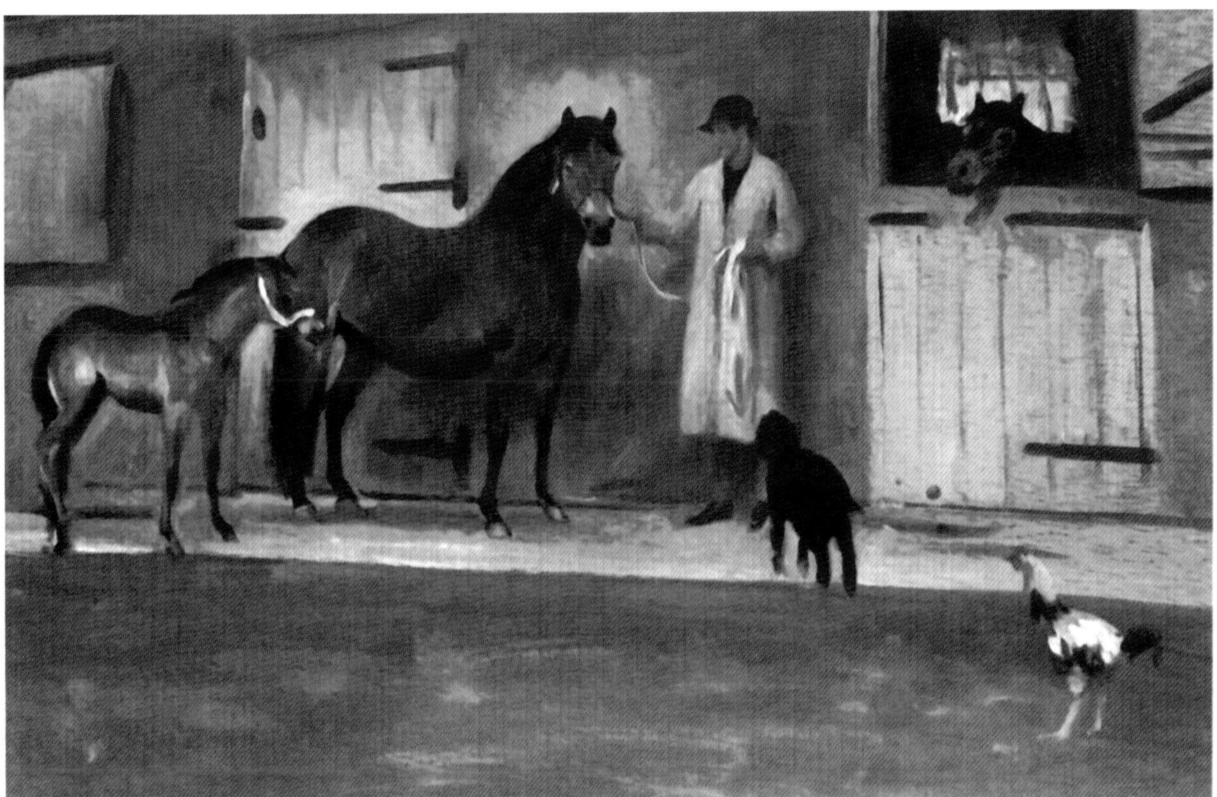

147. Title of painting: Miss Mary Gordon Etherington with Black Spaniard, Foxglove, Aconite, poodle and heckler at Newland 1940. Photo: © Estate of Sir Alfred Munnings, Dedham, Essex. All rights reserved, DACS 2017.

stationary group of ponies against the sky, others lower down the slope, their foals lying basking in the sun, whisking curly tails, unconscious of Bampton Fair and crowded trucks of ponies going where?...........Where are the ponies? To locate them the day before was the thing. Seeking for a clue to their whereabouts, I would ride out in quest of ponies, asking whoever I met: "Have you seen any ponies?" "Yes, somewhere over the hill this morning, near the lane to Molland Moor" – or "I see'd one lot down below the common by Landacre."

Then I would gallop over and round the hill to find them. So well did I know each herd that I recognised them a way off by this mare or that stallion. Imagine thousands of acres of Withypool Hill and common alone, where a man on foot could wander all day never seeing a pony. All the while they might be grazing near by just out of sight. Seeing a herd at Landacre in the evening, I was sure of finding them in the vicinity next morning. Myself on one horse, Bayfield on another, we faced the wild with bag and brushes... "A pony! a pony! my kingdom for a pony," I sang out after an hour's fruitless search – Bayfield, well away on my left, scanning hill and hollow, whilst I, with field glasses, swept the moor. "Where the h—l are the little somethings?" I would say. "Ah well, they're about; we'll come on'em shortly," was the soothing reply. "Ride, and look down the slope to your left," said I. Not a sight of a pony. Then, just as I thought of seeking another herd, Bayfield sat pointing. "Where?" said I "There," said he, still pointing, "there's one; an' where there's one, the rest'll be, too," was his wise remark.....Day followed day with the ponies, weather permitting a warm old overcoat for me. The smell of heather the company of the ponies, taking no heed of my presence; small birds about me, a colony of rooks or a pair of ravens passing above. A precious day would pass in a combe to the sounds of running water and sheep; sweet scents of gorse in the warm air – the little foals resting at full length on the short turf in the sun. When I wanted them on their feet I walked nearer and touched them. Once when doing this a small, dark-brown mother, her ears laid flat, her eye wild, her mane flying, suddenly charged me. Before I could turn and fly, her teeth struck my knuckles, knocking the box from my hand – thought I, what strength and weight in a small compass!'

Double-trouble – Exmoor Pony Twins

The Twins, Bampton Fair

148. Twins at Bampton Fair from the book Horses and Ponies – a book of sketches *published by Country Life; undated but thought to be around the late 1930s.* Lionel Edwards © FRWS - London.

The first recorded instance of twin Exmoor foals comes from the 1930s. The famous artist Lionel Edwards has left us his drawing of these twins as he sketched them on the day they were sold. Fred Milton recalled them as having been born on Withypool Common.

Looking back through the Stud Book, we find that another Withypool mare 23/6 had two foals registered to her in 1950, a colt and a filly, but the registrations show two different sires!

Twins were seemingly produced, again on Withypool Common, in 1980. Red Bay was seen to have two colt foals with her, both of which she suckled and raised successfully. However, later in their lives, DNA tests showed that they were not in fact twins. One explanation is that Red Bay had in fact adopted a foal whose dam had died. Whilst not common, this can occur. If, however, they were genuine twins, the foals must have become muddled up on inspection day.

We can be absolutely sure though that twins were born in 1989 and, remarkably, there were two sets that year. However, both instances brought home how dangerous this can be for both mare and offspring. Eighteen-year-old mare Cinderella, belonging to Hilary Pittam of Llandysul, Wales produced twin colts, both of which were born dead; tragically, Cinderella herself died as a result. In Cumbria, fourteen-year-old Lofteleis also gave birth to twins, one of which died.

Since then, only one set of twins are on record: Anchor mare Aurora gave birth to twin fillies Grouse and Gull in 2011. Both survived initially but Gull had to be put down before a year old. Nature has not designed ponies to have multiple births as a rule.

The Exmoor Mounties

In 1939, with Britain at war with Germany, battalions of Local Defence Volunteers were created. On Exmoor, some of the volunteers were on horseback and became known as the Exmoor Mounties. All manner of horses and ponies provided the mounts for this 'cavalry unit', a few of them pure-bred Exmoor ponies.

In his book *Exmoor in Wartime*, Jack Hurley tells us:

> *'Exmoor made LDV history. In May a correspondent to* The Times *had suggested that horsed patrols offered the best means of covering large tracts of hills and moorland, and that members of local hunts would know every yard of the ground. On Exmoor, action had anticipated suggestion. From among personnel associated with the Devon and Somerset Staghounds had sprung a mounted patrol which by August numbered about fifty.'*

The Exmoor company consisted of four platoons at Withypool, Winsford, Simonsbath and Exford. Night-time patrolling often meant riding considerable distances. The company set up rifle ranges for shooting practice and even had a large area at Exford for practising grenade throwing.

In 2000 I traced Bill Rashley, aged 83, one of the Withypool Platoon, who was living in Molland. I visited him and spent a fascinating time hearing about the Mounties 'from the horse's mouth' so to speak. At the time the mounted Home Guard was formed, he was living in the nearby village of Twitchen and he told me they were formed *'to protect the moors'*. Nearly all the men were farm workers and one was a tractor driver. Back then, they received 7s 6d (37.5p) a week plus their food.

Bill recalled:

> *'When we started as Exmoor Mounties we were laughed at. We began at Sandyway before there were any uniforms but later we looked very smart. Our patrol area was Five Barrows to Withypool Common and the Ansteys. It was just on Sundays and Thursday nights. We met at Sandyway and had a pint first. Then we would drill on Three Corner Allotment and do fire-watching. One Sunday we practised trying to capture Westwater Farm. There were four of us with three rifles and one sten gun. One of us held the horses.'*

149. L -R: Stan Jarman and Bill Rashley outside the Sportsman's Inn at Sandyway. Photograph by R.L. Knight, Barnstaple.

Bill said he had memories of being very cold, especially when out between 2 and 4 a.m.; of charging and falling off; of the platoon being called out when an air balloon escaped; of his troop meeting up with three other troops on the Common; of having to take part in parades on foot. He also told me, *'We were out on patrol once when a plane appeared out of Long Holcombe but it was OK, it was one of ours.'*

He also told me about training on the Filleigh rifle range plus training to put fires out and to capture things from infantry. For the latter, they went by Land Rover to Emmetts Grange near Simonsbath and the Withypool and Exford platoons then competed on Fyldon Ridge.

> 'Our motto was "Look, Duck and Vanish."'
> Bill Rashley

Bill Rashley said:

> *'There were twelve in our Sandyway troop. Stan Jarman – he fell off twice one Sunday! Joe Sinkins from Willingford rode a very dark pony,*

150. The Withypool platoon at the Sportsman's Inn at Sandyway, headed by Captain Chichester and Sergeant Bill Westcott; then, L-R Stan Little, Fred Little, Albert Hutchins, Tom Carter, Joe Sinkins, Edwin Thorne, Stan Jarman, Bill Hutchins, Bill Rashley, Les Carter, Warder Bray and grandson John Bray, aged about nine.

a cross. John Bray from Winsford was our mascot.'

Bill recalled that they rode all sorts of ponies – he borrowed a cross-bred one and also rode his bike sometimes as did Stan. He remembered getting a pony shod one day in exchange for coupons.

In 2003 I located Stan Jarman in South Molton. His family came to Exmoor from Bristol when he was sixteen. He was in his twenties when he joined the Local Defence Volunteers and was soon asked to become one of the mounted section. He rode an Exmoor cross that he borrowed from his employer Mr Delbridge of Blindwell. He told me:

'We went on patrol on Sunday afternoons, meeting at the pub at Sandyway and patrolling around Withypool Common. Sometimes we had to do dawn patrols too. To begin with, we didn't have uniforms but eventually these were provided, except for britches, and we got rifles too. Everything had to be given back at the end of the war. We were going to have our own rifle range, down Sherdon Lane near Sandyway, but it never happened. Each month we went to Castle Hill, near Filleigh for training.'

Stan recalled when there were American soldiers camped at Cuzzicombe Post on Molland Common. The Home Guard was invited to supper at the camp and they had rides on the American tanks.

These riders of the moor seem to me almost a perfect example of what the Home Guard should be. I mean of course, in spirit for we cannot all go riding horses across romantic moors. Few of them have ever been soldiers. For farmers must till, not fight. But they have a few old cavalrymen to teach them the essence of the thing.

Dudley Barker

151. From the Daily Herald, *2 September 1940.*

I also interviewed 89 year-old John Blackmore in 2003, a near neighbour at Oldways End. During the war, he lived in Withypool but was in a different patrol, along with Jack Clatworthy, the Reverend Michael Etherington (Mary's brother) and Charlie Westcott. He recalled:

'We rode out at daybreak with 12 bore shotguns tied to our backs. Our first patrol was Withypool to Westwater, Hawkridge, Old Barrow, Lords Plantation, Porchester Post, Brightworthy Barrows and home.'

John told me that he rode a large crossbred pony, Jack a hunter, Charlie an even bigger horse and Michael had ridden his sister's grey cob, Moonraker.

Although none of this patrol rode true Exmoor ponies, according to Charlie Westcott the stallion Prime Minister, bred by Sir Francis Acland, was one of just a few pure-bred Exmoors that served in the Exmoor Mounties. After the war, Mary Etherington bought Prime Minister and this photograph comes from her collection.

152. Prime Minister, a pure-bred Exmoor that served in the Exmoor Mounties. Photo: the Mary Etherington Archive.

Film of the 'Mounties'

There is a film of the Sandyway 'Exmoor Mounties' in Barnstaple Museum's collection. It was filmed by Mr Carpenter who was the manager of the Odeon Cinema in Barnstaple. When he died, the film was sent to his daughter in Australia; she realised its importance in terms of local history and sent it to Barnstaple Town Council for the museum. Staff at the museum contacted Herbert Geen and Arthur Bray in North Molton who were able to identify people in the film.

Westcountry TV took an interest in the story and featured an excerpt from the film plus interviews with Herbert Geen, Arthur Bray, Stan Jarman and Bill Rashley. The commentary over the excerpt was taken from a newspaper article 'Exmoor Mounties will get their Men' and read by Herbert Geen.

The Exford Mounted Unit

In Birdie Johnson's Exmoor Oral History Archive, John Edwards told how his father was in charge of the unit in Exford. They were a mounted unit because of patrolling moorland at night, looking for parachutists.

John says:

'It was absolutely dotty really. They couldn't have done any good.'

John recalled that his father and the patrol went out one evening and built a horse shelter, near Warren or on Hayes Allotment.

'A great event it was ... They had to have some sort of shelter for these poor horses, having to stand for two or three hours. The horses were hunters and ponies, whatever the particular person owned.'

He also remembered his father's story of how coming back from evening drill one night in the pitch black along the lane, they heard the sound of lots of feet in boots running and thought it was German soldiers. They fled into the hedge and hid only to find that the invaders were ponies! The herds could stray down the lanes before the days of cattle grids.

World War II – Dark Times

Pony Rustling

In March 1940, meat rationing was introduced in Britain and free-roaming stock became targets for those involved in black market dealings. All but twelve of the Acland herd, then owned by Frank Green, were stolen. The story handed down is that the ponies were driven into one of the lanes, trapped and loaded onto lorries. Apparently they were tracked as far as Carlisle but no trace of them was found after that.

HORSEFLESH BLACK MARKET

Ponies from Dartmoor and the New Forest are being stolen and slaughtered for the "black market" in horse flesh, it was stated at Ealing, London, Food Control Committee to-day.

A trader said that hitherto there had been a prejudice in England against eating horse flesh, but people were now beginning to demand "this wholesome food."

153. From The Dundee Evening Telegraph, *25 November 1941.*

Seemingly this event was not reported in the local papers. Nor has anyone been able to add any detail during my collecting of local people's memories. Perhaps, as it has been suggested that the theft could not have been successful without local help, it was all kept quiet at the time.

The only local story I know of that relates to the theft of the ponies was recounted by a visitor to the Exmoor Pony Society Unit at a show: the elderly gentleman told how when he was a boy, he rode his Exmoor pony to school and then, on returning home, the pony was put out on Winsford Hill to graze overnight. He remembered very clearly how one morning during the war, his beloved pony was nowhere to be found.

The Open Road

After areas of open moorland on Exmoor were enclosed, animals were kept separated and prevented from straying by means of gates across the roads that crossed enclosures. In her article in *The Little Horses of Exmoor* in 1947, Mary Etherington wrote:

> *'The threat to-day is probably greater than it has ever been. There are two main reasons for this: the demand for horse meat and the destruction of the common gates. The long queues outside the horse-meat shops in London answer the questions " Where are the ponies going ?" " Can they be brought back ? " but the gates are really the main cause of the trouble. If motor drivers had not been allowed to ruin Exmoor as a stock- rearing district, many young mares and stallions would have been left on the hill and the fact that those which were sold became meat would not have mattered, the breeding stock would have been maintained. Motor drivers will not open and shut gates which were put up to prevent stock straying off the commons. The result has been that thousands of acres of valuable grazing have been lost and the country has been robbed of food which was so badly needed.'*

A report in the *Somerset County Gazette* in January 1948 stated:

> *'Without gates or grids the ponies can range from Dulverton to Porlock and it has become almost impossible for farmers to keep ponies on the hill.'*

154. Mare and foal on Molland Moor, one of the many enclosures crossed by roads.

Denmark

The earliest records of Exmoor ponies being exported to Denmark are to be found in the first edition of the Exmoor Pony Society Stud Book. Mrs Lise Rønnow bought the mare Conkerbell from Mary Etherington's herd in 1943. Then, in 1951, she added geldings Red Squirrel and Dormouse, from the Royal (Dick) Veterinary College's herd 90; in 1954, mare Heatherbelle from Lilo Lumb's herd 78; in 1955, another herd 78 mare Blondie and a gelding Ashley Kestrel from Mrs Edgar in Surrey and, in 1956, another mare, Rainbow from Herd 32 at Highercombe, Dulverton. Then in 1964, Lise imported the Herd 8 stallion Clayford Horner, bred by Alice Sanders and Helen Dashwood and the mare Moss Petral from the Deans in Cumbria.

The Exmoor ponies were for use in the riding school she and her husband had established at Virum near Copenhagen. Iben Tjelum was first a pupil at the riding school in 1976 and then an instructor in the '80s and he recalled:

> *'The first Exmoors she imported had names that were hard to pronounce for young Danish children, thus she translated them into Danish. I recall a Røde Egern (Red Squirrel) and a Hasselmus (Dormouse), whereas the mares Slippers, Whitsun, Rainbow, Blondie, Whimsy kept their English names. Both Red Squirrel and Blondie were more chestnut in colour, than the more common bay colour of the others. At a certain time, she imported a stallion as well: Clayford Horner, or just Horner, as we called him. He was such a good boy, and if placed after a gelding when we went hacking, you wouldn't notice that he was a stallion. He was darker than the others. Unfortunately he refused to cover the Exmoor mares! He was more interested in the New Forest mares, which gave Mrs Rønnow a couple of halfbreeds.'*

When Lise Rønnow began breeding Exmoors, the Exmoor Pony Society created a Danish section in its Stud Book. In the introduction to the 1963 first edition it says: '*The Society's star will be used in the case of Denmark*' but no rules and no higher height limit were mentioned as was the case with the Canadian section. Mrs. Rønnow's herd was named Herd D and she registered two foals, a filly in 1958 and a colt in 1960, both sired by Tademus, a Herd 2 stallion.

155. Lise Rønnow (driving) and pupils from her riding school on a 'trek' in 1964.
Photo: the Mary Etherington Archive.

156. Clayford Horner. This picture was on the front of the 1966 E.P.S. Newsletter.

There were other Exmoor ponies imported into Denmark in 1965. Halling Nielsen and a landowner called Lassen, from the island of Funan, visited Exmoor and bought two male ponies (Candyman and Lucky Boy from Herds 10 and 85) and seven female ponies (Anchor mare Crystal, Belle Heather and Moor Minstrelle, from Herd 10, Hollowcombe Rose from Herd 16,

Un-named from Herd 54 and Bracken and Un-named from Herd 85). These ponies were released onto the island of Tærø.

When Helen Poulsen visited Tærø in 1991, a farmer she met told her that he thought the Tærø project had been intended as part of a larger scheme aimed at establishing herds in France and Sweden as well. He also recalled that the last branded mare had died in the winter of 1990.

The original stock released onto Tærø were left to fend for themselves, inhabiting a strip of the coastal land all around the island. There was, as far as can be ascertained, no interference in terms of the ponies' breeding and survival. Eventually this led to the population reaching 17, including a large number of males, and considerable fighting between them. During the 1990s, this was remedied by removing many of the ponies, leaving just the dominant stallion and one of his sons plus the mares. Most of the ponies removed were relocated to Sweden.

In 2003 some of the ponies on Tærø were relocated to Klise Nor on the island of Langeland, a nature reserve run by the Danish Forestry Commission. Their leaflet states:

> *'The Exmoor ponies on Klise Nor come from a small island, Tærø, between South Zealand and Møn. In the mid 1960s a devoted researcher group imported two flocks of Exmoor ponies from remote areas in Great Britain. One flock grazed on the Hallandsås, the other went to Tærø. The intention was to backcross the Exmoor pony to the original wild pony. The project had to be abandoned though. The ponies on the Hallandsås were sold, but the ponies on Tærø were left to their own devices.'*

John Theilgaard gave me a recent update and wrote:

> *'The smaller area in Klise Nor (25-30 ha) were only a test, to see how it would work out with the ponies. In 2006 they put some of the the ponies from Klise Nor, and a shipment from Tærø, out in a much bigger area (110 ha) called Gulstav. In this area there are somewhere between 50 and 80 horses, depending on the time of year. Every year 20-25 ponies are sold off. There are still 10-15 ponies in Klise Nor, but only stallions.'*

The last significant export of British-bred Exmoors into Denmark was of five ponies in 1977 to Mr Petersen and to Mr and Mrs Bock. Mrs Bock has organised the Danish Exmoor Pony Society with rules for registration and inspection and its own stud book.

157. Exmoor ponies on Langeland in 2008.
Photo: John Theilgaard.

'An Exmoor Lane'

by Sir Alfred Munnings

Grey leaden clouds, slow moving overhead;
The trees and fences dripping as I pass;
A robin singing; berries turning red;
And underfoot the rank and sodden grass.

And all is shrouded in soft, misty rain;
And spattering drops are falling through the beech;
Still puddles lie along the rutted lane
In long, light streaks of grey which curve and reach

Between the fences, 'neath the rainy sky;
And calm, unbroken silence spreads around,
Save for the far-off rook's and jackdaw's cry
And sound of ceaseless rain upon the ground.

But hark! I hear the sound of unshod feet;
And ponies come in sight ten yards ahead.
We stare at one another as we meet;
And suddenly there's silence like the dead.

With pricked-up ears, bright eye and flowing mane;
The older ones amongst them seem to say,
'You cannot stop us coming up the lane;
For centuries we've used this right of way'.

Those hurrying feet are stayed. We stand and stare!
Then, as I draw aside to let them go,
The leader dashes by – an ancient mare,
And all the rest with mane and tail aflow,

Go charging by in vigorous life and strength;
Bright, startled eyes and forelocks blowing back;
Sturdy and stout, they gallop up the length
Of the long lane towards the moorland track.

And as I watch them galloping away;
The rain and dying bracken all forgot;
I feel how weak am I, how strong are they:
Theirs is a life of freedom, mine is not.

158. Herd 12 on gathering day in October 2012.

They disappear and leave me where I stand,
Alone and wondering at the passing sight,
As seen a hundred times in this wild land –
And often on a dark and eerie night

When folk are fast asleep and many snore,
You hear the hurried sound of unshod feet,
Of ponies as they change from moor to moor,
All rushing through the narrow village street.

They know no bounds, they wander where they will;
They graze beside the stream that babbles by;
When days are hot, they stand upon the hill –
A silhouetted group against the sky.

And in the spring the little foals are born;
And there they lie, all basking in the heat
Of some gorse-scented, blazing April morn,
Upon the close-cropped grass where ponies' feet

Have trodden on their way across the moor
Down to the running stream year after year.
A venerable grand-dam going on before
The stallion always bringing up the rear.

Exmoor Pony Targets in WWII?

On Exmoor, the story is told that one of the reasons that the Exmoor pony population was so decimated during World War II was that American troops had used the live ponies for target practice. However, the more people I asked about this, the less actual facts seemed to emerge. I quickly gained the impression that if this happened, it was by no means on a large scale.

The source of this story may actually have been the famous artist Sir Alfred Munnings, who lived at Withypool during the war years. In his autobiography *An Artist's Life* he wrote the following:

'21st August 1944: in the most perfect weather we wandered on the moors round Larkbarrow. Then as the Sheriff lost his pocket book ....we spent the whole of Sunday retracing our steps. His high office took him away on Monday and so, with three mounted friends and the shepherd from Tom's Hill, I made another search. All we discovered was a dead and decaying Exmoor pony that had been hit by long-range shell fire from American artillery who have been using the moors this year.'*

(Note: * Munnings and his friend the High Sheriff of Somerset.)

Roger Burton notes in *The Heritage of Exmoor*, regarding Larkbarrow:

'It was not until the war in Europe was over that American troops stationed on Gallon House Allotment (behind the old inn), with nothing better to do, fired salvo after salvo in the direction of the farm.'

So, perhaps Munnings regaled neighbours and visitors with this story of this pony casualty and, over time and with embroidered repetition, this gave rise to the idea that American troops had figured largely in the pony population crash. The targets for the American gunners were actually remote farm buildings; the pony died through being in the wrong place at the wrong time. The image conjured of American soldiers deliberately aiming at Exmoor ponies is probably far from the truth.

***

159. The ruins of Larkbarrow Farm.
Photo: Catherine Dove/ENPA.

John Pile, farmed at Hallslake Farm near Brendon during the Second World War. His memories are recorded in *Unforgotten Exmoor*, Volume 1 by David Ramsay and give us the following insight into how efforts were made to avoid killing stock:

'During the war years the main thing I did was to clear the common before the rocket firing started. Father and I would both do it; I had the Cheriton Ridge and father would do the Hawcombe and Badgeworthy area of Brendon Common. Jack Edwards was in charge and used to come up and tell us when the next firing was due to start. Sometimes we'd have to be up there at 5 a.m., 6 a.m., that sort of time, and we'd get the whole place cleared of stock. We'd set off on a pony with a good dog. 'Twas mainly Exmoor ponies at that time on Cheriton Ridge. I'd go up to the upper end and drive them all back towards the farm and try to calm them down until the firing started. Of course when the firing did start they stayed back of their own accord! We were paid by the government each time we cleared the common, and I think I spent all my share at the dances!'

Regent's Park Zoo, London

When the Second World War ended in 1945, Mary Etherington realised that the Exmoor Pony breed was in grave danger of extinction. Just 50 ponies, only six of them male, made up the surviving registered population. As well as rallying the local herd owners to re-instate their herds and start breeding again, Mary decided that the British people should be made aware of the threat to their indigenous breed. She set her sights upon London Zoo.

The Zoological Society of London located mention of her purchase of ponies in 1945 but could not find any photographs. Within her own collection of photographs there was, however, an old negative showing two ponies with a camel looking over the wall behind them (see *'Exmoor Ponies – Survival of the Fittest*, Baker, Halsgrove, 2008). We do know the identity of these ponies: the stallion was Caractacus bred by the Westcott family and the mare was Foxglove from Mr H. Williams' herd. The ponies were exhibited for four months in 1946 before returning to Exmoor.

It seems likely that Sophia Best (see page 70 - 71), a member of the Zoological Society of London and friend of Mary Etherington had helped arrange for the Exmoors to be on display.

Mary Etherington held a tea party at Hawkridge village hall – exact date unknown but probably during the mid to late 1940s. Perhaps this was part of her campaign to get local people to commit to helping re-establish the breed.

GETTING ACQUAINTED.
Foxglove, a wild Exmoor pony and latest recruit to the Children's Corner at the London Zoo, is introduced to an old hand, a tame fox. These ponies are rapidly becoming extinct. Only about 50 are left on Exmoor.

160. Newspaper cutting – publication unknown.
Photo: the Mary Etherington Archive.

Above: *161. Foxglove.*
Photo: the Mary Etherington Archive.

Right: *162. From* The Dunkirk Evening Observer *(Dunkirk, New York) 25 February 1946.*

PONIES MAY BE SAVED

The Exmoor ponies, shyest of British animals and hardest to train, are threatened with extinction, according to a group who have started a campaign to save them. As part of the movement, two of the ponies are being exhibited at London's Zoo. A zoo official explained: There are supposed to be only about 50 Exmoor ponies left. They are usually muddy in colour and are so wild that children are not allowed to see them at close quarters.

EXMOOR PONIES

Hawkridge Visitors at Zoo

On May 18th a party from Hawkridge, Exmoor, visited the London Zoo. Dr. G.M. Vevers, the superintendent, arranged for them to be taken round the gardens, and they were given tea in the grounds.

They were shown the Exmoor stallion and mare housed in one of the large cattle sheds, where they have been on short loan, to allow the public to see the pure-bred Exmoor at close quarters. The fact that the Zoological Society has exhibited these ponies establishes their claim to be the only native breed that has been preserved in its aboriginal state. The society does not accept any animal which is not a wild species.

Dr. Vevers said: "We have been very interested in having these animals at the London Zoo. They have caused a great deal of interest and we hope that the impetus given to the breed will help to get them re-established on the hills of Exmoor and that the breeders who have preserved the feral type in spite of so many difficulties, will now be encouraged to increase their herds." Earlier in the afternoon the Hawkridge party was shown over the Houses of Parliament by Sir Waldron Smithers, who has done a great deal to help the Exmoor pony breed.

A talk on Exmoor ponies by Miss Mary Etherington was included in the light programme in "The World and His Wife" on May 20th.

163. *From the* North Devon Journal *30 May 1946.*

164. *Five adult ponies and a foal attended the Hawkridge Tea Party.* Photo courtesy of Margaret Rawle.

Lilo Lumb 1900-1974

Lilo Lumb was the founder of Herd 78 in 1947. She purchased two Acland mares from Frank Green, Old Ashway and Heatherglow. She also bought Brackenbell, Brackenmaid and Dunkery from Sidney Westcott. To begin with, her ponies ran with the Westcotts' ponies and their stallion Crackshot I; she then bred her own stallion, Heatherman, who was extremely successful in the show ring. Her favourite mare was Heather Dewdrop, a very small pony.

Born Annie Isobel Lumb, in Rose Hill, Huddersfield, she was known as Lilobel, which in time became shortened to Lilo. She went to boarding school at Priorsfield in Goldaming, Surrey.

Lilo developed a passion for riding, driving and hunting and hunted all over the world when travelling with a good friend from her school days. She made several visits to Australia.

She first visited Exmoor to watch friends play Polo at Dunster, staying at Porlock. She began hunting on Exmoor, which meant frequent visits, and so just after WWII she bought 'Riverside' in Wootton Courtenay. She knew Sir Alfred and Lady Munnings who had for a time lived in the cottage at the end of the drive to 'Riverside'. She was passionate about hunting and for a time was Master of Minehead Harriers.

Lilo farmed 'Riverside' with help from Frederick Crockford who lived in 'Riverside Cottage'. She ran Red Devon cattle, sheep and kept a number of hunters. Lilo also had her Exmoor Pony herd right from the start. She was very interested in breeding hunters, particularly crossing Exmoor mares with a small Thoroughbred stallion but as well as, rather than instead of, breeding pure Exmoors.

Lilo was a very active member of the Exmoor Pony Society, serving on the Committee and as an Inspector and a Judge; she was Society President three times. She showed her Exmoor ponies and also Hackneys.

Lilo's niece, Wendy, visited 'Riverside' regularly as a child and shared her aunt's love of the ponies. Lilo Lumb never married and when she died in 1974, she left the farm and the pony herd to Wendy (by then married to Geoff Vint); Wendy also served as an inspector and President of the Exmoor Pony Society. Herd 78 continues to this day, now with Wendy's daughter Joanna Webber. In 1984 the prefix 'Dunkery' was introduced for herd 78 foals.

165. Lilo Lumb with Bracken Sunrise, probably at the Bath & West Show.
Photo: the Exmoor Pony Society Archive.

166. A postcard of the children's zoo at Noorder Dierenpark in 1958; these may be two of the Exmoor mares with their foals. Photo: courtesy of Freddy Elzinga.

Noorder Dierenpark – North Holland Zoo

The first Exmoor ponies to go to Holland were exported in 1947 to the North Holland Zoo at Emmen. The four fillies were: two un-named from the Milton herd plus Silvertail and Miss Muffet from Herd 27 owned by Mr S. Sloley at Lower Blacklands, Withypool. All were by the Herd 48 stallion Bradymoor. The colt was from the Westcotts at Hawkridge.

A report, possibly from the *Somerset County Gazette*, quoted Mary Etherington:

> *'The ponies were shipped, by the Batalier Line, from London to Rotterdam. They caused quite a stir at the London docks, where they proved beyond a doubt that Exmoor ponies really are wild. This is the first time that the breed has been acquired by a foreign zoo, but in recent years Exmoor ponies have been exhibited at the London, Edinburgh and Bristol Zoos.*
>
> *Two West Country farmers, Mr. C. Westcott (Somerset) and Mr. S. Tucker (North Devon) were invited to travel with the ponies and introduce them to their new quarters. A large crowd assembled at Rotterdam to watch the ponies being unloaded after a rather stormy crossing … Mr. Westcott and Mr. Tucker spent a few days in Holland, where they were most hospitably entertained and returned to London by air. They reported that the ponies had settled down well and that a great deal of interest was being taken in the breed.'*

Noorder Dierenpark opened on 27 May 1935 and was the realisation of the Director William Oosting's childhood dream. He had been inspired by the Hagen Tierpark in Hamburg which had pioneered displaying animals without bars between the animals and people. Around five thousand people attended the opening of William Oosting's zoo and visitor numbers quickly grew. One of the areas within Noorder Dierenpark was the Jeugdhoeve, the children's zoo, and it is thought that the ponies were on display there.

Unfortunately, there seem to be no records mentioning these early exports to Holland in the zoo archives but they might just possibly have still been alive when the zoo faced declining numbers of visitors in the 1970s and major changes were made during a programme of innovations. Whether they were part of the transformed zoo is not known. Noorder Dierenpark once again ran into financial difficulties in 2015 and temporarily closed. It was re-opened as Wildlands in 2016.

The Breed Show

The Exmoor Pony Society annual Breed Show has long been part of Exford Horse Show, held each August. Originally Exford Show was held at the hunt kennels in Exford but then moved to Buckworthy Farm in 1948; the show was held in the field just to the right as you go down the drive to the farm. All the trailers etc. parked elsewhere on the farm and the people and ponies had to enter the show field through a small hunting gate. Eventually Exford Show outgrew Buckworthy and in 1968 moved to Court Farm where it remains today.

For a long time, it was the custom to show Exmoor ponies with a white cotton halter underneath the leather show bridle. Robert Williams told me how using a halter under a bridle had been normal practice at Great Ash when riding out to check the stock:

> *'This was so that if you encountered a sheep in difficulty, you could tie the halter to the hedge whilst you got off and attended the sheep.'*

Perhaps this gave rise to the show fashion and it certainly lasted until the late 1970s with some exhibitors.

Until sometime in the 1970s, foals ran loose beside their dams in the show ring. Apparently, this worked well for the most part as in such an unfamiliar situation, their instinct was to stay close to their mothers.

167. The Breed Show shrouded in fog in 1974. Photos: John Keene.

168. This photograph of Sid Westcott showing a mare with her foal loose, is dated June 1961 so is not the Breed Show. Photo: Exmoor Pony Society archives.

169. The Breed Show at Exford Horse Show on a bright day in 1973 (note the white halter under the bridle on champion stallion Sherryland.)

Michael Lyne 1912 – 1989

Michael Lyne was born at Upton Bishop in Herefordshire. He showed considerable artistic talent from an early age, writing and illustrating two small books about a rabbit and a dog at the age of four! As a young boy he was fascinated by wild animals but once he had a pony of his own (no record of what type) at six, hunting became his great passion. This endured throughout his life and most of his paintings and sketches depict hunting or racing scenes.

He studied briefly at Cheltenham Art School but was largely self-taught. He was a great admirer of the works of Sir Alfred Munnings and Lionel Edwards and acknowledged that they were major influences on his early work. He developed his own style working in both oils and watercolours and held many exhibitions in London, New York and elsewhere in America.

Stella Walker, renowned British Sporting Art historian said:

> *'Time will confirm that Michael Lyne ranks as one of the most important artists of his generation.'*

The high prices his paintings now fetch at auction shows this to be the case.

Like many of the 'sporting artists', he came to Exmoor to paint the Devon & Somerset Staghounds, and discovered the free-living Exmoor ponies. This scene of a herd heading off to avoid the approaching hunt is the only painting of Exmoors by Michael Lyne that I have seen to date.

170. One of three colour plates from The Wilfrid Pickles Gay Street Book *published in 1949 by Latimer House. This is a children's story book. The colour plates were specially painted for the book and included for the children to 'cut out and put them up in your den'.*

Note: Wilfrid Pickles O.B.E. 1904-1978 was a popular radio broadcaster and actor, appearing on television and in films. His career started in the 1930s and ended in the early 1970s. The other two colour plates depict Dartmoor and New Forest ponies.

Edinburgh Zoo

When Mary Etherington relocated her ponies to Edinburgh in 1950 (see page 81), she rented a field adjoining Edinburgh Zoo. Writing about the history of the Exmoor ponies in pony trekking, Professor Barry Leek referred to the ponies still being beside Edinburgh Zoo in 1956:

> *'The ponies were kept in a field behind Scotus Academy that was the undeveloped extension of Edinburgh Zoo. Three ponies were already broken, Fisherman, Lorna Doone and Puss Moth.'*

As the newspaper cutting shows, the zoo also had one of her mares with a foal on display for a time. The mare was Foxglove and the foal was Richard Strongbow, not registered in the EPS Stud Book.

Is it my imagination or could the keeper pictured below be television presenter Johnny Morris? The BBC did film him at Edinburgh Zoo for the children's programme *Animal Magic* in the 1960s.

Exmoor pony Foxglove and her foal Richard Strongbow find a temporary home at Edinburgh Zoological Gardens, while Miss Etherington carries out her research work on the origin of the domestic horse.

171. From Scottish Daily Mail, *15 February 1950.*

Right: *172. These are assumed to be Edinburgh Zoo keepers with the ponies.* Photo: The Mary Etherington Archive.
Below: *173. Possibly television personality Johnny Morris with one of the Exmoors in Edinburgh Zoo.* Photo: The Mary Etherington Archive.

Canada

The first record of Exmoor ponies travelling to Canada is of those imported by Ian McDonald of Brussels, Ontario on 15 May 1951: the ponies were stallion Battlecry and mares Needlegun and Swallow, all from Herd 2. Needlegun was a daughter of Foxglove, the mare exhibited at Regents Park Zoo in London five year earlier. For Swallow, this must have been a dreadful experience as she apparently gave birth on the dock just before being loaded onto the ship.

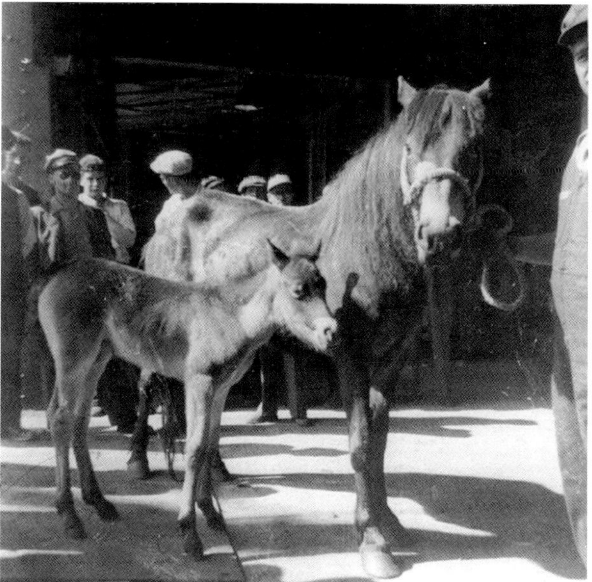

174. Swallow and Holly awaiting loading at the docks. Photo: The Ian McDonald Archive, courtesy of Neil Gowing.

In October 1958 another stallion, Stoodleigh Lad from the Westcotts' Herd 1, and four mares were imported by E.M. Davies of Montreal. Two mares went to Allan Mitchell in Quebec and two to Mrs Holmes of Inverary in Ontario. Later, Stoodleigh Lad was sold to Ian McDonald.

During 1958, discussions were pursued with the British Exmoor Pony Society regarding the formation of a Canadian Branch and the first edition of the U.K. Stud Book included sections for both Canada and Denmark.

Ian McDonald (Herd A) was very impressed with the versatility of his Exmoor ponies and considered them unbeatable for rounding up his cattle. They coped well with winter conditions and he trained a pair to pull a sleigh, as pictured in my previous book.

Ross Hoggart, at Clinton, registered foals in Herd C, beginning in 1960 and with the prefix Ponyshoes. That year he imported a Herd 23 stallion (he named Wincombe), two un-named mares from Herd 6 (subsequently named English Gem and Miss Noggart), two mares from Herd 23 (English Joker and Patricia's Pet) and Mary Jane

175. Ian McDonald with stallion Battlecry (right) and probably mare Swallow.

176. Ian's daughter Susie dressed ready for the Santa Claus Parade, Brussels. Photos: The Ian McDonald Archive, courtesy of Neil Gowing.

from Harold Heard's Herd 85 (who came in foal to the Miltons' stallion Forest). However, English Joker was in fact male! – see page 80.

Dorothy and Tony Griffiths of Toronto imported two more ponies in the 1960s – Hawkwell Pride of the Moor from Herd 12 and Fair Lady from Herd 23.

Herd E was located at Timbertop Farm, Don Mills in Ontario, owned by the Fowler family but managed by Mrs Vimy Siegrist. Her daughter Judy rode Sandy, offspring of Needlegun and Battlecry, and when Judy was seven they were jumping fences over three foot high out foxhunting.

Anne Holmes was Secretary of the Exmoor Pony Trekking Section whilst at the Royal (Dick) Veterinary College in Edinburgh. After qualifying, she returned to Canada with plans to have Exmoors of her own:

'I managed to locate 3 ponies in Ontario and 7 in Kentucky, USA. The three in Ontario were the stallion imported from the UK - Hawkwell Pride of the Moor, aged mare Ponyshoes Rosetta and their last filly Devon's Snow Rose. I contacted Earl and Becky Majeske from Nonesuch, Kentucky. They had a breeding pair, Devon's New Decade (stallion) and mare Cat Ballou and 5 of their foals. They graciously agreed to sell me the oldest filly Lynton of Nonesuch who duly arrived in Ontario in the Autumn of 1990.

Now I needed a stallion. Peter Dean had Marius available whose bloodlines were unrelated to anything previously imported into Canada. When Marius arrived in the US, a relative and I drove to collect him. The quarantine staff said when they were taking Marius off the plane he broke free from his handler and went running down the grassy edge of the runway. He was always a sweetheart and remains to this day one of the easiest ponies to handle that I've owned. The Gowings sent Tabitha to me for breeding to Marius and it is quite a feeling to look at the three ponies in your field and know they are the only breeding stock in the country!

In all I have raised 37 foals of my own and two Thoroughbred Exmoor crosses. I've had mares come from the US to be bred and sold ponies as far as Alberta Canada and California USA.'

177. Hawkwell Pride of the Moor.
Photo: Dorothy Griffiths.

178. L-R Rosy (possibly Ponyshoes Rosetta), Bonfire (a Thoroughbred-Exmoor cross) and Ginny.
Photo: Vimy Siegrist.

179. Stallion Marius at home in Canada.
Photo: Anne Holmes.

Germany

The first instance of Exmoor ponies being imported into Germany seems to have been in 1952, when the Herd 2 stallions Tom Faggus and Carbineer and mares Dabchick, Chaffinch and Devonian were purchased by the German Government's Isernhagen Stud. It is probable that the German zoologist Hermann Ebhardt, who knew Mary Etherington and James Speed through the International Pony Breeders' Federation, was involved in arranging this.

Once in Germany, Tom Faggus was released to run with the Dülmen herd of ponies. Dülmen is a medium sized town in the north-western state of North Rhine-Westphalia, about 50 kilometres from the Dutch border. It gives its name to the Dülmen pony and is called the 'town of the wild horses'.

The origin of these ponies is supposed to be from an originally wild population that was under such threat in 1847, due to industrial expansion causing loss of habitat, that Duke Alfred von Croy established a sanctuary for them on his land a few kilometres west at Merfelder Bruch.

The fenced enclosure at Merfelder Bruch is about 3.5 square kilometres in size with grassland and meadows, coniferous, birch and oak forests, heathlands and marshy areas. Today about 350 Dülmen ponies are free-living on the reserve.

If the animals that were rescued in 1847 were of truly wild European stock, then that would suggest they were Tarpans. The Konik pony of Poland is thought to be similar in appearance to the wild Tarpan. If one looks at photographs of the Dülmen ponies today, they seem to be little changed – but all is not what it seems. The photographs of the Dülmen ponies from 1952 show a very different appearance, with clear indications of significant introduction of genes from horse and other pony breeds; Timor ponies, Thoroughbreds, Arabs, Welsh Cobs, Hackney horses and Clydesdales all get a mention in some breed descriptions.

180. Mary Etherington possibly bidding farewell to one of the 1952 shipment to Germany. Photo: the Mary Etherington Archive.

Most significantly, it would appear that such introductions had diluted their ability to live naturally and Tom Faggus was introduced into the herd specifically to reinvigorate the population with hardiness and primitive characteristics.

181. Tom Faggus (middle, facing) with the Dülmen mares in September 1953. Photo: Klaus Ebhardt.

Within the Mary Etherington Archive there is a report sent to the Speeds in 1953 that details the visit of a Mr Glitz, the estate manager for the Duke of Croy at that time, accompanied by the Ebhardt family. (Hermann Ebhardt published scientific papers on the dentition of Exmoor ponies in the 1960s.) The visit was to assess the first crop of foals sired by Tom Faggus, who was running with seventy mares. The report writer recorded:

> *'"Please do not move out of the cars!" says Mr. Ebhardt, "I shall give Tom Faggus a call!" and he begins to neigh. Cautiously the pony herd begins to approach the cars. At first dams only could be seen, – but suddenly stand he – the sire – in front of them all! Tom Faggus is no more the young, elegant stallion of three years we saw last year. Now he is a strong four years old master of the herd, and promises to be a stronger one next year. When the first car door has been opened however, Tom Faggus frightens away his mares.'*

The new home for Carbineer and the mares was the 'Hannover Tiergarten'. This deer park was created in 1678/79 by Duke Johan Friedrich for hunting and was stocked with wild horses and wild boar as well as deer. In 1799, the public were given access to the Tiergarten for recreational use. Unfortunately, by the end of WWII, all the stock were gone, having been eaten during periods of food shortages. The Exmoor ponies that arrived from Herd 2 in 1952 were part of re-stocking the park and 'three wild horses' also came from Dülmen.

About 150 kilometres south of Hannover is Sababurg Tierpark which also had its origin as a hunting reserve. In the 1500s, Count Wilhelm IV, who was very interested in natural sciences, had the land enclosed with a 5 kilometre long and 3 metre high stone wall. He stocked the area with cattle, deer, chamois, moose and reindeer. However, by the end of the 1700s, much of the forest and its animals were gone and the land reclaimed for pasture. Efforts to revive the Tierpark began after WWII but it wasn't until 1973 that it was opened to the public, a project led by zoologist Hans Georg Picker.

Exmoor ponies were chosen by Hans Picker to represent the wild European pony in a 14 hectare enclosure shared with bison and deer and adjoining that of Przewalski Horses. The first Exmoors, stallion Hannibal and mare Halla, came

182. Two of the fillies arriving at Isernhagen on 16 February 1952. Photo: Hermann Ebhardt.

183. Carbineer at Isernhagen on 16 February 1952. Photo: Hermann Ebhardt.

184. L-R: Mr Hinze with halters, Klaus Ebhardt with Dabchick and Mr Mettke with Chaffinch at Isernhagen on 16 February 1952. Photo: Hermann Ebhardt.

185. Exmoors at Sababurg Zoo, probably in the 1990s. Photo: courtesy of Sandy Roedde.

186. Stallion Golden Sparrow, born in 1993 in Germany. Photo: courtesy of Sandy Roedde.

from Heiligenstadt near Hannover. Both were by Carbineer and out of Dabchick, presumably bred at Hannover Tiergarten. Two years later, four more mares were imported from Cumbria: Cardunneth, Breckney and Kellah from Herd 14 and Molinia from Herd 37.

After 1982, the Sababurg herd stallion changed to Heristal, a son of Hannibal out of Cardunneth and then in 1989 they bought a seven year old stallion from Michael Schäfer called Little M.

The Sababurg foundation stallion Hannibal had never been registered in the English E.P.S. Stud Book, and so none of the subsequent Sababurg-bred Exmoors were eligible for registration, although undoubtedly a pure-bred herd with detailed breeding records. However, in 1996, with the purchase of an Anchor mare Gypsy and the stallion Golden Sparrow, bred by Rainer Willmann in Germany, registration of their progeny in the English Stud Book began. A further registered stallion Ernie was purchased in 2003.

Dr Michael Schäfer, a German vet, perhaps first became interested in Exmoor ponies when he attended the meeting of the International Federation of Pony Breeders in Edinburgh in 1953. On this or a subsequent trip, he also visited British breeders to take anatomical measurements of their Exmoors for his comparative research into pony types.

Michael Schäfer became particularly interested in comparative behaviour and to aid his studies he acquired some Exmoors; he also imported seven Sorraia horses from Portugal and for a long time had the world's largest group of these endangered horses. He also studied Fjord Horses that were being crossed with Konik ponies in breeding-back experiments in Bavaria.

Michael Schäfer's Exmoors came from Peter Dean's Herd 14 in Cumbria (mare Whinnetley) and from author Anthony Dent's Herd 67 in France (stallion Epona's Musketeer and mare Jemima). From these imported Exmoors Michael Schäfer bred three colts and two fillies, all but one from the pairing of Epona's Musketeer and Jemima.

Deutsche Exmoor Pony Geslleschaft

Over two autumns, in 1990 and 1991, Rainer Willmann and his wife bought 21 ponies, six from Herd 23 on Withypool Common and the rest from the Anchor Herd, for various new homes in Germany. The full story of how these newly imported Exmoors were dispersed in Germany was written by Rainer Willmann in the E.P.S. Newsletter of 1998.

This new wave of imports, together with increasing interest in Exmoor ponies, led to the idea of forming a German Exmoor Pony Society to ensure that there was a system for the registration of their progeny. The 'Deutsche Exmoor Pony Gesellschaft' came into being in 1995. In the tenth anniversary edition of its newsletter 'Epona',

DEUTSCHE EXMOOR-PONY GESELLSCHAFT e.V.

187. The German society's logo.

founding President Rainer Willmann and then President Lutz Keller looked back:

'When the German Exmoor Pony Society was founded in 1995, a year-long exchange with the Exmoor Pony Society in England, the internationally recognized breeders' association, had preceded it. The aim was to make sure that everyone who would like to be friends of Exmoor ponies and want to contribute to the preservation of this rare breed would speak with one voice. This is perhaps also due to the few enthusiasts who imported Exmoor ponies to Germany in the 50s, 60s and 70s under the then much more difficult circumstances, and who were tirelessly pointing out the special status of this rare horse.'

The German Society adopted the same rules for inspection and Stud Book registration as its parent Society in the U.K. They also created a 'genealogy book' to record all the pure-bred Exmoors (and their descendants) that had been bred in Germany but were unregisterable. British inspectors have made annual visits to Germany to inspect the foals and German inspectors have also been trained.

A German Accent

For some years a German ex-prisoner-of-war, Paul, worked for the Clayford Stud just outside Dulverton, on Exmoor. The Stud was jointly owned by Miss Alice Sanders and Miss Helen Dashwood, who were active members of the Exmoor Pony Society, both serving as President in 1959 and 1969 + 1978 respectively. Amongst the ponies they bred was Clayford Bracken Sweetie, who was later purchased by Creenagh Mitchell and shown for a time by me. Miss Dashwood told Creenagh that Paul could not pronounce 'Sweetie' and so called the mare 'Sveetie'. Exmoor ponies have good memories and once roaming on Withypool Common, Sweetie would ignore us unless she heard us call 'Sveetie'.

188. Paul showing another Herd 8 mare Clayford Bracken Rosie at Exford Show in about 1976.
Photo: Exmoor Pony Society Archive.

Crystal Palace Zoo

Having exhibited ponies at Regent's Park Zoo in 1946 (see pages 101-102), Mary Etherington brought Exmoors to London again in 1953 to live at the Crystal Palace Children's Zoo. The zoo had been opened in 1951 (to coincide with the Festival of Britain) by author of children's books, Noel Streatfield. It was intended to give pleasure to London's children who had endured the years of World War II.

The ponies were both on display and available to give pony rides. The exact number of ponies involved is unknown but certainly at the start included the mares Aconite, Moccassin, The London Mare and Speedwell, all from Herd 2. Aconite seems to have arrived with her foal Acorn who was then registered into the London County Council Parks Department's Herd 50. The London Mare must have arrived in foal as the following year Minnow was born there.

189. Aconite and Acorn 'en route from train to horse box'. Photo: the Mary Etherington Archive.

190. In the background, Exmoor mare Moccassin with Shetland and Donkey companions. Photo: courtesy of Doreen Witney.

The adult Exmoor ponies were on loan to the zoo and lived alongside some Shetland ponies, also used for giving rides, and one Icelandic Horse.

In 1950, Mary Etherington had also loaned ponies to another London park, Maryon Wilson Park in Charlton. It is thought that some Exmoors were also running in Epping Forest around that time; Epping Forest was under the control of the Corporation of London. Perhaps these ponies also belonged to Mary.

Returning to Crystal Palace, the Exmoors were bred from and a further six ponies were registered into Herd 50. Some of these home-bred foals were kept at Crystal Palace and some sold. The last filly, Tansy, was born in 1959 and was purchased by equestrian writer Anthony Dent who later sold her to Exmoor pony breeder Pat McElligott. Pat bred the stallion Frithesden Beacon, who was out of Tansy.

Pat told me about visiting the zoo with Anthony Dent only to find it closed. Anthony scaled the railings and successfully found a keeper to let Pat in and show them the ponies. She also bought Moccassin from the zoo and recalled paying £10 for her including delivery. Moccassin adored Pat's stallion Skyman and monopolised him. She lived until over 30. According to Pat, the other original ponies eventually went back to Mary Etherington in Scotland.

191. Doreen with foal Witan Chester (not registered).
Photo: courtesy of Doreen Witney.

192. L-R Arrowhead and Oakapple.
Photo: courtesy of Doreen Witney.

In 2002, responding to my appeal for information in a local paper, Doreen Witney made contact and provided a first-hand account of her time as a keeper, then Doreen Newman:

'In 1951-52, for the Festival of Britain, the then London County Council decided to renovate the old racing pits beside the Crystal Palace motor racing circuit. At the same time they opened a Pets Corner in Battersea Park to link with the Festival on The Embankment and the Pleasure Gardens in Battersea Park. They needed a base for the initial intake of animals.

I answered a local advertisement for seasonal staff for various tasks and with experience of livestock etc. We started with a few Exmoor ponies, some Shetland ponies, an Icelandic, goats, Soay and St. Kilda sheep, various birds, four gorgeous Husky dogs, squirrels and mice.

As mere females doing manual work, County Hall never told us anything. A lorry or van used to arrive and a driver would bark "Paddock this" or "Cage this". I loved the Exmoors I had to make and break – most challenging! Oakapple, Arrowhead and Moccassin were my first three. Moccassin, with his sway back, was already there when I joined; Oakapple and Arrowhead arrived some time later. All I had to do was "Break Em".

The mare Acorn was normally at Battersea Park but I believe she was mated to Chester – again, we were not told these sordid details! But I do recall vividly the sad day I took my two boys Oaky and Arry Sparry to Kings Cross Station on route to a riding school in Yorkshire I believe. That would be in the early 60s.

In the late 50s, I was made Supervisor and moved into the house on the edge of the park. I retired from the zoo in 1964, reluctantly I must say. These were, without doubt, the happiest years of my working life. I have so many happy memories.'

193. Mary Etherington and local children with her ponies at Crystal Palace Children's Zoo in 1953. She had brought them by train overnight from Scotland. Photo: the Mary Etherington Archive.

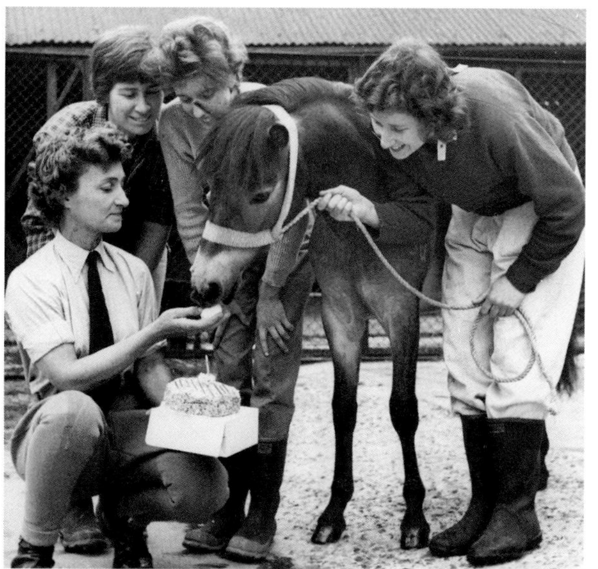

194. Left: Doreen, Pat Adcock, Yvonne Franklin and Georgina MacMahon celebrating the first birthday of Witan Tansy (named Topsy in error in the 2000 edition of the EPS Stud Book). Photo: courtesy of Doreen Witney.

Linda Brittin, a ranger at Crystal Palace Park, told me in 2002 that the original zoo had a variety of animals including an elephant that had been presented to the Queen and came to the zoo as the donors thought that the Queen lived in the Crystal Palace. At one time the zoo bred pedigree Huskies and puppies were exported all over the world.

Linda worked in the zoo from 1982 and then in its later guise as the children's farm; the farm closed in December 2000. The Park remains home to Grade 1 listed Victorian dinosaur figures and also the National Sports Centre is located there.

Above: *195. One of the foals bred at the zoo.* Photo: courtesy of Doreen Witney.

Left: *196. Oakapple (left) and Arrowhead.* Photo: courtesy of Doreen Witney.

The Edinburgh Exmoors Meet Roy Rogers

Roy Rogers was known as 'King of the Cowboys'; he starred in *The Roy Rogers Show* on television in the 1950s with cowgirl Dale Evans and his famous horse Trigger. In 1954 he brought his show to an Edinburgh theatre.

Lesley Wilkie wrote in the 2007 Exmoor Pony Society newsletter:

> *'Granny's flat overlooked Grange Court in Edinburgh, where Tom Hillock looked after the Dick Vet Exmoor ponies ... Because the stables were so central, we had a few famous names for bed and breakfast. Roy Rogers' horse Trigger bedded down with the Exmoors. We rode out round the Kings Park a couple of times and had the privilege of sitting on Trigger in the stable yard. I had an invitation to the Kings Theatre to see the show and there saw the magnificent sight of Trigger, Roy Rogers and Dale coming down the main carpeted stairway of the theatre. What a thrill. I will never forget the beautiful saddle and show outfits worn during the performance.'*

It had been thought that, whilst in Edinburgh, Roy Rogers had made a celebrity appearance at the convention of the International Pony Breeders Federation (I.P.B.F.) but that actually took place in 1953.

197. Roy Rogers meets an Exmoor foal. Photo: George Outram & Co. Ltd., Glasgow.

Note: these photographs were given to Mrs Debbie Davey, owner of Exmoor Herd 21 by Mrs Celia Eriz whose father, Mr Broustead, was a Secretary of the I.P.B.F.

198. The delegates visited the Speed's Exmoor ponies (Herd 2) in the grounds of Edinburgh Zoo on 25 February 1953. Photo: George Outram & Co. Ltd., Glasgow.

A Pony for Princess Anne

In 1954, the Exmoor Pony Society committee decided that it should present Her Majesty the Queen with an Exmoor pony for Princess Anne, then aged two, to ride when she was old enough. Miss Lilo Lumb offered a four-year-old mare she had bred called Heathermaid. Heathermaid's initial training was undertaken by Miss Helen Greenwood of Porlock, after which she was sent to Messrs. Horace Smith for finishing.

The mare was eventually handed over to the Queen in November 1954. E.P.S. Minutes of December 1954 record:

199. Heathermaid during training.
Photo: courtesy of Joanna Webber.

200. Little Cloud was bred by Miss Pam Taylor and is held by Mrs Poffelt with rider Philip who was normally confined to a wheelchair. Thought to be in the 1970s.
Photo: *Kentish Times.*

'The pony was duly handed over to Her Majesty the Queen at Windsor in November last. It was hoped that the President and Miss Lumb could have been present but the Crown Equerry informed the Secretary that he was commanded to convey to the Society, Her Majesty's grateful thanks and appreciation for the gift and much regretted that, owing to the pressure of Her Majesty's many engagements, it was impossible to arrange a formal handing over in advance.'

Heathermaid travelled by train to Wolferton Station (often called the Royal Station, being the closest to Sandringham) on 10 November 1954 and was turned out at Appleton: presumably this was the parkland near Appleton House on the Sandringham Estate.

The intention of the gift was that Princess Anne would one day ride Heathermaid but on enquiring, I was told that the Princess Royal had no memory of this pony at all. However, a letter from the Crown Equerry to Captain Bill Fellowes in November 1954 in the state office at Sandringham stated that the Queen will *'most probably give it away to some child in the district who may like a pony.'* No doubt Heathermaid was just one of many horses and ponies presented to the Queen for her daughter.

Her Majesty the Queen was due to visit the Royal Bath & West show when it was held in Plymouth (this was probably in 1958) and the arrangement was made that she would come to see Miss Lumb's Heatherglow, the dam of Heathermaid. Unfortunately, Heatherglow was a pony that was liable to kick and Charlie Westcott told Lilo Lumb not to let the Queen too close to Heatherglow in case she kicked. In the excitement of the royal visit, Lilo and Charlie forgot all about it but fortunately the mare behaved perfectly.

Princess Anne's first meeting with an Exmoor pony was probably, as pictured here, when she opened an all-weather surface paddock for the Margery McClure School for Handicapped Children near Chislehurst in Kent.

Fisherman

201. Thought to be Alex Moore and Ian Brown with Fisherman (left) and friend. Photo: the Mary Etherington Archive.

Fisherman was born on Exmoor in 1943, sired by Caractacus and out of a Herd 1 mare. He was registered into Herd 2 belonging to Mary Etherington. He was amongst those ponies she took to Edinburgh (see page 81), presumably a gelding by then. I 'met' Fisherman in 1976 when I was given his skeleton; he has lived with me ever since. Naturally, I wanted to know more about this pony and past students of the Royal (Dick) Veterinary College were able to help.

Alex Moore told me:

> *'My association with Exmoor ponies started when I went to the Dick Vet and met Mrr and Mrs Speed. The ponies they had ran on a hill property not far from where I lived in Fife and I used to help rounding up and breaking and handling the ponies for Mrs. Speed. Fisherman came on the scene when Mrs. Speed asked me and another student, Ian Brown, to undertake a trial pony trek using Exmoor ponies. This must have been in the spring of 1955 and we started from the Speed residence in Hillend and did a round trip through Perthshire via Comrie and Lochearnhead, and finally back to Hillend. I think we covered somewhere in the region of 12 to 15 miles a day; we carried all we needed with us and relied on the goodwill of local farmers for shelter for man and beast overnight. The idea was just to demonstrate that this activity was both practicable and enjoyable, and indeed from*

202. *Barry Leek riding Fisherman.* Photo: the Mary Etherington Archive.

203. *Barry Leek and Fisherman meeting up with fellow Herd 2 member, the stallion Tademus.* Photo: the Mary Etherington Archive.

memory pony trekking did become very popular around this time.'

Barry Leek, who became Professor of Veterinary Physiology in Dublin, added to Fisherman's story:

'I did of course develop a very close and special relationship with the Speeds. I spent a lot of time with them, sometimes in Edinburgh but mostly at their cottage on the Fordell Estate. On the second Sunday of the autumn term each year, the Speeds hired a bus and I took a party of Freshers to see their pony herd at Kelty, followed by a visit to the cottage where a grand cold meat salad was served on wooden plates.

To publicise, I suppose, the merits of the Exmoor pony, the Speeds presented an Exmoor to the present Duke of Buccleuch, then as a four year old son of the late Earl of Dalkeith. I remember me, and other students, half lifting, half dragging this pony up a long line of steps into the Conservative Headquarters in Newington, Edinburgh.'

Barry has particular memories of riding either Fisherman or Lorna Doone on a Student Rag Day in Edinburgh:

'On Student Rag Day, the first Saturday in May 1955, the Speeds lent our class deerskins but I was the only one with a pony. The deerskin covered a pair of swimming trunks and was held on with a couple of large safety pins. In the morning I collected in the area around the stables, including riding into the Newington post office, where I could reach over the grill and collect from the post office staff directly. Some of the customers were a bit apprehensive at finding themselves around the back legs of the pony but it was so bomb-proof that there was no danger. In the afternoon the rest of the class collected at Edinburgh's West End to await the arrival of the parade proper coming down from Tollcross. Meanwhile we worked the crowd, collecting their pennies. All was going well until some clown threw a banger (firework) behind the pony. Naturally it took off at a mighty pace along the open Princes Street that had been cleared by the police in readiness for the parade. We had not gone very far when I was conscious of the loss of one of the safety pins. With one hand I was trying to hold the edges of the deerskin together. With the other hand I was holding a collection tin and a pair of reins, whilst underneath me was a pony who was enjoying the freedom of the open road performed now at a good gallop. This was kept up for the 1 mile length of Princes St. as far as the East End (Waverley).'

204. *Barry Leek on Student Rag Day 1955 riding either Fisherman or Lorna Doone.* Photo: courtesy of Colin Warwick.

Hope Bourne 1920 – 2010

When Hope Bourne died in 2010, she left all her paintings, drawings and sketches to the Exmoor Society, numbering around 2000 items; 166 were of horses or Exmoor ponies.

As well as an artist, Hope was a wonderful illustrator and that came from her talent for observing the world around her. Many of her depictions of Exmoor ponies carry detailed notes.

One of the subjects she was fascinated by was the variation in colour of the ponies' coats. She wrote:

> *'Light has a considerable effect upon the appearance of pony colour. All ponies look darker on a grey or cloudy day, or in the shadow. Rain especially makes the coats look dark, almost black. On a sunny day the coats appear lighter and brighter – the sunshine brings out the latent golden-red in the colouring.*
>
> *The direction of light also has some effect on the colouring. When the sun strikes across the quarters the mealy parts of the body are emphasized. When the light falls from the direction of the forehand the colour appears harder and less graduated.*
>
> *Age also affects the coat-colour. Foals are born a light mealy colour and gradually darken as they grow older. Yearlings, usually show a great deal of mealyness about the underparts of the body, but after this age the colour begins to harden.*

205. *'Chummy – an Acland-bred pony. At Ferny Ball – six years old, and third day under saddle!' is written beside this photograph, which was probably taken in the late 1950s.* Photo: The Hope Bourne Bequest/Exmoor Society.

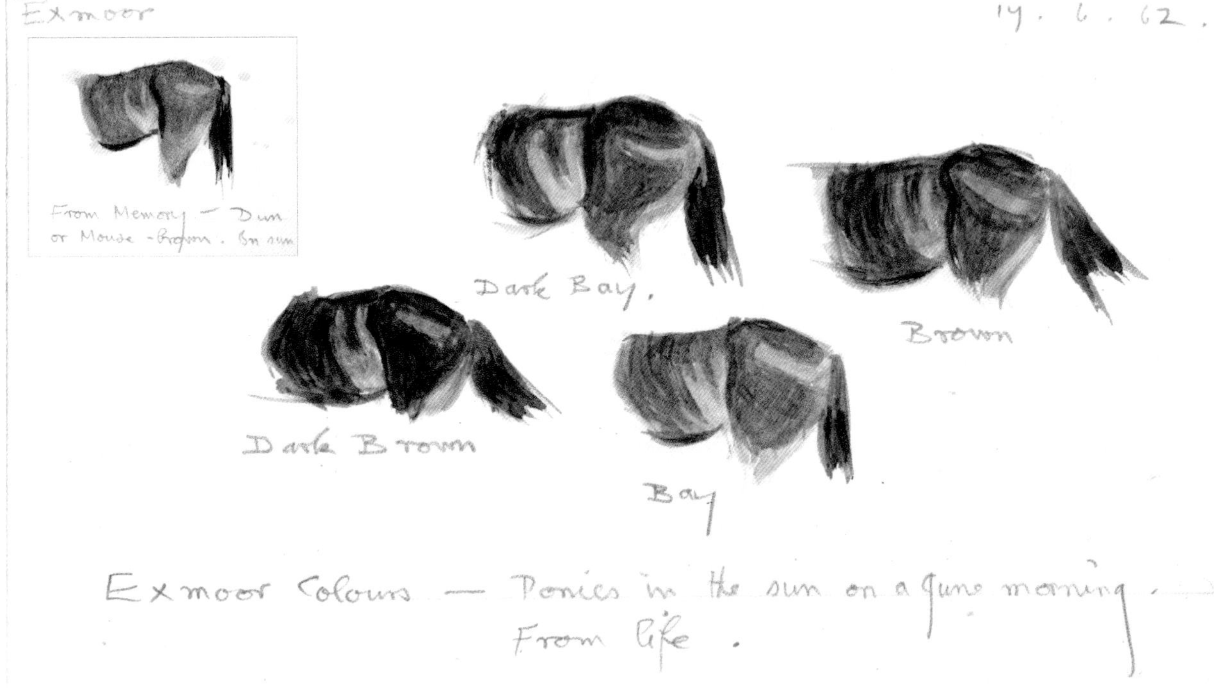

206. *Hope's 'colour chart' for Exmoor ponies. Two items from he Hope Bourne Bequest/Exmoor Society.*

207. One of the most complete annotated illustrations Hope left. This is thought to be Little Lucie bred by Joy Etherington and born in 1955.
The Hope Bourne Bequest/Exmoor Society.

208. Hope's watercolour of the zebra-striped foal during its first week.
The Hope Bourne Bequest/Exmoor Society.

Stallions, whether red or brown, tend to be a rich strong colour.

The season of the year also makes a marked difference to the coat. The winter coat, with its flatness and lack of gloss, shows up the native colouring very distinctly – dark sooty upper parts, russet flanks, and light mealy underparts. The fine glossy summer coat usually has a harder, less graduated appearance, with the mealyness hardened into a tan shade.

Though the Exmoor pony colour is officially divided into bay, brown and dun, these three classifications are really only variations of the one native colour, and each tends to merge into another to such a degree that any real division is not possible.'

Hope recorded a most unusual foal that was born on Withypool Common in 1957 from registered parents. It was born with stripes! Hope said that the stripes were visible for its first week of life but then faded away. She painted the foal again six months later and it had no stripes; its solid coat colour was Exmoor dun – as shown on the previous page.

There is one other record of a partially striped Exmoor foal from the 1981 E.P.S. Newsletter:

'Miss McElligott writes that Frithesden Owlman was born with zebra stripes on his legs and neck but they disappeared at about six months.

I have also been shown photographs of one Exmoor pony that appeared to have thin dark stripes in its coat as an adult.

Norway

Edvin Kjell Thorson, owner of a riding school in Oslo, imported several Exmoor ponies in 1958. He bought a stallion named Forester II with four mares and began breeding Exmoors.

Forester II, a dark bay pony, was born in 1954 on Withypool Common into Herd 23 owned by Fred Milton. He was straight from the moor and unhandled.

The Exmoor Pony Society Stud Book, in its original 1963 edition, also records that three Milton mares were sent to Norway. The mares were 23/43 and 23/46 born in 1956 and 23/47 born in 1957. The fourth mare may have been 23/48. They were named in Norway as Raggy, Gry, Fröya and Daisy; Raggy was also unhandled.

The last pony from that breeding line (Wilma) died in the middle of the 1990s.

The riding school is today run by Eline Falch, granddaughter of Kjell Thorson, so a third generation is still interested in Exmoors. Today they have one Exmoor mare, Myras Api, born in Norway out of Kingsby Holly, a mare Louise Rundell imported into Sweden from Mary Hannah's herd in Somerset in 1999.

David Brewer told me that in about 1962, Fred Milton welcomed a visitor from Norway to Weatherslade, who wanted to purchase four mares and a stallion for the Norwegian Government. They were to be used for moving light artillery in the mountains. David transported the ponies to Oslo and they were then transferred onto a tank landing craft to make the final part of the journey up a fjord to where they were going to be trained. Apparently, the project was not a success and the ponies were sold on to private owners.

The Exmoor Pony Society Stud Book also records that three ponies were exported by Pat McElligott to Norway in 1964, to 'Gundersen'. These were two Anchor colts, Tipsy and Volucris plus a Frithesden filly, Velvet.

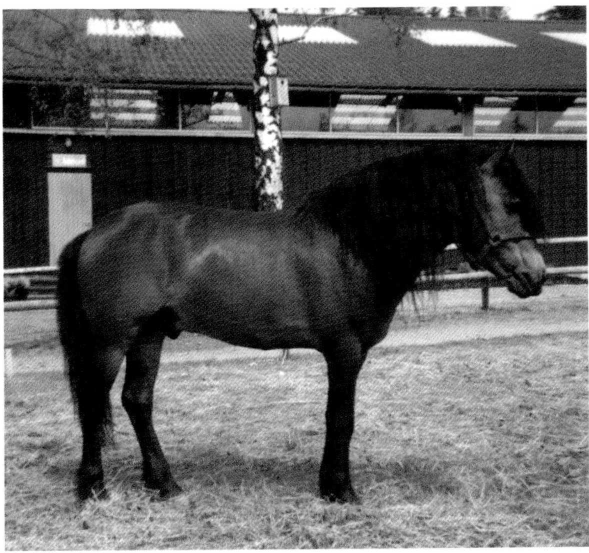

Above left: *209. Forester II at EKT Rideskole og Husdyrpark, Oslo.* Photo: Eline Falch.

Above right: *210. Sissel Thorson Falch holding Exmoor pony Myras Api carrying grand-daughter Maya Dorothea Falch Bargus.* Photo: Eline Falch.

Right: *211. The riding school's logo.* Photo: Eline Falch.

Brendon Pony Fair

E.R. Delderfield devoted a chapter of his book *Exmoor Wanderings* to gatherings and pony fairs. Writing in 1959, he tells us:

'On the Monday following the round-up, Brendon Pony Fair – a miniature and forerunner of Bampton Fair – takes place. This is another custom that has come down hundreds of years. The Sale is held in the paddock beside the Staghunters Hotel, and from mid-morning the ponies start arriving. The droves are small ones which are owned by the individual farmers. They have had time to look them over and decide which they are keeping and which are to be returned to the Moor. The Auctioneer takes his place at 2 o'clock. As one wag put it: "Not a bit of good 'im trying before, us wouldn't come out to listen to 'un till closing time." So, when the Bar shuts, the sale commences. Now and then a pony takes fright and in desperation dashes into the ring of onlookers, scattering them like chaff and, to the huge delight of the "safe" section of the crowd, someone is often bowled over in the melee.'

Brendon Pony Sale was originally held at Cheriton Farm, and moved to the Staghunters Inn in 1923 or 1924 due to fears about Foot and Mouth disease.

212. 'Brendon Pony Fair, where the unexpected always happens.' From Exmoor Wanderings *by E.R. Delderfield.*

Below: *213. From the* North Devon Journal *29 October 1936.*

Unforgotten Exmoor Volume II includes the memories of Jim Sanders. His father was a bidder at one Brendon Pony Sale:

'One time, I remember, he bought me a pony at Brendon. This pony, if he took it into his head, would set off like a bullet from a gun. Nothing would stop him, he just took off, charged at gates, knocked them down. Father and I went to collect this pony and I rode him back. Well we got to the top of Ilkerton and that's when he suddenly took off. I clung on, I can tell you! I was about twelve, thirteen at the time. Cor, he could travel when he galloped – one of the fastest horses I ever rode.'

BRENDON PONY SALE

The Annual Sale of Ponies at Brendon, which is always on the Monday preceeding "Bampton Pony Fair" took place on the Stag Hunter's Yard, on Monday. Several changed hands.

The sale was conducted by Mr. Tattersall at very satisfactory prices.

Dobbs (Cockram Dobbs and Stagg, South Molton). It is interesting to note his Grandfather, Mr. Frank Dobbs, conducted the first sale of the Exmoor Ponies at Brendon over 60 years ago, and in those days and for many years after the sale was held at Cheriton. But some years ago during a Foot and Mouth Disease scare the venue was changed to the Village where it has since been held.

Sweden

The first exports to Sweden seem to have taken place in the late 1950s with two mares, Sweetapple and the other un-named, being purchased from the Williams' Herd 48; where in Sweden and to whom they went isn't known. Then around 1965, five filly foals (Bell Heather, Clayford Badgeworthy, Lorna, Moor Mistral and another un-named) and a colt foal (Lucky Boy) were sent as a combined shipment from the Westcott Herd 10, Milton Herd 23, Heard Herd 85 and Sanders & Dashwood Herd 8. Four years later, Hawkwell Nova and Rainbow, also female, were exported to Sweden. There were also three other fillies or mares – Heatherbell, Whirlwind and one un-named – sent out either before or just after the 1969 exports.

Hawkwell Nova's original Swedish owners are unknown but she lived in Smaland, Southern Sweden. Louise Rundell met Nova for the first time in 1980 near Stockholm and bought her. Nova proved a very good child's first pony and taught many children to ride at the Rundell's riding school at Vårgårda in Western Sweden. She calmly carried Vårgårda's Saint Claus through the town with thousands of people on the pavements. She is also very caring with disabled riders.

During the 1970s, Swedish buyers acquired three mares from the Deans' Herd 14 plus a mare and a gelding from the Anchor Herd. Then in the 1980s, stallions Hawkwell Tizzy Whizzie and Quartz plus four mares from various breeders travelled to Sweden. Taking the ponies to Sweden was literally far from plain sailing as Yvonne Campbell and David Brewer described in the E.P.S. 1990 Newsletter:

> *'Early September and the veterinary work started, with weekly visits taking swabs, blood tests, sketches of each pony which had to be triplicated, working out how long the tests were valid for as by mid September Scandinavia was closed for the movement of equines due to the flu ... We then had a sailing date for 28th September but three days earlier the ferry caught fire!*
>
> *We were then booked to sail on October 1st ... Bad news; rough weather at sea and the Captain would not take us.'*

214. *Hawkwell Nova.* Photo courtesy of Louise Rundell.

215. *Quartz with Yvonne Campbell at the Exford Stallion Parade in the late 1980s.*
Photo: courtesy of Ruth & Dai Thomas.

The ponies finally left Harwich on 8 October. David delivered the them to Vårgårda on Tuesday the 10th; he wrote:

> *'The only time I had any qualms on this trip was the next morning when they were turned out in a small paddock with only two strands of electric fence between them and the rest of Sweden. They galloped up to and touched one and true to their Exmoor intelligence they had it sussed straight away. After being in stables or horse box for ten days it was great to see them galloping and playing in their new home. Exmoors are, in my experience, not a problem except that they get bored. If in lairage for long it gets very expensive when buckets are used as footballs.'*

216. Apple's Original at Exford Show in 2015 with Maddy Buttner; he was shown by breeder Louise Rundell. Photo: Stefan Rundell.

217. Vildrosens Poppy.

In the 1990s, there were ten more British mares and a gelding imported into Sweden plus the stallions Heathpool Marischal and Octavius and colts Arum and Waltersgay Herb Christopher.

Breeders in Sweden also imported some Exmoor ponies from the Danish island of Tærø: one male in 1972; one male in 1981; four males and a female in 1991. Subsequently, one of the colts had to be put down as he was completely impossible to handle; two colts were gelded and broken to ride and the mare was bred from.

In 1989 Svenska Exmoor Avelsföreningen was recognised by the Swedish Pony Breeding Association. As a daughter Society of the British E.P.S., the British inspection system and registration rules are used and some members have trained in the UK as inspectors. As with Germany, David Brewer played a key role in encouraging the Swedish breeders and owners to ensure that, wherever possible, the ponies they breed are eligible for the UK Stud Book as well as being registered in Sweden.

As it turned out, it was very important that the Swedish breeders took this path because some ponies have now been exported from Sweden back to Britain. Maddy Buttner's aim is to breed ponies from the Herd 12 bloodlines that exhibit the breed features particularly well, especially the fleshy rims of the toad eye. This has meant locating ponies that are as closely related as possible to Herd 12's foundation animals. She found that some of the key ponies for such a breeding programme were not in the U.K. but in Sweden. Since 2010 she has imported mares Vildrosen's Poppy from Johanna Björling Nyqvist and Nutina from Lisbeth Sjostrand and now also has stallion Apple's Original, from Louise Rundell.

Whilst the number of Swedish members is not large, the enthusiasm of the Society is boundless as with the German Exmoor Pony Society. Each year there is a big Nordic Equine Event and this has been attended by the Swedish Society on many occasions. For example, in 1992, as well as an exhibition stand, there was a display in the arena by Quartz and Widdenhill Lucky Acorn; Louise Rundell and Lucky Acorn also appeared on television. The following year Robin Rundell and Hawkwell Nova displayed the Exmoor's talents as a children's riding pony and Annita Jansson on Lucky Acorn gave a jumping demonstration.

(In 2016 the Society changed its name to Exmoorponnysällskapet [Exmoor Pony Society] as Svenska Exmoor Avelsföreningen meant Swedish Exmoor Breeding Society and some Exmoor owners were deterred from joining because they were not breeders.)

Love and Marriage – 20th Century

Back in 2008, I met a lady from Glasgow who was married to an Icelander she met in Argentina. That's unremarkable in today's world but when riding or driving a pony, or walking, were the only means of transport, finding romance was usually closer to home.

Muriel Hooper recounted stories of both her father John and grandfather Arthur relying on their ponies for transport for themselves or girlfriends; see page 76.

Presumably in those days ponies also conveyed brides and grooms to and from church but to date no stories of this have emerged. However, more recently, Exmoor ponies have played a part in the weddings of a number of Exmoor pony owners.

In the 1950s and 1960s Mrs Lise Rønnow imported Exmoor ponies into Denmark (see pages 97 - 98) and when the Head Girl at her Stud got married, three Exmoors provided the 'guard of honour'. Unfortunately the names of the happy couple and the riders are not known.

In 1973, Exmoor pony Throstle attended the wedding of Helen Tait to Trevor Ogilvie and was in fact a wedding present; Helen was involved in looking after the Royal (Dick) Veterinary School's herd of Exmoors for several years, and as their wedding gift they gave her the 23-year-old mare.

218. Left to right: Clayford Horner (stallion), Blondie and Carpet Slipper in Denmark. Photo: Exmoor Pony Society Archive.

219. Helen, Trevor and Throstle.
Photo: Exmoor Pony Society Newsletter 1974.

Gate-Crashing

In May 1961, Brian Chugg (a founder of the Exmoor Society) rescued a cross-bred pony on The Chains. Here is his account.

From afar, I noticed that a pony, a mare and foal it became clear, was standing in a gateway. She failed to change her position as I got closer. Reaching the spot, I gasped: the animal was trapped across the gate with its forelegs on one side and hind-legs on the other and the top cross-bar was indenting her abdomen behind the ribs. By now it was mid-morning; evidence on the ground suggested that she might have been there for more than 12 hours. I took a few photographs. It might take hours to walk to get help. Clearly, immediate action was required.

The gate was about 20 inches open at ground level, enough to allow the foal through, but not the mare. The weight of the pony inclined her end of the gate slightly out of perpendicular. I conjectured that the foal, now on the far side, had ventured through the gap. The mare, obeying her maternal instincts, had attempted to leap the gate but had failed and had got herself into a painful if not injurious position. It would be impossible to move the pony without lifting gear. Another solution arose in my mind ..... *dismantle gate under the pony where she stands.*

After examining the construction I decided to attempt to detach the upper strap-hinge using the multi-purpose pocket knife which I carried. Using stones as wedges, I was gradually able to separate the hinge from the woodwork. The gate was now held only by the lower strap-hinge and anchored by the weight of the pony itself, which, as I was working alongside, had stopped kicking. The foal remained close and occasionally, sought nourishment from the mare.

If leverage could be brought to bear on the upper gate, the lower ironwork might now be wrenched off. I applied my weight. The pony seemed to understand, she helped by pulling herself forward with her forelegs.

If her end of the gate rose into the perpendicular and then beyond, she would go with it. This was the dangerous part. Would her legs be injured? Mental geometry had already indicated that was barely an inch to spare. There was a crunch, then a thud as the gate fell forward onto the ground under the belly of the animal.

I had the satisfaction of seeing her take a few faltering steps, but then she seemed to recover more quickly. A final photograph showed the mare, trailed by her foal, in the middle distance. I don't know what happened afterwards. But someone, on doing the round later in the day, would surely have been annoyed to find that one of the gates had been 'vandalised'.

220. *The mare was trapped, straddling the gate.*
Photo: Brian Chugg.

221. *The foal was able to feed through the gate.*
Photo: Brian Chugg.

The Beswick Exmoor Pony

Between 1959 and 1984, the famous Beswick factory created a series entitled 'Ponies' which included all the British native mountain and moorland breeds. They were modelled by Arthur Gredington, Beswick's chief modeller at the time. Gredington apparently preferred to work in isolation and it is said he only visited the factory to deliver his latest models for appraisal.

In 1961, Gredington focused on the Exmoor breed and the stallion Heatherman, bred by Lilo Lumb, was chosen as the subject. Heatherman, a many times champion, was 12 years old at the time. Heatherman is pictured on page 20.

Gredington was the first Beswick ceramicist to use named breed champions as models. He worked closely with R.S. Summerhays, who had written to Beswick suggesting that models of horses and ponies that were truly lifelike and naturally posed would be very popular. Beswick responded by inviting Summerhayes, a past President of the National Pony Society, to suggest which breeds to include and to be involved in the designing. He wrote about this experience in 'The Horseman's Year', saying:

> *'This was something that I could never have visualised, but which proved to be quite the most fascinating work I have ever been associated with in my long life with horses.'*

He described the process of refining one of the models:

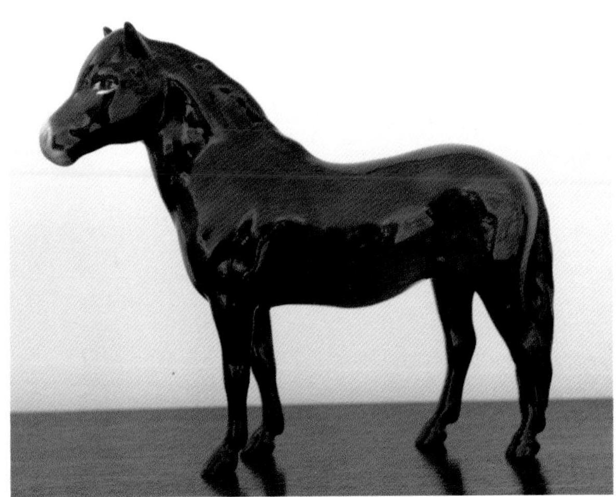

222. Exmoor pony Beswick model No. 1645 was sold to Exmoor Pony Society members at £3.15s.0d (£3.75 today) when first issued.

> *'When the damp clay model was put before me ... its head was most noticeably that of a horse. I mention this because it was an early instance of the skill of the modeller, when with a little off here, a certain shaping there, one or two other touches, the horse's head was changed magically to that of a pony.'*

Summerhayes also contributed a written description of each breed of pony for the Beswick sales brochure.

Pottery Models
of
Mountain and Moorland Ponies
by **BESWICK**

Above: 223. *Front cover of the sales brochure issued by Beswick in the 1960s. A copy is held by the Stoke-on-Trent Archives.*

Right: 224. *The Exmoor pony page from the sales brochure.*

Images reproduced by permission of Dartington Crystal.

Exmoor

Dartmoor and Exmoor are near neighbours and each owns a famous breed of pony, but each is quite unlike the other. Both are the same size, although the Exmoor allows another inch for the stallion. These ponies have short thick and pointed ears and favour a deep and rather broad chest and carry a close hard coat, beautifully bright in summer. The Exmoor's chief characteristic is the entirely distinctive colour. It has a "mealy" muzzle, and round the eyes (they call them "toad-eyes") and inside the flank, we find the same unusual colouring. The only colours allowed are bay, brown and dun, and there must not be a single white hair and as for toughness—a glance at the model will show this—and the mealy markings. An Exmoor carrying an adult will gallop with the best when the Devon and Somerset Staghounds are running !

Model No. 1645. Height 6½″

Odds and Ends

225. Riding class at Exford Show in 1960. L-R: Simpkin/Karen Witt; Little Lucie/Anne Bullen; Jeremy Fisher/John Heard; Tabitha Twitchet/Wendy Rawle. Tabitha Twitchet was the dam of the three other ponies. Photo: courtesy of Anne Williams (née Bullen).

'Joy Etherington wanted to enter Little Lucie in the ridden class at Dunster Show. When asked how she would transport her there, Joy said she would ride her all the way from Withypool to Dunster, some 18 miles. However, passing through Allerford, they met a herd of pigs which got Little Lucie very excited and she arrived at the show snorting and very worked up and "skimming the daisies". It was the only occasion she beat her brother Jeremy Fisher in a ridden class.'

As told by Anne Williams (née Bullen)

Owing to their hardihood, sweet temperament, sure footedness and capacity for hard work they are much sought after as chidren's hunters and for farm work – particularly in their native country. For the refined and responsible work of drawing invalids' chairs and governess carts they are excellent and inspire the greatest confidence, as their mannerisms are the acme of refinement and gentility.

From the *Bristol Times and Mirror*, 28 October 1920
'Wild Pony Driving on Exmoor' by Alfred Vowles

Stan Jarman, one of the WWII 'Exmoor Mounties' told me about his sergeant Bill Westcott:

'When Bill was out shepherding, he would sleep out on the moor. He made his pony lie down and slept up against him.'

The Society's booklet (translated into Italian) and a large photograph of the stallion Caractacus were exhibited at an exhibition in Verona March 12th - 20th 1967. This was arranged by the British Agricultural Export Council and the National Pony Society.

From the 1967 E.P.S. Newsletter.

An Exmoor foal became trapped in a bog. Its mother whinnied and another mare joined her. Then they both kicked it from underneath and raised it up; then they pushed it out of the quagmire. The foal was fine and galloped off.

I have no record of who told me this story.

226. Herd 12 foals on Codsend Moor where the body of local girl Molly Phillips was found in a bog in 1929.

United States of America

Exmoor ponies were first sent to America in the nineteenth century, as this report from the *Reno Evening Gazette's* 'Horse Notes' on 27 March 1888 shows. When talking to David Brewer about Exmoor exports, he said that some Exmoors were sent to the southern cattle rearing states in the late 1800s/early 1900s but there was no way of knowing whether they were from pure-bred or crossed herds.

Mr. D.E. Branham, Litchfield, Miss., writes: "I have lately purchased some fine Exmoor ponies which I intend to keep for breeding purposes, among them a stallion I consider one of the best."

227. From the Reno Evening Gazette *1888.*

The first record of a registered Exmoor being sold to the United States is to be found in the first edition of the Exmoor Pony Society Stud Book; notes about purchasers were included in the registration details back then. The first colt born into Herd 48, owned by Harry Williams of Great Ash, was gelded and exported in 1931.

To date, I have found no other instances of American imports until much more recently. Melissa Coyner takes up the story:

'I got my first pony, Barley, around 1974. I was told he was an Exmoor, but he was not branded, so it couldn't be confirmed.

In 1980 I went to England for a summer college class, and decided to see the Exmoors in person. The Mitchells, owners of Knighton Farm, kindly let me stay with them. It was there that I saw Knightoncombe Dark Dagger H8/9, a lovely filly. I thought it would be a worthwhile endeavor to bring her to the US and start a breeding program. The Exmoor is such an important, historical breed, and I hoped that I could help the breed become better known and increase their numbers. As I was only 19 at that time, my enthusiasm was greater than my knowledge!

Once Dagger was in the US, I found that there were no other Exmoors in the US. Zero. There may have been one imported into Colorado years before, but that was it. And while Canada once had a thriving breeding herd, those ponies had dwindled down to a few scattered individuals. Rather than import the Canadian ponies, I decided to go back to England in 1982 and brought back our foundation stallion, Casewick Aristotle, the filly Avocet and Anchor filly Talisman. I named my farm "Withyfield

228. Melissa with her first Exmoor, Barley.
Photo: Bernie Coyner.

229. K. Dark Dagger at Gatwick Airport ready for loading onto her flight to California.
Photo: Creenagh Mitchell.

230. *Sierra Sky Pilot at the Kentucky Horse Park.*
Photo: the Exmoor Pony Society Archive.

Farm," in honor of Withypool, England, where Dark Dagger was born.

Since there was no breed association in the US, The American Minor Breeds Conservancy (now the American Livestock Breeds Conservancy) helped me set up a registry within their organization. That registry was later dismantled, and no other registry in the US has taken its place.

Over the years, Withyfield Farm produced only 9 foals, as I quickly ran out of time, money and talent, and discovered that ponies didn't have the marketability in California that horses did. I still have four ponies: Talisman, Avocet, and two of Avocet's foals, Chaparral Lily and Desert Calico (or, as we refer to the bonded sisters, "CallieLily"). Three of our foals went to Laverne Harris in Washington state. She has included the ponies in two of the books she has written. One of the ponies went to a breeder in New York state; upon the death of the owner, the mare went to a breeder and Exmoor advocate in Connecticut. A gelding was donated to the Kentucky Horse Park in 2000, but they sold him to a private owner.'

The Philippines

This extract from the *Western Morning News* shows that there was interest from America in sending Exmoors even further afield to the Philippines. (See page 24 for India.)

Mr. R. V. Le Bas stated that he had received applications for Exmoor ponies from the Philippines, India, and elsewhere overseas. American buyers wanted to have some Exmoor stallions sent to the Philippines, but as it would have cost £200 to send them there they were not sold.

231. *From the* Western Morning News, *9 May 1930.*

Bampton Fair 1974 – 2014

The pony sales at Bampton Fair, behind the Tiverton Hotel (now The Quarryman's Rest) came to an end in 1985, mainly due to public disquiet regarding the welfare of wild ponies put through such a stressful experience. Then, after nineteen years without ponies being sold at Bampton Fair, there was a call for a pony sale to be re-introduced on a small scale as part of efforts to return the Fair to its roots. As part of the renaissance of Bampton Fair, a striking logo was designed with an Exmoor pony as its focus.

However, in the intervening years, moorland breeders on Exmoor had changed to selling their foals direct from their farms. One or two 'tested the market' when Bampton's pony sale was revived in 2004 but did not revert back permanently to using this traditional means of selling their stock. After ten years, the new pony sale proved unsustainable.

232. *Bampton Fair logo.*
Bampton Charter Fair.

ONLY HOLDERS OF GRAND STAND CATALOGUES WILL BE ADMITTED TO BUYERS' STAND

BAMPTON FAIR ANNUAL SALE

— OF —

EXMOOR PONIES AND SUCKERS
HACKS, HUNTERS AND COBS, &c.

— ON —

Thursday, 31st Oct., 1974

YARD CATALOGUE

PRICE 10p.

DOBBS, STAGG, KNOWLMAN & Co.
AUCTIONEERS, VALUERS & ESTATE AGENTS
SOUTH MOLTON, TIVERTON, Devon, and WELLINGTON, Somerset
Telephone: South Molton 2263/4

NOTE—NO CHILDREN ADMITTED WITHOUT THEIR PARENTS

Printed by S. W. LYDDON, Tower Printing Works, South Molton.

PARTICULARS OF ENTRIES:

About 30 Hunters and Cobs, &c.

About 300 EXMOOR, DARTMOOR and other PONIES and SUCKERS

viz.:—

Consignment No.	1.	Tiverton Ponies	50
	2.	Simonsbath Ponies	25
	3	Withypool Ponies	30
	4.	Culbone (Doone Country) Ponies	30
	5.	Hawkridge Ponies	40
	6.	Porlock Ponies	45
	7.	Dartmoor Ponies	30
	8.	Cornwood (Dartmoor) ...	25
	9.	Western	25

SALE TO COMMENCE AT 10.30 a.m. PROMPT WITH THE HUNTERS, &c.

NOTICE TO PURCHASERS:

The Purchaser, when he has paid for his Ponies must show the Delivery Note to the Vendor or Vendors from whom they were bought, when his purchases will be handed over to him.

ALL HORSES AND PONIES MUST BE REMOVED FROM THE SALE YARD BY 5.0 P.M.

233. *and* 234. *Bampton Fair pony sales in 1974, photographed on my first visit.*

235. *Yard catalogue for Bampton Fair in 1974.*
Reproduced courtesy of Stags.

Knightoncombe Royal Mantle (Fred)

Fred first made his mark by demonstrating how strong Exmoor ponies are, carrying Tom Summersgill on a 'mini Golden Horseshoe' ride organised by the Dulverton East hunt in the late 1970s. Fred's performance established him as the pony at Knighton that could be ridden by anyone and led to something of a career in front of the camera.

His international debut came about when a Tibetan student of film, Tsedup Karko turned up at Knighton in 1998; he asked Creenagh and Bob Mitchell if he could camp close to the farm and borrow an Exmoor pony to play the part of a Tibetan pony. (Honestly, I am not making this up!) He was making a film contrasting Tibetan nomadic life in the past and present; Fred and another Mitchell pony were used to depict the 'old ways'.

Fred was also recruited for a programme made by UK Today, for transmission internationally. The production company wanted to film a gathering for their programme on Exmoor ponies; the call went out for people to ride Exmoors on the Withypool gathering. Sue Burger came down from Yorkshire to take part and was lent Fred, who in the end proved to be the only Exmoor amongst the gatherers that day. Sue wrote about their day in *Going Native* magazine Winter 1993/94:

237. Sue Burger and Fred bringing Herd 23 down Kitridge Lane at the end of the Withypool Common gathering.

236. Tom Summersgill riding Fred on a 'mini Golden Horseshoe' with Dulverton East hunt.
Photo: the Creenagh Mitchell Archive.

> *'For the past four years I have been very fortunate in being lent a pony (an Exmoor of course) to ride on the Withypool Common gather. My steed for three of those years has been Knightoncombe Royal Mantle (Fred to his friends) … Fred and I enjoyed a pleasant ride along the bottom edge of the Common … Seemingly from nowhere, another group of ponies appeared at a canter, heading straight for Fred and me through the heather. Between the riders and foot followers, we turned them and they plunged down the hill, splashed through the river and headed up Bradymoor … It was at this point that Fred spied his quarry and the brakes became somewhat less than effective. I've never been quite sure whether he wants to catch the ponies or join them. Withypool Common is his home and for a proportion of each year he is living with these very ponies.'*

A few years later, the BBC planned a feature about Exmoors for their programme *Country Tracks*. They arranged to film at Knighton and for the presenter to ride Fred out on the moor accompanied by Kate Heightman on her Exmoor pony. They filmed the two riders talking about the breed as they rode.

All went well until the director got over-ambitious and asked whether the ponies could go faster and canter back towards the farm. Fred duly obliged but one of the stirrup leathers broke and the presenter 'unintentionally dismounted', fortunately without injury. Fred was the complete gentleman, stopping immediately and waiting for his rider. Although only shaken, the presenter returned to the farmhouse in the land rover and filming was over. Kate and I walked the ponies back to their stables.

Fred also participated in the advancement of science. Lindy Mitchell was training to be an animal chiropractor and had to undertake a final year research project. Her plan was to investigate the angles of leg bones in Exmoors and Icelandics and try to explain why Icelandics tölt and Exmoors don't. I was her research assistant for the field work i.e. measuring the angles of the bones. She would locate the ends of the bones and I would apply white sticky dots and then we would measure the angles. We brought in Fred out of the field to be our first subject and Lindy started. After a short while I realised that she had her head resting on Fred's side and was shaking with laughter. Eventually she managed to speak 'I can't find any bones!' – Fred, like all Exmoors, was a good doer. As other Exmoors proved equally difficult, in the end her project focused on Icelandic Horses alone.

Over the years Fred was ridden by many visitors to Knighton, as part of a short-lived pony trekking experiment and also by visiting friends. He also spent time with Gill and Reg Stanton at their trekking stables in Withypool village. Fred constantly demonstrated the versatility of the Exmoor pony, taking everything in his stride; he was also living proof of the contribution geldings make in the world of Exmoor ponies.

Fred lived to a ripe old age and ended his days at Knighton.

During one of many chats with Fred Milton, he told me that when ponies were relied upon for all manner of transport, this included one's final journey – that coffins were once taken to Withypool church by pony and cart.

When his own time came, Fred's funeral was held in Withypool village hall, as he was not a member of the Church of England, but his burial was to be in Withypool churchyard. After the service in the hall, the coffin was taken by motorised hearse the short distance through the village but he was accompanied by an Exmoor pony. Bob Mitchell had brought Knightoncombe Fred to pay his respects. As one of the mourners recalled,

> *'As we came out of the hall and saw pony Fred escorting Fred's coffin it was a very emotional moment.'*

238. Another religious occasion – the Reverend Robin Ray, reading the prayer and blessing that he wrote especially for the departure of the Native Pony Pilgrimage in 1998. His 'mobile pulpit' was pulled by Merlin and driven by Peter Farmer.

The Royal Worcester Exmoor Pony

239. The Royal Worcester Exmoor Pony. Photo: Museum of Worcester Porcelain.

The Royal Worcester Exmoor mare was sculpted by Bernard Winskill in fine bone china and issued as a limited edition of 500 in 1975.

Bernard Winskill was born in Wigan and his childhood experience of working at Lord Dudley's stud gave him an enduring love of horses. He trained at St Martin's School of Art in London and then specialised in sculpture at the Kennington School of Art. In 1968, he became a designer and modeller for Royal Worcester.

240. Octavius. Photo: Debbie Davy.

When Royal Worcester decided to create an Exmoor pony figurine, they contacted Peter Dean in Cumbria to find a model for the sculpture. Although the finished product was an Exmoor mare, it was in fact the stallion Octavius who Bernard Winskill used as his reference animal.

Bernard worked from his studio in Axminster, Devon, regularly visiting the factory in Worcester to monitor the production of his models.

When the limited edition came out, the price was around £300. The gift shop in Ilminster, where I was living, proudly displayed one in its window, probably in the hope that my parents would buy it for me! However, as a real Exmoor foal only cost about £30, they bought me Moorland Daisy, an Anchor filly instead. Good decision!

Birth and Childcare

A visitor to the Exmoor Pony Society 75th Anniversary exhibition at Exmoor House in Dulverton in 1996 told me the following delightful story, probably from around 1925-30:

'I've come to live in Dulverton again recently. I was born in Dulverton and the day after my birth, my parents took me by pony and trap up onto Winsford Hill and laid me in the heather to bring me good luck.'

From Wales comes a story of an equine perambulator! In 1977, Exmoor pony Aztec was bought as a birthday present for eleven-year-old Penny Jenkins. He came from a council house garden in High Wycombe but it is thought that he was originally from Withypool Common. Later, when Penny was away at college, he went on loan to Kay Birkett. Kay takes up the story:

'I inherited a hill sheep farm from my father in West Wales. In 1989, my husband Graham and I moved to the farm from Buckinghamshire and our daughter Arabella was born in 1990. Originally, I carried Arabella in a baby chest carrier but as soon as she could sit up, I strapped her into a wicker basket saddle on Aztec, so she could come with me when I checked the sheep each day. Aztec was amazing, plodding up and down the hills. Arabella has continued to ride but will always remember Aztec, her first pony. I wish there were more like him. When Arabella moved on to other ponies, Aztec stayed with us and entertained visitors; he was great, especially with those who couldn't ride.

Aztec's moment of fame was appearing in the Welsh film 'Tan ar y Comin' starring Edward Woodward that was filmed locally; it was the story of Tim Boswel, a young gipsy who lives an idyllic life travelling around Wales with his grandfather.'

Aztec lived until he was 32 years old.

On the west coast of Scotland, Debbie Davy's Exmoor ponies also helped with transporting young sons Richard and Philip:

'We frequently used ponies to get our sons over the hill when they were small, especially if there was snow or awful weather. I do remember on one occasion in a snowstorm leading one pony with one of the boys on her and another pony tied to her tail following with the other boy on her and the snow being so bad I could hardly see the second pony when I looked round.'

241. Graham with Arabella on Aztec, the 'Exmoor perambulator'. Photo: Kay Birkett.

Stuck in a Rut

In the late 1970s, Creenagh Mitchell was establishing Herd H8 at Knighton Farm just outside Withypool. She purchased three ponies from Miss Helen Dashwood, one of which was Clayford Candy, pictured here in some considerable difficulty.

Driving across the open moorland above Knighton, Creenagh stopped in surprise at the sight of just an Exmoor pony head seemingly set upon the ground amongst the patches of snow. It was Candy who was very much alive but thoroughly stuck.

The road down to Knighton has a drainage ditch running alongside it. The ditch starts out very shallow but, as the road climbs up a slope, it deepens and is a dead end. Candy had obviously entered the ditch and for some reason kept walking along it only to find there was no way out ahead.

Whatever Creenagh and Bob tried, Candy would not walk backwards and so in the end Bob had to fetch a spade and he dug a ramp in front of her – no mean achievement considering how frozen the ground was. Then, without a backward glance, Candy walked out and trotted off to rejoin the herd.

So, a happy ending but it could have been very different had there been heavy snowfall as they might not have seen her.

Other Hazards

I once watched two young foals on Withypool Common playing with a large piece of agricultural plastic and possibly ingesting pieces that ripped off its edges.

Elsewhere, a pony unfortunately encountered a piece of barbed-wire, presumably left behind after fencing the enclosure's boundary. The wire cut deeply into her lower leg just above the foot. Despite being taken in-ground and given veterinary treatment, she could not be saved.

Beware of Adders

Another pony had an unfortunate close encounter with an adder on Withypool Hill. Lindy Mitchell discovered Knightoncombe Linnet with a large swelling on her face and obviously very unwell. Linnet was transported back to the farm for veterinary treatment. Happily, Linnet came through the experience but it was some time before she was well enough to rejoin the herd on the Common.

Fortunately, I have only heard of one case of a pony on Exmoor being fatally bitten.

242. Clayford Candy – well and truly grounded!
Photo: the Creenagh Mitchell Archive.

243. Knightoncombe Linnet showing the large swelling under her eye. Photo: the Creenagh Mitchell Archive.

The Poole Pottery Exmoor Pony

In 1870, Jesse Carter started manufacturing architectural and garden tiles in Poole, Dorset. Later, under the control of his sons, Poole Pottery developed into a major producer of domestic and ornamental wares attracting many different designers and artists. In 1921, the pottery was taken over by the Carter, Stabler and Adams partnership and throughout the twenties and thirties a distinctive Poole style was established.

In 1972 Sales Executive Colin Day met Barbara Linley Adams, a well-established sculptress and ceramic artist, at a trade fair in Atlantic City. She had trained at the Slade and Central School of Arts in London before studying pottery design in Finland at the Helsinki School of Industrial Art. Her career had taken her to both Australia and America by the time they met. As a result of their meeting, she returned to England and became a modeller for Poole Pottery.

Poole's Dorset clay suited her detailed style of sculpting and she produced a highly distinctive range of stoneware sculptures of birds and animals, producing well over a hundred different figures between 1972 and 1983.

Having sculpted her design for a figure, she would finish the first cast personally, adding the highlights and applying iron oxide to provide the detail. This was then used within the stoneware department as the standard to which the clayware finishers worked.

It was in 1980 and 1981 that she turned her attention to the pony world and sculpted the heads of four of the British native breeds: the New Forest, the Shetland, the Welsh Mountain and the Exmoor.

Although she officially retired in 1983, Barbara continued working from her studio in Budleigh Salterton, Devon, sometimes on commissions for Poole Pottery. She died in 1995.

244. The Poole Exmoor head measures 10 cms in height, excluding the wooden base and has a matt finish.

245. Barbara Linley Adams at work.
Photo: Mike Murless, courtesy of Leslie Hayward.

Winter Journey to Withypool and Back

By Frances Spottiswoode.

246. Exmoor ponies on Molland Moor. Photo: Neville Stanikk.

There you stand with mealy muzzles and frosted backs
Close to the high beech banks of White Post Gate.
The sharp sun giving rays of living warmth
That even I can feel.
You stay there; don't follow me
As I wind and climb my way
To bleak and lonely Sandy Way.

Downhill now to Cradditch Moor through Woolcombe Gate
To Brightworthy's rusts and green, soft tipped with morning frost
Shelving oh so steeply down to Knighton Combe.
Your cousins will be somewhere there
On another wild terrain
But doing much the same.

Round Portford Bridge where bullocks eat their hay
And I am very near to start another day.
Back now with snow filled winter clouds
Allowing shafts of late noon sun throw golden light
On moor, field, wood and narrow road.

Where are you now, my morning friends?
Deep down sheltering in some coombe perhaps;
I know no more where you will be
Than you will know of me.
And so at Knowstone I arrive
With horse and children in the drive.

The Falkland Islands

In April 1982, Argentina invaded the Falkland Islands, a British territory in the South Atlantic. The Falklands War that followed lasted ten weeks, with Argentina surrendering in June.

Once the war had ended, the Falklands Appeal Fund was established in Britain to raise funds to help the islanders rebuild their lives. Mr Steve Whitley, the veterinary surgeon for the Islands suggested to General Mills, who was in charge of the Fund, that sending animals to both replace the limited number of stock that perished and expand the populations of livestock in the Falklands would be a significant help. The Trustees agreed and allocated a budget of £170,000.

This led to the planning of a shipment of farm animals and pets to be donated to the islanders by the Appeal Fund: these were cattle, sheep, pigs, goats, horses, ponies, sheepdogs, cats and parakeets. The Falkland Island Association Newsletter reported in November 1983:

> *'It was a comparatively simple matter to obtain animals which were to be direct replacements for those lost in the fighting, but the offers of gifts from the various breeders and societies had to be placed with farmers who were prepared to accept them. As the numbers grew, it became apparent that chartering a ship was likely to be the most economic way of transporting the animals for which farmers were prepared to pay. The Trustees agreed that all transportation costs and ancillary charges would be borne by the Appeal and that ex-farm prices only would be charged for animals which were not replacements for battle casualties.'*

An animal transportation ship, the *Dina Khalef*, was organised for the voyage to the Falklands and quickly became labelled 'Noah's Ark' by the media.

One Falklands resident, Mrs Lynn Blake, asked if some Exmoor ponies, including a stallion, could be part of the shipment; she wanted to breed riding ponies.

The request came to the Secretary of the Exmoor Pony Society, Ken Walker, and he put the word out to breeders. Melanie and Bob Wright owned a 2-year-old licensed stallion, Knightoncombe Gold Spangle (Horace) and had two other stallions; they agreed to sell him to the Crown Procurers who were dealing with all the purchasing.

The Ministry of Agriculture, Fisheries and Food (MAFF) then took control and Melanie and Bob faced a mass of form-filling and bureaucracy plus lots of veterinary checks on Horace. All was completed satisfactorily and so the day came when Horace was collected from their home in South Molton. Melanie tied a name tag into his mane and also included a letter to his new owners in with all the documentation. She recalled:

> *'At that time there was no indication as to whether we would ever hear of them again.'*

247. Horace at Little Chartres Farm, West Falkland in 1991. Photo: Frances Hall.

So it was that a total of eleven Exmoor ponies made their way to Poole in Dorset to embark on their five week sea voyage. The ponies were: stallions – Knightoncombe Gold Spangle, Frithesden Linnaeus and Hawkwell Holly; mares – Cara Calla, Cracrop, Kano, Kellet, Kittiwake, Kiwi, Musk and Tallulah Bankhead. They were taken to Whitsbury Manor Farm Stud near Fordingbridge in Hampshire, to await transfer to the docks at Poole. They joined two Arab mares, three Welsh cobs, two Welsh ponies and two Dartmoor ponies that were also to leave on the 'Ark'.

Then on Tuesday 22 September, L.E.P. (Bloodstock) Ltd. transported all the horses and

248. Tallulah Bankhead and foal and Musk, with Dave Gray at Goose Green before they went to Sea Lion Island. Photo: Alan Mills.

ponies to Poole docks for loading onto the ship. Several film crews and many journalists were there to see the animals enter the Ark. Two vets had volunteered to accompany the animals to the Falklands; they and the R.S.P.C.A. officials checked that conditions on the ship were suitable and loading began. Lindy Mitchell, from the Knightoncombe Stud, was present that day and recalled:

> *'The ponies were led up the ramp onto the deck and it seemed as if their pens were constructed around them.'*

The *Dina Khalef* finally left Poole with 220 animals on board, 21 of them pregnant. The ship passed Madeira seven days later. Just off Brazil they had to take on water and repair a breakdown; then they had to weather a force 8 gale. 'The Ark' finally reached its destination on Saturday 29 October after 35 days at sea. All the animals were unloaded at Port Stanley.

The Exmoor ponies stayed at Port Stanley for a few days before travelling on to their new homes. Melanie Wright reported that Mrs Lynn Blake had sent her a telegram a couple of weeks after the ship berthed to say that Horace had arrived safely at her farm on West Falkland. In a later letter, Lynn reported that to reach Little Chartres Farm, Horace had taken another three day boat ride and then walked 18 miles being led by another horse. She was delighted with him and felt that her plan to breed children's ponies was taking shape. He was a little difficult to catch and so he was temporarily in a four acre paddock but due to be released onto 7000 acres with some mares.

Melanie remembers that Lynn's plan was to use Horace with her horses to inject some toughness into resulting riding ponies.

In 1991, whilst serving in the army, Frances Hall was posted to the Falkland Islands for a four month tour. In her spare time she went in search of the Exmoor ponies from 'Noah's Ark':

> *'Travelling around the islands is rather difficult, either cross-country by Land Rover, by helicopter or by light aircraft'.*

She visited Kittiwake at Johnson's Harbour who was living amongst a herd of farm horses. She flew to Little Chartres Farm and saw Knightoncombe Gold Spangle and some of his first cross progeny. Another visit was to Saunders Island where she found Kellet; this mare had been brought to the island by raft from her previous home on Keppel Island. Frances also had news of Musk and Tallulah Bankhead on Sea Lion Island and Cara Calla who was living at Blue Beach Farm, San Carlos, the site of the military cemetery. She learnt that Hawkwell Holly and Frithesden Linnaeus had both been used for breeding and Kiwi was still at Dunbar Farm.

The mare Cracrop was living at Port Stanley and Frances was able to ride her

> *'using traditional saddlery of a folded blanket, saddle free with a whole sheepskin strapped over the top'.*

Frances reported in the 1992 Exmoor Pony Society Newsletter that all the Exmoor ponies were living out all year round on unlimited rough grazing. They weren't requiring extra feeding generally and appeared to have adapted to their new home.

249. Frances with Cracrop at Port Stanley in 1991. Photo: courtesy of Frances Hall.

Fetching and Carrying

Whilst the days of Exmoor ponies being relied upon for all manner of transport are long gone, there are still occasions when Exmoor residents return to pony power. When heavy snowfall blocked the road from Knighton Farm to Withypool, Bob Mitchell recruited Knightoncombe Royal Mantle (see page 134) to accompany him to the village and carry home the groceries.

In April 2010, Threeshires Little Plum, had a very important duty – to carry the ashes of her owner Jean Ellice, Lady Laird of Glengarry, to the family burial ground on the south side of Loch Garry in Scotland. Led by ghillie Steven MacKenzie, Plum had to follow a highland piper, who played throughout the journey, but she took it all in her stride. As Miss Ellice's ashes were interred, Plum neighed – coincidence or understanding?

250. Bob Mitchell returning with provisions, assisted by pack pony Fred. Photo: from the Creenagh Mitchell archive.

251. Plum undertaking a final service for her owner. The baskets were normally used for carrying grouse down from the hills. Photo: Vivian Taylor.

Annie Dent

Annie Dent, whose photograph of Alma Swan's stained glass panel adorns the back cover of this book, bred Exmoor ponies at Harthill Stud in Dorset between 1980 and 1996; her herd was H30 and prefix Semley.

In 1984, she photographed her husband Neville and friend Sandy, walking the Ridgeway long-distance path, with two of their ponies, Rowanberry and Fabian serving as pack ponies. Jack Hargreaves met the expedition and this was featured in his series 'Out of Town'.

253. Neville Dent and Sandy Sinclair at Waylands Smithy on the Ridgeway Path in 1984. Photo: Annie Dent.

254. 'The Hooligans' – two of Annie Dent's ponies found having fun after escaping into the woods near Hart Hill. Photo: Annie Dent.

252. Annie Dent – self portrait.

Annie has photographed horses and ponies of many breeds in a variety of locations; in addition to Exmoors, Hackneys and the horses of the Camargue in France have particularly attracted her. Her portfolio is far from limited to the equine world though and Hungarian Vizslas, flowers, tall ships, Venice and the Canadian Rockies have all featured recently in her work, providing the basis for a number of exhibitions.

I asked Annie to tell me about her approach to photography:

> *'I have always been fascinated by looking at something as the camera sees it, as a 'real' image, then visualising an alternative version and gradually working towards that interpretation of the scene.*
>
> *My aim is to create arresting images that can also be lived with and returned to with renewed interest and pleasure. For the past thirty years or so, Exmoor, it's landscapes, its magic and its inhabitants (both two and four legged) have been an inspiration, helping me along the road to the fulfilment of my aim. Above all the ponies, both those that still give me goose-bumps at every new moorland sighting and my own beloved little group that provided so much fun and pleasure during the 1980s and '90s.'*

The Netherlands

The first Exmoor ponies to be exported to Holland were shipped in 1947 – see page 104 for their story. After a long gap, further interest came from Dutch conservationists in the 1980s when managing nature reserves with grazing animals was becoming popular in many European countries.

In 1983, *It Fryske Gea*, a regional conservation association in the Friesland area, imported stallion Knightoncombe Dark Spectacle and a mare. They also bought two mares from Dr Voorhoeve from Zeeuws-Vlaanderen in the south-west of Holland; they were already living on a nature reserve 'Het Zwin'. The mares were very hard to catch and had to be sedated; the vet involved noted that 'normal horses' would not be able to run, as the Exmoors did, with such a high dosage. Eventually, the ponies were loaded and taken to Ryptsjerksterpolder reserve in Friesland. Dr Voorhoeve had imported these mares a few years earlier. Later, he sold *It Fryske Gea* a mare and a gelding, the progeny of these mares.

In 1984, Dark Spectacle and his three mares moved to the Dellebuusterheide reserve. Another stallion, Larkus, and a mare were purchased from the Knightoncombe herd and, together with some daughters of Dark Spectacle, were released onto Ryptsjerksterpolder.

It Fryske Gea acquired more Herd H8 ponies in 1987 for Bakkeveense Duinen reserve. Hopes of breeding their own stallion were not realised and so two sons of Dark Spectacle joined the group.

On Dellebuusterheide, after a few years the oldest son of Dark Spectacle successfully challenged his father and took over as dominant stallion. Ultsje Hosper, director of *It Fryske Gea* at that time, recorded that Dark Spectacle was chased out of the herd. However, he wouldn't accept this and often fought with his son. Finally he was fatally injured in one of these fights. Up to the year 2000, all breeding stallions on the Dellebuusterheide were sons of Knightoncombe Dark Spectacle.

The Dutch Exmoor pony population owned by *It Fryske Gea* grew steadily during the 1980s and 1990s, with home-bred additions. Other organisations such as *Ecoplan* and *Foundation Taurus* also began using Exmoors in 1996 and 2000 respectively. Five stallions were purchased from Britain in 2007.

255. Exmoors at Nieuw Woelwijk, near Hoogezand-Sappemeer in the northern part of The Netherlands in 2007. Photo: Debbie Davy.

In 2008, these three organisations and other individuals formed the *Samenwerkingsverband Exmoorpony* (the Dutch Exmoor Pony Co-operative) and, in order to avoid inbreeding, started a Dutch Stud Book. They have adopted the U.K. rules for registration except that they exclude ponies with sweet-itch. Members have also imported Exmoors from Germany, mainly from Sababurg Zoo.

In 2016, a further four stallions and ten mares were imported into Holland from the U.K. in order to introduce some new bloodlines into the Dutch Exmoor pony population.

Quarter-Horse x Exmoor

Hilary Pittam, from Llandysul in Wales, has several times put Exmoor mares to Quarter Horse stallions. Here she explains about her 'Quexmoores':

'I had bred various crosses over the years mainly using Thoroughbreds. When Leanne, my daughter, was about 8 we had Anonymouse (Nonny) and wanted to breed a first cross as a larger pony for her. I was looking for a pretty, small Thoroughbred so we went to the local stallion parade in Cardigan. As each one came through Leanne was saying "This one Mum?" and I kept saying "Smaller and prettier!!" After a while a voice came from a lady sitting behind us, "If that's what you want, come and see mine". She wouldn't tell us more but gave the address which wasn't too far away.

Quite soon we went to visit and the stallion turned out to be a Quarter Horse called Lunre Lucre. We instantly fell in love with him – pretty, laid back and immensely strong. We were given a demonstration of him galloping towards us, down a steep hill with only a wire fence between us. He stopped in his own length literally at the fence. Amazing! Anyway we arranged to send Nonny and so Moonmouse (aka Mouse) was born.

She was a rather bolshie foal with a mind of her own, but Leanne adored her and eventually rode her to some success. Soon after, we acquired Mystery from the disbanding of the local wildlife park. We knew she was purebred but unregistered, so there was little point in breeding Exmoors from her. She was unbroken with an unregisterable Exmoor foal at foot. We called him Major as John Major had just won the election!! He was later sold as a riding pony.

Anyway, we decided to send Mystery to another Quarter Horse. She was very sweet but not the most beautiful Exmoor. However, over the years she produced almost identical 14:2 ponies who all went on to become stunning and successful, mainly eventers. Some are still competing. Thus the Quexmoore was born.'

256. Mouse, the 'Quexmoore' as a foal. Photo: Hilary Pittam.

257. Hilary Pittam's daughter, Leanne, on Mouse, her Quarter Horse x Exmoor. Photo: Hilary Pittam.

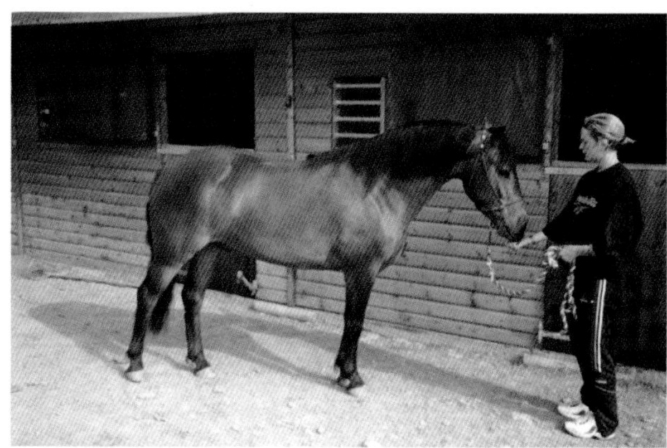

258. Special Edition, by a Quarter Horse sire out of Exmoor mare Mystery. Photo: Hilary Pittam.

The Will to Live

In 1995, Haddon Erica gave birth to a filly foal out on the open moorland of Haddon Hill. At just three weeks old, the foal disappeared. A search party scoured the area and surrounding farmland but there was no trace of the foal. Eventually the search was called off. Sometimes if a weak foal dies, its body is taken by scavengers, so such a disappearance is not unheard of.

It was therefore quite astounding when news came through that the filly had been found, on adjoining farmland, some eight days after it became lost. In hot and dry conditions, without water other than dew and receiving no sustenance from its mother, this remarkable little pony somehow managed to cling to life. Few would have given much for her chances past day three or four. No surprise then that she was subsequently named Lucky.

Weak and dehydrated, she was taken to David and Sandra Mansell's for veterinary attention and nursing. The vet spent over an hour holding up a saline drip at over waist height, quite a feat of endurance that soon had a positive result.

The filly's mother, although totally unhandled, was brought in from the moor to see if she could be reunited with her foal, but she proved to have no milk, having dried up in the very hot week without suckling. So she was returned to Haddon Hill and the hourly bottle feeding continued. Slowly the emaciated little figure began to fill out. David's overriding memory is of a mealy muzzle dashing to him when he called her around midnight, downing two bottles of milk, and then rushing back to the mare and foal she was living with. The Mansell's mare, Viburnum, and her colt foal Pinkery Juncus (Rush), had been brought back from East Anstey Common to keep the filly company and undertake the important task of ensuring that the foal realised she was a pony. Often bottle fed foals become so humanised they almost lose understanding of their equine identity.

260. Penny Beattie riding Haddon Lucky on an Anchor Herd gathering day. Photo: Tricia Gibson.

259. Haddon Lucky with her dam Haddon Erica during the attempt to reunite them. Although the mare accepted Lucky, her milk had dried up. Photo: D. Mansell.

The vet came daily for about the first week, during which she developed some fluid on the lung and was running a high temperature. Again, Lucky responded to treatment and gradually became stronger. By four months old, she was grazing and eating hay and cool mix.

Meeting Haddon Lucky some years later, when she was being shown at Exford Show by owner Penny Beattie, there was no hint of the ordeal she had survived as a foal – she was a charmingly friendly, much-loved riding pony.

Lusitano x Exmoor

About twenty years ago, when her granddaughter was born, the elderly wife of a cattle farmer in Churchill,Worcestershire bought a just weaned Exmoor filly with an Anchor brand at a dubious sale. Her idea was that in four or five years time the filly would be a lead rein pony for the child. She proceeded to turn Bracken out with the cattle and not touch her for the next three years! She then decided that she would break her in, although her experience with horses had been limited to hunting a few times in her youth. Bracken had other ideas: she was almost impossible to catch and when cornered, she kicked her owner who didn't touch her again. Bracken's future was not looking good but the lady on the farm next door, a qualified B.H.S. Instructor, bought her, thinking that she would be able to break her in. She also failed dismally and sent her to a local man who specialised in 'naughty ponies'. He sent Bracken back after eight weeks with no charges as he couldn't do anything with her either.

At the time one of Janet Hakeney's Lusitano colts (Negatiw, pet name Tiga) was three years old and not very big. Janet was persuaded to cover Bracken with him. Due to her owner's domestic problems, Bracken stayed with Janet and in due course gave birth to a colt, named Rincewind, the following year. Janet was asked to let Tiga cover Bracken again before she returned home. The Exmoor mare was confirmed in foal, but when Janet tried to organise Bracken and Rincewind's return, she was told that their owner could not have them back.

Bracken's second foal was another colt which Janet named Sonico. As producing the Lusitano-Exmoor crosses had never been her plan, Janet just put them in the fields with her Lusitano youngstock. She said:

'After a while it became obvious what nice ponies the boys were so I put their mother back in foal again and Urna, a filly was born. They were like three peas from the same pod … turbo charged Thelwells. Around 14 hands. I started Rincewind under saddle and rode him myself for several months. He was the most fun I had had on an equine-back for years.

Above: *261. Lusitano colt Tiga.* Photo: Janet Hakeney.

Left: *262. Janet riding Rincewind, her Lusitano – Exmoor cross.* Photo: courtesy of Janet Hakeney.

It has to be said that it is a fairly unique cross. The most pure hotblood breed in the Lusitano and the most pure coldblood breed in the Exmoor. Neither breed has been 'tinkered with'. It has produced ponies which biologists would describe as F1 Hybrids – in technical horsey terms they should strictly be called Iberian Warmbloods. They are all registered as part-bred Lusitanos. They are very bright and intelligent and want to work and learn. They are very quick learners. Rincewind is a very jolly, friendly, inquisitive, little person.'

Fay Weldon

'Forget the sweet Exmoor ponies; the devil rides them bareback on stormy nights.'

263. *'The Devil Rides Bareback' by Alma Swan.*

'Exmoor is a cold, wild, cruel place; all heather and bog and grass that snaps and crackles beneath the feet in winter. It's always winter. Forget the tourists, forget the sweet Exmoor ponies; the devil rides them bareback on stormy nights. Listen hard; that's not the howl of the wind, that's the devil shrieking his delight.'

This is a quote from a short story called 'Inspector Remorse' by Fay Weldon from her collection entitled *A Hard Time to be a Father*, published in 1998.

I asked Fay Weldon what experience of Exmoor had enabled her to write so evocatively about Exmoor in winter. She replied,

> *'In the early nineties I spent a winter night with my stepdaughter in a house on the edge of Exmoor. There was a plague of snails, and fog, and even the pretty horses seemed mocking and sinister. Once as a schoolgirl on a walking tour on Dartmoor I got lost, and was terrified: never did nature seem so inimical.'*

The Milton Pony Plough

Following the death of Fred Milton in 1998, I attended the dispersal sale at Weatherslade Farm and purchased two items of pony-drawn machinery, a hoe and a potato ridger that had been used on the farm, drawn by an Exmoor pony. Shortly afterwards, John Milton told me that there was also *'the old pony plough'* still at Weatherslade but it was wedged between the old ash house and a tree. He explained that one day the pony pulling the plough had spooked and bolted; the traces had broken and the plough had hit a gatepost, damaging it beyond repair. The broken plough had been thrown up into the hedge. John said that if I could get it out, I could have it.

Ian and I went to Weatherslade and found the plough. Over the years, the roots of trees had entwined themselves around the rusted metal and it seemed to be stuck fast. Ian was optimistic though and made it clear that I was not going to be of any real help. So I spent a while saying my goodbyes to Weatherslade: to the yard which had seen so many gathering and inspection days; to the small stable where the floor was raised due to year upon year of cutting part of the ponies' tails, the hair mixing with the mud and muck under foot. On returning to the ash house, the plough was free.

264. The old ash house at Weatherslade in 1999.

According to John Milton, Fred's father Charles had the pony plough made sometime between the two world wars i.e. 1919 - 1938. It had been made specifically to be drawn by an Exmoor pony in order to cut drainage channels along the edges of the moor and to plough in places the larger farm horse could not cope with, such as steeper slopes and close to the edge of the fields. It was a made-up design and probably made in a local blacksmith's workshop.

John Blackmore, who was born in Withypool in 1914, told me that there were no workshops in Withypool itself but two in Exford at the time: one was Dick Steer and Son, the other run by Evan and Fred Lock. Evan lived in Withypool and so perhaps his forge was the more likely. Evan had been the farrier while his brother Fred did the other blacksmith work, so the plough had most probably been made by Fred Lock.

265. The plough before removal in 1999.

Physician of Olympus

by Megan Young

He is not my General, nor my King.
Neither my lover nor my God.
Sometimes he is suffering, sometimes glory.
Some would have him bound, some a legend
If he had need of wings.
He has not the heart of a lion,
Yet his blood runs over the fields of war.
He has dragged our dreams through history
And carried the wind of fortune.
One day a nation's idol,
Another, worthless flesh.
To some the face of love, to some a child,
He is everything we wish for but without vice.
He is our graven image and the potter's wheel,
Though, as he walks the earth, we do not kneel.
Yet still he is not humbled, his eye is proud.
With all that he accepts, he is unbowed.
His truth and substance, I would claim my worth
In the breath of the monarch I am privileged to serve.

266. Megan with Hawkwell Harrier (Mac). Mac was a breeding stallion at the Cotswold Farm Park 1993 to 1999. Photo: courtesy of Merrilyn Thomas.

Megan Young wrote the above tribute to the horse in February 1999, eleven years before she died from cancer of unknown primary at the age of just 32. Her mother, Merrilyn Thomas explained:

'I can tell you that the poem "Physician of Olympus" was written at a time when she was deeply involved with the Pentland Exmoors and around the time she bought Mac and so I think that it is highly likely that they (or perhaps Mac) were the inspiration behind this poem.'

Megan qualified as a vet from the Royal (Dick) Veterinary College in Edinburgh. During her first year, she joined the college's Exmoor Pony Trekking Section. She quickly became a very active member of the group. In June of that year, 1997, she was one of the trek leaders at Glendevon: every summer members of the public pay to take part in trekking holidays run by the students. In 2000 Megan became President of the Trekking Section.

In March 1998, Merrilyn had visited Megan in Edinburgh:

'It was very cold and snowy. Megan took me out onto the Pentlands to see the Exmoors. I remember this vividly because she took me in the extremely old Land Rover she had bought with her grant – to my horror! It had no heating and the windows didn't shut properly. We drove up tracks into the hills – it was freezing, I was wrapped up in rugs, scarves and gloves. Megan wore only a fleece. That was my first sight of Exmoors. Then in June I went to Glendevon where Megan was again running the trekking holidays. We celebrated Megan's 21st birthday among the Exmoors.'

In 1999, Megan bought her first Exmoor pony – Mac, a ten-year-old unbroken stallion – from the Cotswold Farm Park. Merrilyn explained:

'I don't recall how Megan found him, but she did and bought him. Again I was horrified. Where was she going to keep him? How would she pay for all this? She stabled him at a small holding just outside Edinburgh. She had him gelded at the vet school hospital and her plan was to break him in and sell him on as a riding pony. In April, after he was broken, he threw her and she fractured a vertebra in her middle back. It was a serious accident but very fortunately there was no paralysis and no long-term damage.

Left: 267. *Megan with two of her ponies in Kent in 2005.*
Above: 268. *Herd 2 ponies on the Pentland Hills.*
Photos: courtesy of Merrilyn Thomas.

She was discharged from hospital after a few days and despite enormous pain very quickly carried on with her studies and her life. She did decide, however, to give up on the idea of riding Mac. He remained with Megan for the rest of her life and died of old age here in Kent about four years after Megan died. We were all very sad to lose him. He was a part of Megan.'

The following year, her last at university, Megan slipped on ice while leading Exmoors on the Pentland Hills: she fractured her upper arm with resulting paralysis of her whole arm. Despite this, she carried on with her studies, caring for the ponies, including Mac, and sat her finals. Fortunately, the nerve in her arm recovered and she regained full use of it after six months, although she had problems with her arm for the rest of her life. Megan's first job required her to move to Kent, accompanied by Mac. Then, in 2005, she set up her own equine vet practice in Kent and brought more Exmoors into her life. Merrilyn recalled:

'One of them was Saffy, Mac's daughter. She hoped to breed from Saffy and in that way keep Mac's line going. Despite many attempts though (including sending Saffy to a stallion on Exmoor) Saffy failed to become pregnant. Then, accidentally, one of Megan's other horses (a Morgan pony) got into Saffy's field and she did become pregnant and gave birth to a foal called Faith.'

She also gave a retirement home to Eeyore, one of the Pentland Exmoors.

In 2002, Megan met Toby and they were married in 2004. They had a son, Amos, in 2008. Toby became very involved with the care and management of the Exmoors.

The Exmoor ponies and her other horses were such an important part of Megan's life: she wrote about man's relationship with the horse in 'This is a Miracle', an essay that she sent to Merrilyn to help her mother understand how she felt:

'Horses are not something we retreat to when life is hard nor hide behind from the rest of the world. It isn't something we imagine in order to justify our obsession. The love of a horse is real, tangible. Anyone with eyes can see it. It is genuine and unconditional and can never be reproduced. It is without artifice and even thought.'

Merrilyn Thomas has interwoven the story of Megan's life and examples of her poetry in the book *Wordsmith – the Gift of a Soul*. Megan's poetry is spiritual yet rooted in her scientific appreciation of the world around her. If I had to explain 'love' to anyone, I would now simply tell them to read this book. I hope my readers will buy it as a donation from each copy sold helps support the charity *Cancer of Unknown Primary Foundation*. www.wordsmiththebook.com

Sue Baker

Stained Glass

This wonderful stained glass panel is the work of Dr Alma Swan, whose illustrations also enrich this book.

Alma's love of Exmoor ponies began in the 1980s:

> *'My interest in Exmoor ponies was sparked originally because I read about their claim to be Britain's original native horse: as a zoologist, my attention was grabbed. At the time I was incubating a rather grand plan to get a Shire mare and breed heavy horses, but at a small summer show an Exmoor walked past me on his way back from the ring and made such an impression. He was like a gleaming, lightly-dappled conker, and his browns-and-cream colour scheme was stunning. I also liked his shape – reassuringly stocky (fellow feeling, probably) and his perky little face and beautiful eyes. That was it. Before long, there was a nine-year-old gelding in the field and, soon after, a three-year-old filly (who later produced two sons). Through all this emerged an enduring friendship with Sue, so the rewards have been tremendous, all from reading a little bit about Exmoors and then seeing that handsome little chappie gleaming in the summer sunshine. I often wonder who he was who started off all this.'*

The 'two sons', Apollo and Mercury, are today part of the Yorkshire Exmoor Pony Trust's 'conservation grazing army'.

Alma kept Exmoor, Shetland, Fell and New Forest ponies and with the involvement of enthusiasts from other breeds, held several special native pony days in Leicestershire through the first half of the 1990s. She made a film about British

270. Alma filming with Desmond Morris on East Anstey Common for her British Native Ponies video.

269. Alma's unique Exmoor pony panel.
Photo: Annie Dent.

Native Ponies and was founder and Director of the British Pony Centre in Leicestershire until a move to Devon.

Alma's career was firstly in academia: she was a Lecturer in Zoology at the University of Leicester. In 1985 she moved into into science publishing. Most recently, she has been a leading international advocate for Open Access (to published research).

In addition to her array of professional skills, Alma is an artist and calligrapher. She works in a variety of media and, hard though it is to believe, the Exmoor pony panel was her first major project in stained glass; it is a greatly treasured part of my collection.

I asked Alma to write about making the panel:

> *'I learned to work in stained glass by attending evening classes for a couple of years. It's a lovely craft and, despite the fact that I almost always had sticking plaster on at least one of my fingers, the glorious colours and effects of sunlight streaming through the finished products made it a very rewarding hobby. Initially I used pre-designed templates but when I felt ready to start creating my own designs, what better subject than Exmoor ponies? The colours of their coats and the different hues of the Exmoor environment were perfect for depicting in glass. I do remember deciding to do this panel for Sue for Christmas 2002 even though that self-imposed deadline was nearly upon me. No doubt there were more sticking plasters than ever at that time!'*

Takhi x Exmoor

The Takhi is another name for the Przewalski Horse, also known as the Mongolian Wild Horse. This Takhi x Exmoor was an unplanned cross-breeding occurrence: born in 2007 in The Netherlands, a Takhi colt had broken out the previous year onto an area where a herd of Exmoor ponies was living free.

Przewalski Horses have 66 chromosomes whilst all other true horses have 64 but it has been shown that the offspring of this cross have 65 chromosomes and can be fertile.

271. The mare in the foreground is a cross between a Takhi stallion and an Exmoor mare. Photo courtesy of Debbie Davy.

Exmoor x Konik

These crosses between an Exmoor stallion and Konik mares were born in the Netherlands in about 2008 and were also unplanned. They came about when there were not enough of either breed alone to graze a particular area and so a mixed group was used. Interestingly, since then the Dutch reserve managers have focused upon breeding pure-bred Exmoors as they don't interact with visitors to reserves, whilst Koniks have proved less shy.

272. Exmoor x Konik ponies. This cross produced some individuals with more upright manes than either of the breeds involved.
Photo: Henri Kerkdijk-Otten.

Love and Marriage – 21st Century

In June 2009, Rebecca Taylor's brother drove her to the church to marry her fiance, Ken Brooks. After the ceremony, Becky found that pony-power had replaced horse-power:

> *'I had kept hinting to Ken it would be nice to have a horse and carriage but he pooh-poohed the idea.To my surprise, when we left the church, David Faulkner met us with a bottle of champagne and the pony and trap was waiting … Ken had arranged it all in secret as he had met David when helping me show our colt at Exmoor shows.'*

Becky was at the Royal (Dick) Veterinary College from 1988-1993 and involved with the Exmoor Pony Trekking Section. She ended up leaving college with Exmoor pony Netherwood Rupert and had bought Twolads from Herd 14 as a foundation brood mare. Rebecca and Ken now also have driving pony Twolads Hector.

Exmoor ponies just had to be in attendance when Jackie Searle and George Ablett were married at Cutcombe Church, Wheddon Cross on 3 September 1996. The ponies were excused transportation duties and had to remain outside the church but were important guests. Jackie's first Exmoor pony was Nobby; she was three when she first rode him and her father, Dr John Searle, drove him to do his house visits in and around Hockley in Essex.

Jackie and sister, Gill Langdon, have been breeding Exmoors at Luckwell Bridge on Exmoor since 1978.

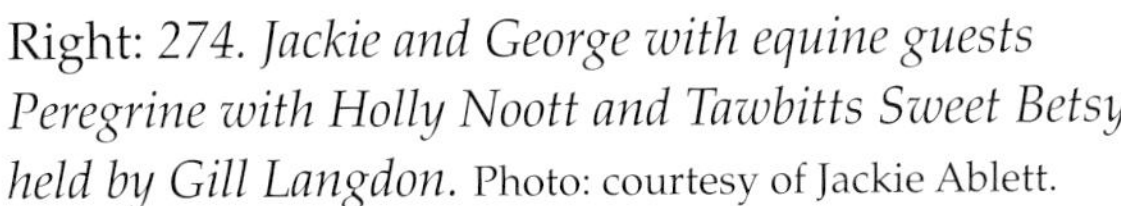

Right: 274. *Jackie and George with equine guests Peregrine with Holly Noott and Tawbitts Sweet Betsy held by Gill Langdon.* Photo: courtesy of Jackie Ablett.

Below: 273. *Kebroyd Votadini providing the wedding transportation for Becky and Ken Brooks in 2009, driven by Kath Faulkner with Helen Faulkner as groom.* Photo: courtesy of Becky and Ken Brooks.

Quilting

In 2011, members of the European Quilt Association were set the challenge of designing and making quilts to illustrate 'Celebrating Diversity'. The quilts had to be made up from 20 centimetre squares (blocks) and members of *Contemporary Quilt*, a specialist group of The Quilters' Guild of the British Isles, took for their theme 'Rule Britannia'. The finished quilt was displayed with those from other countries at the Quilters' Guild Museum in York and at the Guild's Festival of Quilts at the National Exhibition Centre, Birmingham.

275. Jane Andreoli in front of one of her full size quilts.
Photo: Annie Dent.

One of the members involved was Jane Andreoli, wife of Kevin, who was the Exmoor Pony Society Webmaster for many years. Jane decided that she wanted to make her design all about Exmoor ponies being ancient Britons.

276. The 'Rule Britannia' Quilt.
Photo: Hilary Gooding.

When Jane decided to take part in the project, she was conscious that a large number of quilters around the country would be submitting their designs and therefore the obvious British icons would probably feature repeatedly in the submissions. She wanted to find something unusual as her subject. After many holidays on Exmoor, and a long friendship with the author, she was well aware of the Exmoor pony and the theories of its antiquity. So what better candidate for representing the essence of Britain?

Jane explained to me that she had already been interested in depicting standing stones in some of her textile pictures:

> *'large structures such as Stonehenge seemed to hint at gateways into other worlds.'*

To make her quilt block Jane firstly printed off a photograph of a gathering onto ordinary paper and selected a group of ponies small enough to fit within her square with room for the stones around them. Then she started with a square of calico on top of which she placed thin wadding. Next came a collage of printed materials for the sky, ground and stones plus the cut-out ponies. The final layer was organza and then Jane machine quilted through it all and machine stitched the words 'Ancient Britons' and 'Exmoor Ponies'.

277. Jane Andreoli's block 'Ancient Britons'.
Photo: Hilary Gooding.

The unusual theme and quality of execution resulted in Jane's submission being one of those selected for the final quilt. At the end of the project, the quilt was dismantled and the blocks returned to their creators; happily, 'Ancient Britons' was then given to me.

Exmoor x Haflinger

278. *Haflinger mare Cindy with her Exmoor cross filly Izi.* Photo: Hans Hovens.

Hans Hovens and family live in the Netherlands and have a selection of horses and ponies including Exmoor, Friesian and Haflinger breeds. Hans studied biology at university and went on to spend four years working for the Foundation Reserves Przewalski Horse in Hustai National Park in Mongolia, co-ordinating ecological research. Since returning to Holland, he has worked for the Province of Utrecht and three Dutch environmental consultancies. He is president of 'Alliance Exmoor' and 'Fauna Consult' founded in 2000.

280. *Exmoor stallion Anchor Brandy.* Photo: Hans Hovens.

279. *Hans Hovens with Friesian Horse, son Baer with Haflinger mare Cindy and wife Grietje with the Exmoor x Halfinger foal Izi.* Photo: Paul op het Veld.

In 2016, an accidental encounter between Exmoor stallion Anchor Brandy and Haflinger mare Cindy, resulted in an Exmoor x Haflinger filly foal, Izi. Hans said:

> *'She looks a lot like an Exmoor, but has longer legs and no "dorsal stripe" (I know Exmoors do not have a real dorsal stripe i.e. a black stripe on the spine, but they have a dark brown spinal stripe in summer coat).'*

Hans Hovens and Toon Rijkers co-authored a paper entitled *'On the Origins of the Exmoor Pony: did the wild horse survive in Britain?'* which was published in *Lutra,* December 2013.

This is not 'The End'

So many people have been Exmoor pony chroniclers and contributed to this book through their written words, images or conversations; some I have met and known but many others were long gone before I was born. It is immensely satisfying that I have played my part in this timeline of recording the Exmoor pony world. Others must take up the baton and, of course, are already doing so whenever they write about or photograph the Exmoor pony.

Chronicling is a constant,
it's just the chronicler who changes.

However, my own task is not yet completed. The material I have included here, plus more (I didn't have space for), needs to be properly safeguarded for the future. To this end I have embarked upon creating The Exmoor Pony Archive. This will be a fully catalogued archive of my collection of documents, photographs and films, all stored in acid-free boxes. When completed, this physical archive is to be given a home with The Exmoor Society in Dulverton, in their environmentally-controlled archive room. I am enormously grateful to the Exmoor National Park Authority for funding the purchase of storage materials and to The Exmoor Society for accepting it into their care. As I assemble the Archive, I will be scanning everything. I hope that eventually much of the material will be available online for those who cannot visit Dulverton.

However, even the completion of this project will not be 'The End'. Personally, I will continue to dig around for further glimpses of the ponies' past. Most importantly, it is my heart-felt wish that others will add to the Exmoor Pony Archive, particularly those Exmoor families who have collections of photographs and papers that relate to the moorland herds. It is so easy for such material to deteriorate over time or to be completely lost; scanning and placing copies in the Archive would be a priceless legacy for those who come after us.

I am also hoping that over time, we will be able to identify the people and places for the many photographs that have no information accompanying them. So it will be important to ensure that local people get the chance to see such material.

Finally, if whilst reading *The Exmoor Pony Chronicles*, you have spotted any factual errors, or can add to any of the stories I have told, or have your own stories to record for posterity, please get in touch.

Sue Baker

Address: 16, Battleton, Dulverton, Somerset, TA22 9HT. Email: sue@horsebeasts.f9.co.uk

281. One of many items in the Mary Etherington Archive that has nothing written on the reverse. However, after using it in an article in 2001, it was identified as having been taken outside Chittlehamholt School (which closed in 1948). Bill Heard is holding the pony and the boy far left is Robert Baker; the two girls are Margaret Guard (left) and Muriel Wright.

Index

A

Acland: Family, 15-16, 24, 33, 47, 49; herd, 17-18, 20-21, 29, 33, 36-37, 44, 60-61, 95-96, 103, 112, 121, 125,
America, 109, 131-132; Soldiers, 94, 100,
Arab-Exmoor Cross, 38-39
Artists, 22, 62,64, 68-69, 90, 92, 106, 121-122, 153
Ashway Side, 36-37, 60-61
Auctions, 14, 27, 32, 34-35, 37, 54, 73, 79, 124
Australia, 29
Authors, 62, 149

B

Bampton Fair, 13-14, 17, 21, 25, 28, 30, 32, 35, 37, 41, 52, 54-59, 70-71, 73, 78, 82-83, 88-89, 91-92, 124, 133
Bath & West Show, 85, 103, 118
Best, Sophia, 70-71, 81, 88-89, 101
Beswick Model Exmoor, 20, 129
Births, 92, 108,
Bison, 84, 111
Black market, 96
Bogs, 38, 72, 75, 130, 149
Books, 62, 64, 68-69, 132
Bourne, Hope, 121-122
Brands/Branding, 32, 61-63, 87
Breed Show, 105
Brendon Pony Sale, 56, 124
Burial, 135, 143

C

Canada, 80, 108-109, 131
Cattle grids, 95-96
Celts, 7-9
Chariots, 7-10
Childcare, 137
Colours, 48, 97, 121-122, 153
Conservation, 37, 71, 145
Courting, 76, 86
Crockford Family, 45-46, 74
Crossbred Ponies, 13, 23-24, 28-29, 36, 38-40, 53, 55-59, 62, 94-95, 103, 128, 131, 142, 146, 148, 154, 157

D

Danish Exmoor Pony Society, 98
Denmark, 97-98, 108, 127
Dent, Annie, 144
Dent, Anthony, 112, 114
Droving, 13-14, 56-59, 73, 82
Duchess of Hamilton, 33
Dülmen herd, 110
Dunster Show, 85, 130
Dutch Exmoor Pony Co-operative, 145

E

Ebhardt, Hermann, 110-111
Escapes, 82, 87
Etherington,Mary, 19, 63, 70-71, 81, 86, 90-91, 95-97, 101-102, 104, 107, 110 114, 116
Evans, Daniel, 21, 34-35, 37
Ewart, James Cossar, 40, 71
Exford Show, 46, 50, 53, 61, 105, 113, 126, 130
Exmoor Mounties, see Home Guard
Exmoor National Park Authority, 85, 87, 158
Exmoor Pony Society, 14, 17-19, 21, 24- 26, 42, 46-53, 55-56, 61 70, 80, 84-85, 97, 103, 105, 108, 113, 118, 126-127, 130-131, 141, 156
Exports, 19, 23-24, 29, 80, 97-98, 104, 108-113, 123, 125-126, 131-132, 141-142, 145

F

Fairs - see Pony Fairs
Falkland Islands, 141-142
Film, 10, 14, 95, 134, 137, 153
Fisherman, 83, 107, 119-120
Fortescue Family, 15-16, 21, 48-49
Frozen ponies, 77
Funerals, 135,143

G

Gatherings, 14, 18, 55-58, 124, 134, 147
German Exmoor Pony Society, 112
Germany, 59, 93, 110-113, 145
Gipsies, 83
Green Family, 60-61,
Grey Exmoors, 37, 44, 48

H

Haflinger-Exmoor Cross 157
Helme, Eleanor, 62, 71
Hern, Dick, 50-51
Home Guard, 19, 46, 76, 93-95, 130
Horse meat, 61, 96

I

Illustrators, 68-69, 121
Improved Exmoors, 28
India, 24, 132
Inspections/Inspectors, 14, 18-19, 26, 46-48, 53, 61, 84, 87, 92, 98, 103, 113, 126
Intaglio Ring, 11
International Federation of Pony Breeders, 110, 112, 117

K

Knight Family, 27-28, 39
Knightoncombe Royal Mantle, 134-135, 143
Konik: Pony 110,112; Konik-Exmoor Cross, 154

L

Le Bas, Reginald, 48, 49-50, 84
Leech, John, 22
Lumb, Lilo, 19-20, 97, 103, 118, 129
Lusitano - Exmoor Cross, 148
Lyne, Michael, 106

M

McElligott, Pat 114,122-123
Milton Family, 12-14, 18, 25-26, 32, 43, 51, 54, 75, 80, 92, 104, 123, 125, 135, 150
Mongolian Wild Horse, 154
Munckton, Lt.-Colonel Victor, 51
Munnings, Sir Alfred, 53, 90-91, 99-100, 103, 106

N

National Park – see Exmoor National Park Authority
Netherlands, 19, 104, 145, 154, 157
New Zealand, 23-24
Norway, 123

P

Pack ponies, 43, 143-144
Parkman,Tom, 36-37, 48, 60-61
Philippines, 132
Photographers, 44, 52, 59, 66, 144
Pit ponies, 13
Pitt Rivers, General Augustus 31, 71
Pixies, 72
Poetry, 65, 99, 140, 151-152
Pony Fairs & Sales, 12-14, 17, 21, 25, 27-28, 30, 32, 35, 37, 39, 52, 54-59,

70-71, 73, 78, 82-83, 88-89, 91-92, 124, 133,
Pony plough, 150
Pony trekking, 10, 52, 107, 109, 119 135, 151, 155
Poole Pottery, 139
Population crash, 81, 100
Post round, 76
Przewalski Horse, 154
Pugsley, John Follett, 50, 56

Q

Quarter Horse - Exmoor Cross, 146
Quilting, 156

R

Rabbit-catcher, 75
Racing, 26, 51, 86
Railways – see Trains
Registers & registration, 14, 17- 19, 21, 33, 36-37, 45-48, 55-56, 61, 63, 92, 97-98, 108, 112-114, 126, 131, 145
Riding schools, 97, 115, 123, 125
Rogers, Roy, 117
Romans & Romano-British, 8-9, 11, 31
Romance, 127, 155
Royal Family, 118
Royal (Dick) Veterinary College, 7, 52, 81, 83, 97, 109, 119, 127, 151, 155
Royal Worcester Model, 136

S

School, 13, 20, 46, 75, 96, 158
Scott, Sir Walter, 15-16
Seaby, Allen William ,68-69
Second World War, – see World War II
Secretary (Exmoor Pony Society), 48-52, 56, 84, 141
Shepherding, 12, 14, 19, 76, 130
Shipping ponies, 23, 80, 104
Shows, 53, 74, 85, 103, 105, 130
Smith, Robert, 27-28
Snakebites, 138
Snow, 38-39, 77, 137-138, 140, 143
Songs, 41
South Hill: stallion, 33; enclosure, 36-37, 53
Speed (James and Mary), 7, 70-71, 81, 83, 110-111,117, 119, 120. See also Etherington, Mary
Stained glass, 153
Striped Exmoors, 122
Stud Books, 17-18, 21, 33, 36, 45, 48, 51-52, 55, 60, 63, 92, 97-98, 107-108, 112-113, 116, 123, 126, 131, 145
Sweden, 98, 123, 125-126

T

Tærø, 98, 126
Takhi - Exmoor Cross, 154
Tapp, David, 17, 47-48
Tayler, Richard Kingsley, 66-67
Television, 7-10, 107, 117, 126, 134
The Exmoor Pony Archive, 158
Theft of ponies, 61, 96
Thorne Family, 25-26, 32, 37, 94
Thoroughbred, 53, 79, 86, 103, 109, 146
Trains, 74, 81, 114, 116, 118
Transport, 13, 43, 75-76, 78, 81, 130, 135, 143
Trapped, 61, 77, 96, 128, 130, 138
Twins, 92

U

United States – see America
Unregistered, 19, 55, 113, 146

V

Vowles, Alfred 55-59, 130

W

Walker, Ken, 52, 141
Wallace Family, 61
Wanklyn, Joan, 64
War, 46, 61, 93 96, 100, 113, 141
Watts, Jeanne, 51-52
Weddings, 127, 155
Weldon, Fay, 149
West Somerset Yeomanry, 43
Westcott Families: Hawkridge Westcotts,14, 17-21, 61, 66, 84, 95, 103-105, 118, 125; Porlock Westcotts, 55-56,82
Western Family, 46
Wild Ass - Exmoor Cross, 40
Williams Family, 14, 53-54, 80, 101, 105, 125, 131
Winter, 45, 62, 77, 108, 122, 140, 149
World War II, 19-20, 43, 54, 61, 71, 81, 90, 96, 100-101, 111, 114, 130

Z

Zebra - Exmoor Cross, 40
Zoos: Crystal Palace, 114-116; Edinburgh, 107,117; London /Regent's Park Zoo, 101-102, 108; North Holland Zoo (Noorder Dierenpark), 19, 104; Sababurg, 111-112, 145